Romantic
Jealousy

Other Books by Ayala Malach Pines

Couple Burnout: Causes and Cures
(Routledge)

Career Burnout: Causes and Cures

Experiencing Social Psychology: Readings and Projects
(with Christina Maslach)

The Juggler. A Working Woman: Problems and Solutions
(available in Hebrew)

Psychology of Gender
(available in Hebrew)

How We Fall in Love
(forthcoming from Routledge)

Romantic Jealousy

ॐ

Causes, Symptoms, Cures

Ayala Malach Pines

Routledge

New York and London

Published in 1998 by
Routledge
29 West 35th Street
New York, NY 10001

Published in Great Britain in 1998 by
Routledge
11 New Fetter Lane
London EC4P 4EE

Copyright © 1998 by Routledge

Printed in the United States of America on acid-free paper
Design and typography: Jack Donner

Library of Congress Cataloging-in-Publication Data

Pines, Ayala M.
  [Kina Romantit: Tsilah, shel ahavah. English]
  Romantic jealousy
        p.   cm.
Previously published: New York: St. Martin's Press, 1992.
Includes bibliographical references and index.
ISBN 0-415-92010-8 (pbk.)
1. Jealousy.   2. Jealousy–Case studies.
[BF575.J4P4713   1998]
152.4'8–dc21   97–44734
                                                          CIP

For Israel

Contents

Preface

In the summer of 1978, I flew back to San Francisco from Toronto, where I had attended a convention of the American Psychological Association. On the plane I sat next to Elliot Aronson, one of the leading social psychologists in the country and a dear friend whom I admire greatly. We were chatting about various things when he said, "What do you know about jealousy?"

"Jealousy?" I responded, surprised. He explained, "I was asked to write an article called 'What We Don't Know About Jealousy' for a new behavioral science magazine. The problem is that I don't know much about jealousy—hence the title. But I thought if you were interested in the subject, we could pool our ignorance and have some fun writing the article together." While I definitely had my own personal experience with jealousy, I had never given much thought to it as a subject for study. I knew as much about it as Elliot did, but the offer was such a great compliment that I said yes right away.

The next day, in Berkeley, I went to the university library and did a computer search to find out what had been written about jealousy. There was quite a lot. I buried myself in literature on romantic jealousy written by novelists, poets, philosophers, anthropologists, sociologists, psychiatrists, and psychologists. While the volumes written were enormous, many questions were left unanswered. This was the subject of the article Elliot and I wrote.

Although the magazine folded before the article could be published, I became "hooked" on jealousy and, for the following twenty years, continued to study it. I've worked with jealous individuals and couples in my private practice both in California and Israel and have led jealousy workshops and collected questionnaires from close to a thousand people. I've worked in prison with male inmates serving time for "crimes of passion" and both interviewed and collected questionnaires from female inmates. I've worked with couples in open relationships. I've studied two urban communes practicing open relationships: one in which members succeeded in overcoming their jealousy, the other in which jealousy was a major problem and eventually caused the break-up of the commune. I've also reviewed the extensive and steadily growing literature on jealousy. This book is based on these experiences, research, and clinical work.

The book describes five different approaches to jealousy. The psychodynamic approach, which is particularly interested in delusional jealousy, views it as the result of unresolved childhood traumas. The systems approach views jealousy as the result of the dynamics within a particular relationship. The cognitive–behavioral approach views it as a learned response that when inappropriate can be unlearned. The social–psychology approach views it as a result of cultural forces that determine when jealousy is experienced and how it is expressed. The evolutionary or sociobiological approach views jealousy as innate, the result of evolutionary processes that appear to be different for men and women (Pines, 1992a).

While these approaches are considered by many theoreticians to be contradictory, I use all five of them in my work. I believe anything that helps a person with a jealousy problem can and should be used. This book reflects that conviction.

What the Book Is About

This book is for anyone who seeks a better understanding of romantic jealousy. It was written with three kinds of readers in mind. The first is the clinician who works with people struggling with a jealousy problem. The second is the person who struggles with a jealousy problem or with a mate's jealousy. The third is the intellectually curious person who might have encountered jealousy, either within himself or herself or in another, and is interested in learning more about it. Each chapter should have something for all three types of readers.

A person suffering from a jealousy problem is most likely to benefit from answering *The Romantic Jealousy Questionnaire* (see Appendix B) both before and after reading the book. The questionnaire can also be used by researchers and by therapists working with people with a jealousy problem. It is best to use it both before and after therapy. The intellectually curious reader is invited to answer the questionnaire just for fun.

The first chapter serves as an introduction. It defines *jealousy* and explains the differences between jealousy and envy and between jealousy that is normal and abnormal, chronic and acute.

The second chapter addresses a series of questions (as presented in *The Romantic Jealousy Questionnaire*) that are aimed at helping readers explore their romantic jealousy and compare their responses to those given by over seven hundred people.

The third chapter explores the unconscious roots of jealousy from the perspective of the psychodynamic approach, which views jealousy as a problem in the mind of the jealous individual that is best treated by individual therapy. This chapter shows how childhood events help shape adult jealousy.

The fourth chapter presents the systems approach, which proposes that jealousy occurs within the dynamic of a particular relationship and can best be treated through couple therapy. The chapter shows how couples collude to keep a jealousy problem alive.

The fifth chapter presents the sociobiological approach, in which jealousy is seen as an innate response resulting from evolutionary forces that are different for men and women. The chapter suggests that jealousy may be a universal problem for couples.

The sixth chapter discusses jealousy in different cultures and presents the social–psychological approach. According to this approach, the culture determines when people feel jealous and how they express their jealousy. The social–psychological approach encourages people to make an attributional shift in their explanation for their jealousy from "I'm a jealous person" to "I get jealous in certain situations."

Chapters seven and eight examine the range of responses to romantic jealousy. One chapter discusses people who succeeded in overcoming their jealousy and have established long–term open relationships. The other chapter discusses people who were overcome by their jealousy and committed crimes of passion. Whereas chapter seven presents the views of people who believe that jealousy is learned and thus can also be unlearned, chapter eight presents the view that, under the all–powerful influence of the green-eyed monster, some people can become temporarily insane and commit the most "monstrous" and violent crimes. The chapter provides an opportunity to gain an appreciation for the explosive potential in jealousy and learn how to defuse it.

Chapter nine is devoted to coping with jealousy. It presents the cognitive–behavioral approach, in which jealousy is seen as a learned response that, if inappropriate, can be unlearned and replaced with a more appropriate response. The chapter offers a variety of cognitive and behavioral techniques for coping with a jealousy problem. It also makes reference to techniques inspired by the other approaches presented throughout the book. The goal of all these coping techniques is to help individuals and couples protect their relationships in positive and constructive ways so that something good can come out of their jealousy problem.

My view that jealousy can be a growth–enhancing force is explored in chapter ten and demonstrated through the analysis of an unusual triangle relationship. Beyond the benefits to be gained from each chapter, my hope is that the book as a whole will help readers turn romantic jealousy into a useful signal they can use to improve themselves and their relationships.

A word about heterosexuality and homosexuality. Everything I say in this book about male–female relationships can also be applied to male–male or female–female relationships. I will mention this point again and present relevant examples when appropriate.

I have enjoyed my work on jealousy immensely and loved writing this book. I hope my excitement about the subject comes through.

Acknowledgments

I would like to thank my friends and colleagues who read this book and helped improve it with their thoughtful comments. These include Dr. Gordon Clanton, Dr. Bernie Zilbergeld, Professor Clair Rabin, Dr. Loise Shawver, Dr. Laura Stechel, and Kathy Knopoff (on her way to a brilliant career in psychology). Discussions with Professors Elliot Aronson, Murray Bilmes, Jack Block, and Troy Duster, as well as with Tsafi Gilad and Israel Segal, helped crystallize my ideas about jealousy.

I would also like to thank the team at Routledge that was responsible for publishing this book for their enthusiasm and support. This includes first and foremost Heidi A. Freund, the publishing director. Heidi's warmth and high energy make her a delight to work with. Other people that were a joy to work with are Anthony Mancini, the managing editor; Ilene Kalish, the assistant editor; Ron Longe, the publicity manager; Sarita Sahni, the editorial assistant; and Beth Mullen, who is in charge of rights and permissions.

I owe special thanks to my agent, Judith Weber, who besides being a dear friend is a wonderful editor and an intelligent and insightful reader who helped improve the book greatly both in content and in style. Wanda Cuevas, a member of the Sobel Weber Associates professional staff, also provided valuable feedback and support.

Anne Savarese, my editor at St. Martin's Press, where the book was first published, has gone through every version of the book with a thoroughness I have never encountered before. The result is an invaluable contribution to the book, for which I am extremely grateful.

The greatest thanks, however, are reserved for the people in my private practice and participants in my workshops and research, who opened their hearts to me and shared some of their most painful and difficult experiences with jealousy. This book could never have been written without their contribution.

1

The Green-Eyed Monster or the Shadow of Love?

♾ ♾ ♾

O, beware my lord of jealousy! It is the green eyed monster, which
doth mock the meat it feeds on.
—Shakespeare, *Othello*

He that is not jealous is not in love.
—St. Augustine

Jealousy is the dragon in paradise: the hell of heaven: and the most
bitter of emotions because it is associated with the sweetest.
—A. R. Orage, *On Love*

♾ ♾ ♾

I found myself sitting all curled up in the bushes following every
movement seen through the curtains in her lit-up window. I
knew her boyfriend was there, and the knowledge caused me an
excruciating pain. It was a cold winter night, and once in a while
there was a drizzle. I said to myself, "I know I am a sane, well-
adjusted, responsible adult. What in the world is happening to
me? Have I totally lost my mind?" Yet I continued sitting in those
bushes for hours. I didn't leave until the light in the window was
gone. A force more powerful than myself held me hypnotized
to the light and to her. I never felt so close to madness.

Although I knew that our relationship was over, I still had very
strong feelings toward him. Then, one day, I saw him at the cor-
ner store where we used to shop when we lived together. He was

with this Los Angeles-type bleached blonde, the kind who spends hours choosing her outfit. She had heavy makeup perfectly put on, and every hair on her head was in just the right place. I knew that I looked like a bag lady, my nose was red from a cold, my hair was unwashed and greasy. I think I simply went mad. I went up to him, kicked him in the balls, snapped his hat and ran outside. I got into his car—which for some reason he left unlocked—and started crying. I've never cried like that. I felt I was going out of my mind.

The man in the first paragraph and the woman in the second are describing powerful experiences that have several things in common. The experiences are extreme and unusual, involve loss of control, and result in a sense that one is going mad. Indeed, these are three notable features of jealousy.

What Is Romantic Jealousy?

The word *jealous* is derived from the Greek word *zelos*, which signifies emulation and zeal and denotes intensity of feelings. In this book the focus is not on jealousy in general but on *romantic* or *sexual* jealousy—the jealousy that emerges in the context of a romantic relationship.

The phrase "romantic jealousy" means different things to different people. It evokes a variety of images, explanations, and definitions. Here are some examples: "It's a hard-to-control emotion that results from fear of losing an important person to someone else." "It's a feeling you have when you're afraid you're losing an important relationship." "It's the feeling of being betrayed by someone you trust." "It's when somebody else looks at a person I love the way I do." "It's when you are insecure about your relationship or about yourself, and you feel that you are not man enough." "When you love someone, but the love they felt for you is gone."

What is your definition of romantic jealousy? I presented this question to close to a thousand people and received as many definitions as there were respondents. The definitions I just presented, for example, were suggested by inmates serving time in prison for committing crimes related to jealousy.

Since it seems clear that we can't simply assume everyone knows what jealousy is, I would like to offer the following definition: *Jealousy is a complex reaction to a perceived threat to a valued relationship or to its quality.*[1]

Jealousy is *a complex reaction* that has both internal and external components. The internal component of jealousy includes certain emotions, thoughts, and physical symptoms that often are not visible to the outside world. The emotions associated with jealousy may include pain, anger, rage, envy, sadness, fear, grief, and humiliation. The thoughts associated with jealousy may include resentment ("How could you have lied to me like this?"), self-blame ("How could I have been so blind, so stupid?"), comparison with the rival ("I'm not as attractive, sexy, intelligent, successful"), concern for one's public image ("Everyone knows, and laughs at me"), or self-pity ("I'm all alone in the world, nobody loves me"). The physical symptoms associated with jealousy may include blood rushing to the head, sweaty and trembling hands, shortness of breath, stomach cramps, feeling faint, a fast heartbeat, and trouble falling asleep.

The external component of jealousy is more clearly visible and is expressed in some kind of behavior: talking openly about the problem, screaming, crying, making a point of ignoring the issue, using humor, retaliating, leaving, or becoming violent.

The fact that jealousy has both an internal and an external component has an important implication for coping. Even if people can modify the internal component to some extent, most have relatively little control over it, especially over their emotional and physical responses: "I wish I could be cool and rational about it, but the pain is simply too big." "I stood there like an idiot, blood rushing to my face, and couldn't do a thing to stop it." However, people can be trained to have more control over their thoughts. Actually, the premise of cognitive therapy is that we can change our feelings by changing our thoughts (e.g. Bishay et al., 1996; Dolan & Bishay, 1996a; Ellis, 1996).

People have far greater control over the external component of their jealousy than over the internal component. They don't always realize this (and even when they do, they don't always want to admit it), but they can—if they choose to—talk about their feelings, make fun of the whole thing, cry their hearts out, suffer silently and covertly or loudly and visibly, lash out in anger, get out of the relationship, try to make their mate jealous, or throw dishes. When one feels overwhelmed by jealousy, it is important to remember that while it may be difficult to control jealous feelings, changing the thoughts that trigger them helps keep the feelings in check. Furthermore, most people have significant control over what they decide to do about their jealousy.

The jealous response is triggered when there's a *perceived threat* to the relationship. The perceived threat may be real or imagined (just as the relationship can be real or imagined). If a man thinks that his wife is interested in other men, even if the threat is a result of his own wild imagination, he is going to respond with intense jealousy. On the other hand, if a woman has a close friendship with another man, but her husband feels secure in their marriage and does not feel threatened by this friendship, he is not likely to respond with jealousy.

A couple I saw in therapy provides an example of jealousy in response to an imaginary threat. The husband, a rather plain-looking man, married a beautiful woman thirteen years younger than himself. He was convinced that every man who looked at his wife desired her. Since he did not feel secure in his own attractiveness, he was terrified every time she left the house, thinking that she would find someone else and leave him. His wife was faithful and committed to the marriage; when they first met, she loved the fact that he put her on a pedestal and welcomed his intense attraction to her. With time, however, she found his jealousy increasingly bothersome and suffocating. When the couple came to me for help, she said she needed to get away from him—not because he lacked attractiveness, and not because she had found a more attractive man—but because of his suffocating jealousy.

Another couple provides an example of how not perceiving a threat can act as a buffer against jealousy. The husband in this case was a swinger. He loved swingers' parties, even orgies. His wife did not. For years he used to go to these sexual encounters alone, with the full knowledge of his wife. The wife, for her part, disliked the idea of sexual promiscuity, but accepted the fact that this was extremely important for her husband, and that it was not a threat to their marriage or to herself. After years of this arrangement, the wife had an affair. The husband's way of dealing with it was to befriend her lover and accept him as part of the family. He said the lover wasn't a threat to his marriage. Furthermore, the fact that his wife had a lover made him feel freer to continue his own sexual exploits. Even if one doubts the husband's claim that he felt no jeal-

ousy, it's clear that his response to what is for most people a powerful jealousy trigger was very mild.

A relationship that triggers a jealous response has to be *valuable*.
It can be valuable in different ways. If a woman can't stand her husband and he arouses in her only feelings of boredom or disgust, the
knowledge that he is having an affair is not likely, in and of itself, to
trigger much jealousy. Yet for such a woman, losing her husband to
another woman may threaten her public image, as well as her standard of living and general lifestyle. In other words, the marriage may
not be valuable for her emotionally, but it may have economic or
social value. The following is a case in point. It demonstrates that
jealousy can exist in a relationship that has only extraneous value,
even after that relationship has ended.

A wealthy woman who wanted desperately to get out of her marriage finally managed to do so, at great financial cost. She had to
leave the house to her husband, but said she was glad to do it if it
meant being rid of him. Then, one night as she drove past the house,
she saw a shadow of a woman on the curtain and was overcome by
tremendous jealousy.

Did she perceive a threat to her marriage? Obviously not, since
the marriage was over. Was her marriage emotionally valuable to her
as a love relationship? Obviously not, since she was the one who
worked so hard, and sacrificed so much, to get out of it. Yet she felt
jealous when she saw the shadow of the woman. Jealousy, as noted
earlier, is a response to a perceived threat to a valued relationship or
to its quality. The woman was responding to the threat against her
perception of her relationship with her husband.

In her mind she saw herself as superior to her husband and as
having more power in their relationship. After all, wasn't she the one
who kicked him out of the marriage and out of her life? And here
the worthless bum had already found someone else to be with, while
she was still alone. What enraged her even more was that the two of
them were "in" and she was "out" of "her" house. The other woman
presented a threat not to her actual marriage but rather to her perception of the marriage.

This example illustrates the complexity of the jealous response.
The wealthy woman experienced possessiveness (this was "her"
husband and "her" house), exclusion (they were "in" and she was
"out"), competitiveness (her husband had someone and she didn't),

and envy (she wanted to have a relationship like the one she imagined he had).

For some people, the strongest component of jealousy is a fear of being abandoned: "He is going to fall in love with her and leave me and then I'll be all alone." For some, the primary component is loss of face: "How could you humiliate me in front of everyone by flirting openly with this slut?" For some, the most painful aspect is the betrayal: "How could you, the person I trusted more than anyone else in the world, lie to me and betray me in this way?" For some, the primary component is competitiveness: "If she fell in love with him, he must be a better lover than I am"; or, "How could she fall for this sleaze-ball?" And there are those for whom the primary component is envy: "I wish I were as skinny and gorgeous as she is" or "as successful professionally as he is."

When people describe intense jealousy, they often confuse their response with the degree of threat actually present in the situation. They may, for example, respond as if their mate's "outrageous" flirting at the party indicated that their mate would leave them for that other person, when in fact all that the flirting causes is embarrassment. When they confront the threat realistically ("How likely is it that your husband will leave you for the other woman?"), the intensity of their jealousy invariably diminishes.

Predisposition to Jealousy

Although jealousy appears in different forms and in varying degrees of intensity, it always results from an interaction between a certain predisposition and a particular triggering event. The predisposition to jealousy is influenced by the culture we grow up in; some cultures encourage jealousy while others discourage it. It is influenced by our family background: A man whose mother was unfaithful to his father or whose parents had violent outbursts of jealousy is likely to have far greater predisposition to jealousy than a man whose father and mother felt secure in each other's love. It is influenced by our family constellation: A woman who was outshone by a prettier or brighter sister is likely to have a greater predisposition to jealousy than a woman who was the favorite child in the family. It is also influenced by childhood and adult attachment history: A person who had a secure attachment to his mother will be less likely to become jealous than an anxiously attached person, and A person who was betrayed by a trusted mate is likely to develop a greater predisposition to jealousy in the future.

A predisposition to jealousy may never express itself unless a triggering event brings it out. For a person with a high predisposition to jealousy, such a triggering event can be as minor as a partner's glance at an attractive stranger passing by. For most people, however, the trigger for intense jealousy is a much more serious event, such as discovering that their mate had an illicit affair. For a person with an unusually low predisposition to jealousy, almost no event, short of ending the relationship because of a romantic involvement with a third person, can activate the jealous response.

Throughout the book, as mentioned in the preface, five theoretical approaches to romantic jealousy will be presented. Each emphasizes a different aspect of the predisposition to jealousy (Pines, 1992). The psychodynamic approach focuses on the question, Why do certain people have an unusually high or low predisposition to jealousy? It assumes that the answer can be found in people's childhood experiences. The systems approach asks, What is it about a particular relationship that increases or decreases a couple's predisposition to jealousy? It assumes that the answer can be found in the repeated patterns in the couple's interactions. The behavioral approach asks, What increases an individual's predisposition to behave in a jealous way? It assumes that the answer can be found in learned behaviors. The sociobiological approach asks, How have evolutionary forces of natural selection shaped men's and women's innate predisposition to jealousy? It assumes that the answer can be found in universal sex differences that exist in most human societies as well as in the animal world. The social–psychological approach asks, What effects does the culture have on people's predisposition to jealousy? It assumes that the answer can be found in cultural norms, which define what people perceive as threatening and what responses are considered appropriate.

In the case of some gay couples, for example, as a result of societal and familial pressures, one member of the couple may find it difficult to acknowledge openly their relationship, which decreases the other partner's sense of security and thus increases the predisposition for jealousy. Sharon and Mary are an example.

Mary is a tall, slender, attractive, and elegantly dressed manager in a big public relations firm. Her lover, Sharon, is chubby and less attractive, and works as a lawyer in a small law firm. Mary does not want people in her firm to know she is gay. She feels this will seriously jeopardize her chances of being promoted. So she flirts with men she works with and makes sure she always has a man accompanying her to various social events in the firm. This causes great jealousy in Sharon.

One could argue, of course, that Sharon would have felt the same jealousy if she were married to an attractive and elegant man who didn't take her to company functions and that Mary's flirtations are even less of a threat because Sharon knows she is not attracted to men. Nonetheless, the humiliation caused by having to keep their relationship secret, the feeling of being left out, and the threat that Mary may have a relationship with a man (to make sure people didn't think she was gay) were very difficult for Sharon and caused tremendous jealousy.

Jealousy and Envy

In defining jealousy, it's important to distinguish it from envy. Despite the frequent confusion between the two terms in everyday use, jealousy and envy are very different psychologically.[2] Envy involves two people. The envious person wants something that belongs to the other person and doesn't want the other person to have it. The object of envy can be the other person's mate, a good relationship, a desirable trait such as beauty or intelligence, a possession, success, or popularity. Jealousy, on the other hand, involves three people. The jealous person responds to a threat to a valued relationship posed by a third person. This is true even when the third person exists only in the imagination of the jealous person. Lionel Kreeger summarizes these differences by saying that whereas jealousy has a triadic basis, being concerned mainly with love and fear of loss, envy is contained within a diadic relationship and represents deeply entrenched destructive impulses aimed at the removal or spoiling of desirable qualities in the other (Kreeger, 1992). Envy and jealousy have been described as being keyed to two basic conditions of human existence. Envy is connected with not having, while jealousy is connected with having (Anderson, 1987).

Gerrod Parrott and Richard Smith conducted two experiments to distinguish the experiences of envy and jealousy. In the first experiment subjects recalled a personal experience of either envy or jealousy. In the second experiment subjects read one of a set of stories in which circumstances producing envy and jealousy were manipulated. The results of both studies revealed qualitative differences between the two emotions. Envy was characterized by inferiority, longing, resentment, and disapproval of the emotion. Jealousy was characterized by fear of loss, distrust, anxiety, and anger (Parrott & Smith, 1993).

People tend to mistake envy for jealousy, but not the other way around. Would you tell your husband that seeing him with his old girlfriend makes you envious or jealous? Would you say that you are jealous, or envious, of a friend who has just inherited a large amount of money? Most people would describe themselves in both cases as jealous, although what they actually feel in the second case is envy.[3]

This transposition often occurs because envy tends to have a more negative connotation than jealousy; envy is perceived as less mitigated by love than is jealousy (Joseph, 1986). While jealousy is a response to a threat to a love relationship, envy is an expression of hostility toward a perceived superior and a desire not only to possess the advantage, but in extreme cases to destroy the superior. Leonard Shengold (1994) suggests that envy develops early in life and is characterized by "destructive primal hatred." With age, it becomes modified in intensity and its primal murderous quality lessens. In cases of pathological envy there is a regression to the original primal envy. The person with such pathological "malignant" envy feels with delusional intensity that what the envied one has is not only urgently needed, but has been stolen from them.

If jealousy and envy are so distinct, why do people confuse them so often? Part of the reason lies in the fact that the jealous response includes, in many cases, a component of envy. A man who is jealous because his wife is having an affair with his best friend, for example, is likely to feel envious of his friend's success with his wife. It has been suggested that part of the reason is that envy, which begins earlier in psychic development, with maturation becomes partly transformed into jealousy (Shengold, 1994).

Jealousy and envy indeed seem to originate in different stages of our psychological development. Jealousy originates primarily in emotional experiences children have during the Oedipal stage, when they are about two to three years old. (This point will be elaborated in chapter three, during the discussion of the unconscious roots of jealousy.) Envy, on the other hand, originates much earlier, in the first months of a child's life.

According to Freud, during the Oedipal stage children experience the first stirrings of sexuality. Their sexual urge is directed toward the closest person of the opposite sex. In the case of a boy, that means his mother; in the case of a girl, her father. The boy wants Mother to himself. Unfortunately he has a very powerful competitor: Father. The competitor is bigger and stronger and has other advantages too, so the boy "loses" the contest. Through a similar process, the girl "loses" Father to Mother. When the child becomes an adult, whenever a third person presents a threat to a valued romantic relationship, the old painful wound is reopened and experienced as jealousy (Freud, 1922/1955).

Envy, according to child psychoanalyst Melanie Klein, develops during the period from birth through the first year of life, in response to the baby's helplessness and dependence on Mother. "From the beginning of life, the infant turns to Mother for all his needs," Klein writes. "The mother's breast, toward which all the infant's desires are directed, is instinctively felt to be the source not only of nourishment but also of life. An element of frustration, however, is bound to enter into the infant's earliest relation to Mother, because even a happy feeding situation cannot altogether replace the prenatal unity with the mother." The frustration and helplessness the hungry baby experiences are the roots of envy. The baby "envies" Mother for her power to nurse him or deprive him of nourishment. In his angry frustration, he wants to devour the source of his nourishment and her power—the breast (Klein, 1986, pp. 211–229).

Even if we don't accept Klein's idea that the baby "envies" his mother's power to feed him, we can still accept her idea that the early bond with Mother contains the fundamental elements of the baby's future relationship to the world. When the bond is loving and satisfying, the baby will develop a basic sense of security and trust toward people. When the bond is unloving and unsatisfying, deep-seated insecurity and envy will develop and the baby will grow up to be an envious adult. Whenever envy is triggered in such an adult, it reopens the early childhood wounds with all their destructive power.

Klein believes that jealousy is based on envy, but is different from it nonetheless. Her distinction between the two is similar to the one presented earlier: "Envy is the angry feeling that another person possesses and enjoys something desirable—the envious impulse being to take it away or to spoil it." Jealousy, on the other hand, involves the person's relationship to at least two other people, and "is mainly concerned with love which the individual feels is his due and which has been taken away, or is in danger of being taken" (p. 212).

Envy, as Klein and Shengold describe it, is an earlier, more primitive, and more destructive emotion than jealousy. It is different from the jealous desire to protect the relationship or get the beloved back. When there is a component of envy in a jealousy situation, it is expressed in an impulse to destroy the person who has the advantage—either the rival or the beloved, who has the power to make one happy and chooses not to.

Normal and Abnormal Jealousy

After defining romantic jealousy and distinguishing it from envy, another important distinction needs to be made, that between normal and abnormal jealousy. An analysis of abnormal jealousy leads to some of the most extreme forms that jealousy can take and some of its more dramatic consequences.

Jealousy has produced pain, drama, and tragedy throughout history. A wide range of hostile, bitter, and painful events have been attributed to jealousy: murder, aggression, hatred, lowered self-esteem, depression, suicide and suicide attempts, domestic violence, destruction of romantic relationships, marital problems, and divorce.[4] A nationwide survey of marriage counselors indicates that jealousy is a problem in one-third of all couples coming for marital therapy (White & Devine, 1991).

People who experienced intense jealousy describe it as an extremely painful, "crazy" experience. A woman in one of my jealousy workshops said that jealousy was the most painful thing she had ever experienced:

> I tried everything in an attempt to control it, but nothing, nothing worked. Now the only thing left for me is lobotomy. And believe me, I am tempted. I don't think I can live with this much pain any longer.

Even when people who experience extreme jealousy have enough self-control not to resort to actual acts of violence, they often fantasize about such acts. A woman who saw her ex-husband with his wife, who used to be her best friend, recalls:

> One day, as I was parking my car, I saw them in his new sports car parked right in front of me. It was a car he never let me drive but was now letting her use. Everything went white with rage in front of my eyes. I sat there trying to get hold of myself. I imagined myself putting my car in gear, accelerating, pushing my foot all the way down on the gas pedal and slamming into them at full speed, full force. I could feel the impact of the crash in my body, and hear the sound of metal and glass crashing.... I don't know what force helped me control the urge to destroy everything.

Most people have faced jealousy at some point in their lives, even if they don't consider it a problem.[5] Anyone who has experienced intense jealousy is well aware of its power and potential destructiveness. This helps explain people's great fascination with stories about the wild things some people are driven to do out of jealousy. One such story involves a middle-aged woman whose husband left her for a younger woman. With the help of a friend, the outraged wife kidnapped her rival at gun-point, shaved her head, stripped her naked, covered her with tar and feathers, and released her at the city dump. I read the story in the newspaper and subsequently heard it repeated over and over again, with great delight, by women who identified with the revenge of the deposed wife.

We tend to show more understanding toward people who commit "hot-blooded" crimes motivated by jealousy than we do toward people who commit "cold-blooded" crimes motivated by greed. We feel a certain identification with the betrayed lover who "had his revenge," who dared do something most of us can only imagine as a fitting revenge for an unfaithful lover or a rival.[6]

Even the law in some countries treats "crimes of passion" with relative leniency. In a famous case that happened some years ago in Italy, a man who suspected his wife of infidelity bought a gun and drove all the way from Rome, where he lived, to Milan, where he had reason to suspect that his wife was spending time with her lover. He arrived in Milan, caught his wife and her lover together in bed, shot them both dead, and was tried and found not guilty on grounds of temporary insanity.

Is jealousy a form of madness? Getting back to the examples presented at the beginning of this chapter, one can ask, Is a man who is sitting in the bushes on a rainy night, spying on a woman, sane? What about a woman who kicks a man in the groin, or one who covers another woman with tar and feathers? What about a man who kills two people in a jealous rage?

Jealousy, as these examples show, lies somewhere in the gray area between sanity and madness. Some reactions to it are so natural that a person who doesn't show them seems in some way "not normal." Think, for example, about a man whose wife has just informed him that she has fallen in love with another man, and who says in response, "How wonderful for you, darling."

Other reactions seem so excessive that one doesn't need to be an expert to know that they are pathological. An example is the man who is so suspicious of his loving and faithful wife that he constantly spies on her, makes surprise visits, listens in on her phone conversations, checks her underpants for stains, records the mileage in her car for unexplained trips, and, despite her repeatedly proven fidelity, continues to suspect her and suffer from tremendous jealousy.

While the responses of these two husbands seem completely different from each other, there is an important similarity between them. Both are very inappropriate. In one case the husband is not responding to a real threat to his marriage: His wife might leave him for the other man. In the other, the husband is responding with jealousy when there's no real threat. Indeed, both cases are considered pathological. The first is an example of "pathological tolerance," the second an example of "pathological jealousy."[7]

For most people, even if jealousy produces tremendous pain and distress, it remains an inner experience that does not cross the boundary to violent action. The woman I described earlier, whose estranged husband started dating her best friend shortly after their separation, said:

> I have daydreams in which I go into her apartment with a sledgehammer and start destroying things, furniture, records, windows. I can virtually hear the glass breaking.... These

fantasies have a way of calming me down, even if I know I will
never carry them out.

Does that seem like an appropriate response? What if the other
woman were not her best friend? What if she knew that her husband left her because of that "best friend"? And what if, instead of
imagining the sledgehammer destruction, she were actually to do it?

The more a response seems (in Freud's words) to "derive from the
actual situation" and be "proportionate to the real circumstances," the
more "normal" it is (Freud, 1922/1955). Freud, and modern–day psychologists, differentiate "normal" from "delusional" jealousy. Normal
jealousy has its basis in a real threat to the relationship, while delusional jealousy persists despite the absence of real or probable threat.
The husband who suspects and spies on his wife, despite her faithfulness and devotion to him, presents a good example of delusional
jealousy.

Why would someone "choose" to suffer the incredible pains of
delusional jealousy if there is no basis for it in reality? One explanation is that through jealousy the person is trying to overcome an
unresolved childhood trauma of betrayal. Another explanation
focuses on couples' interactions that help maintain such a jealousy
problem. A third explanation views the roots of the jealousy problem in behaviors that were learned earlier in life and that persist
even when no longer appropriate. An additional explanation, which
will not be discussed in this book, emphasizes the role of different
organic, neurological, and physical disorders.[8]

In addition to the distinction between a real and imagined threat,
another distinction can be made between a "normal" (which is to say,
appropriate) and an "abnormal" (meaning inappropriate, "pathological," "morbid,") response to a jealousy trigger.[9]

Instead of the negative and judgmental connotation implied in
the ordinary usage of the word "abnormal" (that is, crazy, pathological, sick), it is more useful to think of "normal" as a statistical term
that describes what is typical or average. People experience as broad
a range of jealous responses as the range of different physical and
emotional characteristics they possess. The vast majority fall in the
middle range and are thus defined as normal. A small minority fall
in the lowest part of the scale and are defined as abnormally low. A

similar minority fall in the highest part of the scale and are defined as abnormally high.[10]

If we were to consider such a thing as height, for example, most people are of "normal" height, a small percentage are "abnormally" short, and a similar minority are "abnormally" tall. Abnormal in this case does not mean crazy or sick; it simply means the lowest and highest ends of the scale.

The same thing that can be said about height, weight, strength, or beauty can be said about jealousy. The majority of people are in the middle (that is, the "normal") range of the jealousy scale. The few that are at the highest end of the scale, who see a threat even when none exists, are "abnormally" jealous; the few in the lowest part of the scale, who don't see a threat even when it's obviously there, are "abnormally nonjealous."

This point is more than a mere semantic distinction. All too often, people who experience jealousy are so shaken by the intensity of their emotions and the things they find themselves doing or wishing they could do—such as spying on an ex-lover or day-dreaming about destroying a house with a sledgehammer—that they jump to the conclusion "I must be crazy!" This kind of a conclusion is not very useful and is also very likely incorrect. Most "normal" people experience intense jealousy when a valued relationship is threatened.

Actually, from the description of the way jealousy is expressed and treated in different cultures, one may conclude that "normal" is simply that which is considered an appropriate response in a particular culture.[11] No matter how abnormal a certain response to jealousy may seem, chances are that it is (or was) considered normal somewhere.

This is not to say that there aren't cases of abnormal jealousy, which is to say, pathological, delusional, morbid. There are, but they are few and the exception. We hear so much about them precisely because they are truly outside the "normal" range and are therefore particularly fascinating both to the lay person and to the professional.[12]

Most abnormal cases of jealousy have one or both of the following features: (1) they are not related to a real threat to a valued relationship, but to some inner trigger of the jealous individual, and (2) the jealous response is excessive, dramatic, exaggerated, or violent. This may be a good place to introduce the distinction between chronic and acute jealousy.

Chronic and Acute Jealousy

Acute jealousy happens to people who never thought they were jealous when they discover that their partner has been unfaithful. While their reaction is a response to a real event, it is often excessive, dramatic, exaggerated, and experienced by them as abnormal. Indeed, it has been suggested by several writers (e.g. Glass & Wright, 1997; Lusterman, 1995) that the symptoms of many betrayed spouses are strikingly similar to the posttraumatic stress reactions of the victims of emotional, physical, and sexual abuse. The symptoms of posttraumatic stress disorder (PTSD) cluster into three categories: *intrusion,* which involves recounting and reexperiencing the trauma (e.g. traumatic images of the moment of the discovery, obsessive ruminating, flashbacks); *constriction,* which is evidenced by avoidance and numbing behaviors (e.g. loss of interest in other people and the outside world); and *hyperarousal,* which is characterized by physio-logic arousal and extreme hypervigilance (e.g. insomnia, irritability, startle responses) (American Psychiatric Association, 1994).

While the outside manifestations of acute and chronic jealousy may be similar, the cause of the jealous response and its duration are very different. In the case of acute jealousy, the response is extreme, but it is temporary and to a specific event. In the case of chronic jealousy, the individual indicates a predisposition to jealousy that is related to childhood experiences and low self–confidence. This person is likely to experience jealousy even in situations where most people will not perceive a threat.

I would also like to note that some social scientists reject altogether the notion of abnormal jealousy as it applies to the individual. They believe that what is normal or abnormal is defined by the culture and that the individual has little to do with it.

For those who are concerned about whether someone is "abnormally jealous," chapter two and *The Romantic Jealousy Questionnaire* (see Appendix B) may prove helpful. In the latter readers are presented with a series of questions aimed at helping them diagnose their jealousy. Filling out the questionnaire may be interesting even for people who don't have a jealousy problem. It may make reading the rest of the book, and especially the following chapter, more personally relevant.

After discussing some of the extreme forms that jealousy takes as, in Shakespeare's words, "the green-eyed monster," we can move on to a discussion of jealousy as the shadow of love.

Romantic Jealousy as the Shadow of Love

Whatever it is that draws two people to each other will shape the jealousy they may experience. One way to demonstrate this is with the help of an exercise. The exercise is especially recommended for people who suffer from a jealousy problem and for therapists working with such people.

> Think back to the time you first met or got to know your mate, and try to recall as best you can the way you felt. What was it that most attracted you? What was it that made you think (right away, or at some point later) that this was the person with whom you wanted to share your life? What was the most important thing the relationship gave you? Was it a feeling of security? Of being respected and listened to? Of being desired or adored?
>
> Now switch to the present, and consider the primary component of your jealousy, the most painful thoughts and feelings associated with your jealousy. Is it a fear of being abandoned? Is it humiliation and loss of face? Is it loss of self-esteem? Is it a rage at being lied to?
>
> The third part of this exercise is the hardest, the most challenging, and the most significant. Think: Could there be some connection between the things that the relationship gave you initially and the primary components of your jealousy?

Why is it so important to note the connection between what attracted people to each other—the most valuable thing the relationship gave them initially—and the primary components of their jealousy? Because it proves that jealousy is indeed the shadow of love. It also serves as a reminder to people that they didn't just happen to be in their relationship. They chose to be in it. Something in themselves attracted them to their mate. And something in themselves makes them experience jealousy the way they do. That something is their romantic image.

Psychologists have invested a great deal of effort in studying who falls in love with whom.[13] They discovered similarities among couples across a wide range of variables, including personality characteristics, intelligence, values, family background, education, income and social status, sex of siblings, attitude toward parents and happiness of parents' marriage, religious affiliation, tendency to be a "lone wolf" or socially gregarious, preference to "stay at home" or be "on the go," drinking and smoking habits, number of friends, physical attractiveness and various other physical attributes, mental health, and psychological maturity.

Even when two people are similar in several of the traits mentioned in the list, they probably still feel that these were not the "real" reasons they fell in love with each other. Yet, after they made their romantic choice, these were the things that told them that their choice was right. The romantic choice itself—the spark the two people felt—was based on their internalized romantic image.[14]

The Romantic Image

People develop their romantic images very early in life, based on powerful childhood experiences. Parents influence the development of these romantic images in two primary ways: (1) by the way they express, or don't express, love toward the child, and (2) by the way they express, or don't express, love toward each other. One way to discover the romantic image is with the help of the following exercise.

> Think back to the earliest time in your life you can remember. (It maybe helpful to think about a house you lived in, a place you liked to play, or a particular event that sticks in your memory.) Who took care of you? Who taught you the meaning of love? Was it your mother? your father? an older sibling? a grandparent? Who else was important to you as a child? Try to recall as much as you can about these people—not the way they are now, but the way you experienced them in your childhood. What were their most important traits, both good and bad? What was the most notable characteristic of their relationship with each other? What was the most important thing they gave you? What was the thing you most wanted but didn't get? Were they unfaithful to each other? Were they jealous?

The positive and negative features of the people who raised us are the building blocks of our romantic images. But while our romantic image is influenced by our mother, our father, and other people who reared us, there is an important difference between their negative and positive traits. The negative traits tend to have more influence on our romantic image. The reason for this is not, as one psychologist has suggested, that people tend to marry their worst nightmare, but that people seek in the beloved what they did not get from their parents (Bergman, 1995). If a girl's father was unfaithful to her mother, his unfaithfulness will become an important component of the girl's romantic image. If a boy's mother had frequent fits of jealousy, this will become an important component of his romantic image.

As adults, people look for someone who fits their romantic image in a significant way. When they meet such a person, they project their internalized image onto him or her. This is why, when they fall in love, they say such things as: "I feel as if I've known you all my life." This is also why they are so often surprised after the infatuation is over. It's as if they didn't see the person, only the projection of their own romantic image.

The person who fits an individual's romantic image is also the person who is best able to help them work through their childhood traumas. For example, although it would seem to make sense for the woman whose father was unfaithful to look for a man who is sure to be faithful, this is not what usually happens. In fact, a woman like this most often falls in love with playboys just like her father—not because she needs to repeat her childhood trauma, but because only a man who resembles her father can give her what she didn't get from her father. The paradox is that she marries such a man because he resembles her father, yet what she wants most desperately is for him not to behave the way her father did. She wants him—a sexy, flirtatious man with women always flocking around him—to be a faithful husband and give her the security she didn't get as a child. Even if this does not happen, by repeating her childhood trauma as an adult, with some measure of control over her life, she can—and often does—achieve some healing.

The effects of a romantic image are not always that direct and straightforward. A boy who was a witness to his mother's unfaithfulness may choose to marry a woman whose most redeeming quality is her faithfulness. How will he then be able to "work" on his childhood trauma? By suspecting his faithful wife of infidelity. The repeated proof of her innocence helps heal his wound. It shows that, unlike his father, he is the one and only for his wife.

Because the person one chooses to fall in love with has such an important influence on one's inner life, the discovery of such a person is a powerful event. Love can give one's whole life a sense of meaning. When someone gives meaning to your life, the threat of losing that person can be devastating. Indeed, the results of a study on love and jealousy show that people who invest such existential significance in love relationships tend to be particularly sensitive to the threat of their loss (Lester et al., 1985).

Most people have some unresolved conflicts they carry from their childhood. Some have more of them, some have fewer. For some, these conflicts are serious and problematic, for others they are less so. People may experience these conflicts as fears, as vulnerabilities, as insecurities. When they fall in love and their love is reciprocated, these fears and vulnerabilities seem to vanish. They are loved despite their imperfections. It makes them feel safe. But when this love is threatened, the fears and insecurities that they thought had gone forever come back in full force. If this person whom they love—the person who they thought loved them despite their flaws—is going to leave them for another, then there is no hope. Now they may feel insecure even in those things they love in themselves. As glowing as love was, so dark is the shadow of its possible loss.

Even people whose upbringing was loving, secure, and relatively problem-free, and who are burdened by few unresolved conflicts, respond to the threat or the actual loss of love in a similar way. Their response, however, is likely to be appropriate and proportionate to the situation. Because they are not as desperately dependent on their love relationship as is someone who is trying to work through a childhood trauma, they are less likely to perceive a threat when none exists, and an actual threat seems less overwhelming to them. Yet they, too, respond with jealousy when a third person threatens a romantic relationship for which they care deeply.

If even well-adjusted people who had a happy childhood experience jealousy, then we can assume that everyone experiences jealousy at some point in life. This seems a logical conclusion considering the origins of jealousy. All of us were infants once, and as a result we all carry certain vulnerabilities and fears. As loving as our parents may have been, we all were left hungry and cold at times and thus had an opportunity to feel fear of abandonment. Similarly, at one time or another we all have had to compete for the exclusive love of a parent or a caretaker, and have lost. Since these experiences are universal, say psychologists like Freud, then jealousy is universal.

Jealousy need not be the green–eyed monster that destroys people and relationships. Recognizing it as the shadow of love gives couples an opportunity to examine two important questions:

> What is the essence of your love? What was it that attracted you to each other initially, and what is the most important thing the relationship has given each one of you?
>
> What is the shadow that your love casts when it is threatened? What is the threat or the loss that the jealous person is responding to? Even if the jealousy is not grounded in reality, what is it focused on: a loss of love? of face? of self-worth? (Pestrak et al., 1986).

Jealousy has been described as an eruption that can be transcended only through awareness. As people move—with awareness—into the core of their jealousy, they discover ungrounded expectations, projections, envy, loss of self–esteem, and infantile fears and insecurities (Swami, 1983). Other times they may discover extreme ego insecurity, serious hostility, low frustration tolerance, dire love needs, dependency, obsessive–compulsive attachments, misdiagnosing a partner's unloving or provocative behavior, and childhood traumas and conditioning (Ellis, 1996).

These are not "nice" discoveries. In fact, they may be so unpleasant that some people will try hard to avoid them. Yet, avoiding, denying, or even suppressing a problem from consciousness doesn't make it go away. To solve a jealousy problem, a much more effective approach is an open and honest examination of the issues involved. Such an examination can do more than help relieve the jealous person's perceived threat. It can also help enhance the relationship and deepen both mates' commitment to each other. The next chapter offers an opportunity for just this kind of examination.

A Note to Therapists

When an individual, or a couple, comes to therapy with a jealousy problem, it is important first to examine both mates' predisposition to jealousy, including cultural background, family background, family constellation, and experiences with intimate relationships.

In my experience, couples find the definition of jealousy (response to a perceived threat to a valued relationship), the distinction among its three components (cognitive, emotional, behavioral) and between chronic and acute jealousy, and the fact that it is normal and universal very comforting.

This chapter contains several exercises that can be used very effectively in the context of individual therapy, couple therapy, and couple's workshop. One is finding the connection between what attracted the couple to each other originally and what is at the core of their jealousy problem (jealousy as the shadow of love). The other entails identifying the internalized romantic image a person or a couple has and the connection between that romantic image and the jealousy problem.

2

Are You a Jealous Person?

ॐ   ॐ   ॐ

O! What damned minutes tellse he o'er who dotes, yet doubts;
suspects, yet soundly loves!
—*Othello*, III, 165

Thou tyrant, tyrant jealousy. Thou tyrant of the mind.
—John Dryden, *The Song of Jealousy*

ॐ   ॐ   ॐ

Are you a jealous person? When I asked this question of 728 people in three different studies, slightly more than half (54%) answered "Yes, I am a jealous person." Close to half (46%) answered "No, I am not a jealous person."[1]

Nearly all of the people who described themselves as not jealous have experienced jealousy at some point in their lives. Furthermore, their experiences were rather similar to those of the people who described themselves as jealous. But as we shall see, the difference in self-perception between people who define themselves as "a jealous person" and those who do not has far reaching implications for coping.

The Experience of Jealousy

In order to identify the components of the experience of jealousy, the following exercise is recommended:

Try to recall the event that produced your most extreme jealousy. Even if this is difficult, recall the event with as much vividness and as many details as possible. What related incidents preceded it? What was your relationship like prior to it? Where and when did it take place? What was the jealousy trigger? Who was the interloper? When it happened, how did your mate look? How did you feel? What did you think? Ideally, you should recall enough details to be able to reproduce the event on stage or on a movie screen.

Once you have the event firmly and clearly in your memory, try to recall how intensely you experienced each of the physical, emotional, and cognitive (thoughts) components of jealousy presented on the next page.[2] Did you experience the particular component very intensely, moderately, or not at all?

The majority of the people who responded to the jealousy questionnaire (see Appendix B) experienced many of the components of jealousy to some extent and experienced those at the top of each list more intensely than those at the bottom. People who had experienced all the items in the list very intensely, or else didn't experience any at all, belong to that small minority that is either "abnormally jealous" or else "abnormally not jealous." Abnormal, as noted in chapter one, doesn't mean pathological, but outside the middle range where the majority of responses fall.

The guided memory exercise and the jealousy questionnaire can be used by lay people as well as by therapists either in the context of individual therapy or of a jealousy workshop.

It is important to note that the experience of jealousy reported by people who described themselves both as "jealous" and as "not jealous" was similar; the only difference was in intensity. Those who described themselves as "a jealous person" reported experiencing feelings of pain, grief, inferiority, aggression, and resentment "intensely," whereas those who described themselves as "not jealous" reported experiencing them "moderately." In all other cases the differences between the two groups were even smaller. This seems to suggest that despite its complexity, jealousy has some universal and identifiable features.[3]

Components of Jealousy

	INTENSITY		
	Very intense	*Moderate*	*Not at all*
PHYSICAL COMPONENTS:			
emptiness in stomach	_____	_____	_____
trouble falling or staying asleep	_____	_____	_____
nervous and shaky	_____	_____	_____
heart beating fast	_____	_____	_____
loss of appetite	_____	_____	_____
hands sweaty or trembling	_____	_____	_____
blood rushing to head	_____	_____	_____
feeling faint	_____	_____	_____
EMOTIONAL COMPONENTS:			
grief	_____	_____	_____
pain	_____	_____	_____
aggression	_____	_____	_____
rage	_____	_____	_____
helplessness	_____	_____	_____
envy	_____	_____	_____
fear	_____	_____	_____
humiliation	_____	_____	_____
COGNITIVE COMPONENTS:			
thoughts about your inferiority	_____	_____	_____
self–pity	_____	_____	_____
self–blame	_____	_____	_____
possessiveness	_____	_____	_____
resentment	_____	_____	_____
thoughts about being excluded	_____	_____	_____
thoughts about revenge	_____	_____	_____
defeatist thoughts	_____	_____	_____

Situations That Trigger Jealousy

The intensity of people's experience of jealousy, not surprisingly, is related to the circumstances in which it is aroused. The following situations were presented to subjects in my studies. All of them are real situations that happened to real people. Other researchers also found that situational threats predict jealous responses through their effect on the appraisal of threat (e.g. Melamed, 1991; Radecki–Bush et al., 1993).

How much jealousy would you experience when (*no jealousy? moderate jealousy? extreme jealousy?*):

- during a party, your mate is flirtatious and spends a great deal of time dancing intimately and behaving provocatively with someone else?
- your mate spends a great deal of time during a party dancing with someone else?
- your mate spends a great deal of time during a party talking to someone else?
- you are at a party and your mate disappears for a long period of time?
- you are at a party, and for a brief time you realize you don't know where your mate is?
- your phone rings and the caller either says, "Sorry, wrong number," or simply hangs up?
- you call your mate and the line is busy?

Most of the people who answered this question thought they would be most jealous in the first situation—when their mate is behaving provocatively. They thought they would not feel jealous in the last three situations—when the phone is busy, someone hangs up on you, or you don't know where your mate is during a party. If even these last situations cause a jealous response, the person is probably "abnormally" jealous. This can be a temporary condition caused by the recent discovery of an affair or a more permanent condition. If the first situation doesn't cause jealousy, the person is probably "abnormally" nonjealous.

The majority of people who answered the question felt jealous even in situations less extreme than having their mate dance intimately with someone else; for many, such behavior is a good enough reason to get out of the relationship, not just the party. Seeing one's mate spend a lot of time during a party dancing with someone else (even if it is "only because s/he is a great dancer") is enough to make most people jealous. The same goes for seeing one's mate spend a great deal of time during a party talking to someone else (even when it is "only because he or she is working in the same company and it's good politics"). People who find themselves in such situations, and their mate "can't understand" why they are making such a big fuss over an "innocent" dance or conversation, can comfort themselves (and enlighten their mate) with the knowledge that most people would have responded the same way. In other words, contrary to what their mate may think or say, they are not "abnormally" jealous.

Here are some other common jealousy triggers. Would you (or do you) experience jealousy when your mate:

- has a lover?
- has an intimate friend who is single and available?
- has an intimate friend?
- is associating with single available people?
- expresses appreciation/interest in a casual acquaintance?
- expresses appreciation of an attractive stranger passing by?
- expresses admiration of a movie or television star?

Shirley Glass and Tom Wright, who wrote extensively about the trauma of infidelity, note that the severity of reactions varies greatly among betrayed spouses. Some appear to take it in stride and others respond catastrophically. The intensity of the betrayed spouse's traumatic reaction seems to be related to the assumptions that spouse had regarding a mutual commitment to monogamy in the relationship (Glass & Wright, 1997).

Appreciation of a good-looking movie star is not associated with shattered assumptions about the marriage and does not represent a real threat. Consequently, it does not trigger jealousy in most people. People who are jealous even in such a situation are "abnormally" jealous. People who are not jealous even when their mate has a lover either no longer value the relationship or else are "abnormally" nonjealous.

Clearly, the situation most likely to produce jealousy is one's mate having a lover. But it turns out that there are variations even here. Would you (or do you) experience jealousy when:

- your mate announces he or she has fallen in love with someone else and is thinking about leaving you?
- your mate has a serious, long-term love affair?
- your mate has an affair, but assures you it is a result of his or her need for variety and in no way affects your relationship?
- your mate is open to, and frequently has, casual sexual experiences?
- you discover that your mate recently had a "one-night stand"?
- you discover that your mate had a love affair many years ago, when the two of you were already a couple?
- you discover that your mate had a love affair many years ago, before the two of you were a couple?
- you discover that your mate had a love affair many years ago, when the two of you were already a couple, with a person who is now deceased?
- you discover that your mate had a love affair many years ago, before the two of you were a couple, with a person who is now deceased?

Everyone who answered these questions described the most intense jealousy in response to a mate announcing that he or she has fallen in love with another person and is leaving. This is the nightmare that triggers the most intense jealousy, even in situations that don't really pose this kind of threat. The reason is obvious. This situation represents the ultimate threat to a love relationship—its painful, unwanted, and unexpected end. In one of my jealousy workshops, a woman told what happened when she found herself, unexpectedly, in this exact situation:

> My husband came home one night looking very grim. When I asked him what the problem was, he said he had fallen in love with another woman, that he had been having an affair with her for a while, and had finally decided to leave me and go live with her. I went wild. I jumped at him and started hitting his face with my bare hands. He is much bigger and stronger than I am, but there was no way he could stop me. I didn't stop until his face was covered with blood.

Years after the incident, she was still not over it. She shook and sobbed as she was describing it, still unable to comprehend how she, a calm, sane, nonviolent person, could have done what she did. My clinical experience seems to suggest that the situation she was in is the most likely to produce violence. The person who is left for another is pushed against the wall without a recourse to prevent the impending catastrophe. The violence is a response to the helpless frustration, pain, rage, and despair.

For most people questioned, the idea of their mate leaving them for another was almost too much to contemplate. Other situations involving a current affair—even a casual one-night stand—also caused intense jealousy. On the other hand, an affair that happened many years ago, especially if it happened before they were a couple, caused little or no jealousy.

The reason? This kind of an affair no longer poses a threat to the relationship. On the rare occasions when it does—as in the case of the wife who doesn't stop telling her new husband how wonderful her late husband was—it is likely to trigger jealousy. This is true despite the fact that the "other person" no longer presents a "real" threat to the relationship.

A past relationship can cause a "perceived" threat even without such an obvious provocation. A woman described her jealousy when seeing her husband's ex-wife for the first time:

> We were sitting in the football stadium waiting for the game to start when my husband said, "There's Meg," and pointed to a woman who sat across the aisle from us. I felt the blood rush to my head and thought I was going to faint. The fact that they had a terrible divorce that happened before my time didn't matter. All I could think about was that they used to be high-school sweethearts, something we could never be, and that he was madly in love with her in those early days.

Even an affair that happened many years ago with a person who is now deceased can cause jealousy, despite the obvious fact that this person can't possibly present a real threat. This happens when the dead person poses a threat to the quality of the relationship.

A powerful example of just such a situation is described in James Joyce's short story "The Dead" (Joyce, 1969). After a lavish dinner party,

Gabriel is feeling amorous toward Gretta, his wife. But she is distracted; a song played at the party reminded her of a young man she knew in her youth. Gabriel, who wants to get her out of her strange mood so they can make love, is feeling a twinge of jealousy:

> He tried to keep up his tone of cold interrogation but his voice when he spoke was humble and indifferent.
>
> —I suppose you were in love with this Michael Fury, Gretta, he said.
>
> —I was great with him at that time, she said.
>
> Her voice was veiled and sad. Gabriel, feeling now how vain it would be to try to lead her with what he had purposed caressed one of her hands and said also sadly:
>
> —And what did he die of so young, Gretta? Consumption, was it?
>
> —I think he died for me, she answered.
>
> A vague terror seized Gabriel at this answer as if, at that hour when he had hoped to triumph, some impalpable and vindictive being was coming against him, gathering forces against him in its vague world. But he shook himself free of it with an effort of reason and continued to caress her hand.

Gabriel's reason tells him that he has nothing to worry about. Yet he knows full well that the dead Fury (what a great choice of both men's names) has defeated him in the battle for Gretta's love.

Just as a past relationship can still present a threat, embarrassing circumstances in which an affair is discovered can pose an additional threat not only to the relationship itself, but also to the image that the couple presents to other people.

How much jealousy would you experience in each one of the following situations: no jealousy at all? moderate jealousy? extreme jealousy? Once again, these are all situations that actually happened to people.

You discover that your mate has a love affair and

- your mate is extremely indiscreet, a scandal erupts in the middle of a big party, you are cast in the role of the betrayed lover, and are expected to respond?
- your mate is extremely indiscreet, a scandal erupts, you are cast

in the role of the betrayed lover, and hear about it when you are alone?
- everyone else but you has known about it for a long time, but no one has said anything?
- everyone knows about it?
- only you and few close, trusted friends know?
- your mate is very discreet, the three of you are the only ones who know, and they know that you know?
- your mate is very discreet, no one else knows, and your mate doesn't know that you know?

Based on the responses of those surveyed, the worst trigger of jealousy is not the situation in which a scandal erupts in the middle of a big party. A woman who found herself in this situation describes the experience:

> I wanted to leave the party, and since I couldn't find my husband, I decided to leave alone. I went to get my coat, together with some other guests who were ready to leave. I opened the bedroom where the coats were put, with the other guests right behind me. There, on top of the coats, was my husband fucking this slut he had been flirting with all night long.... I felt the blood running out of my face, and my knees started wobbling. But I knew everyone was looking at me and waiting for me to respond. So I just said, "Good night, dear. I'm going home," and left.

Behaving in this cool and collected manner gave her a measure of control in the situation. This, and other people's similar experiences, suggest that in public people are more likely to minimize their jealous responses. The courageous face that they put on helps them control their reactions, at least to some extent, and manage their jealousy better than they would otherwise.

When you discover that your mate had an affair for years and that everyone else but you knew about it, you don't have the comfort that such a public performance can provide. A man who had gone through this devastating experience describes it:

> We were married thirty-seven years and I was sure we had a wonderful marriage. One day I came home early and discovered

my wife in the bedroom with a man I considered one of my best friends. I was devastated. Then I discovered to my horror that this had been going on for years and all our friends and acquaintances knew about it, but no one had said anything. I felt betrayed and terribly humiliated. I could imagine them talking behind my back, laughing.... It was horrible.

This man believed that the situation would have been easier to bear if only the three people involved knew about it. The ease or difficulty in this case are not necessarily related to the level of threat posed by the outside relationship. One could argue that an affair that has gone on for years doesn't pose much of a threat, since everyone, including the unfaithful mate, has tried to protect the marriage by keeping the affair a secret. While the discovery of "the slut on the coats" may be more embarrassing at the time, a long-term secret affair presents a far more serious threat.

Why is our response to such public situations so extreme? The reason is that these situations threaten the public image of our relationship. We are socialized to believe that people fall in love with their "match made in heaven" and live with that one and only, "happily ever after." Part of the pain associated with the discovery that our mate is having an affair comes from the realization that we can no longer apply this idealized image to ourselves. When other people know about the affair, the image of our relationship in the public eye is destroyed. Their knowledge takes away our option of pretending to the world that "everything's fine."

People Who Trigger Jealousy

Thus far we have focused on the different situations that can trigger jealousy. But the effects these situations can have depend on the people involved. It is possible, for example, that the woman who discovered her husband on the pile of coats was able to keep her cool because she didn't consider the other woman a serious rival, but instead a worthless "slut." The man who discovered his wife with his best friend, on the other hand, not only had a serious rival, but the added pain of betrayal by the two people he most loved and trusted.

David DeSteno and Peter Salovey (1996b) studied the effect the characteristics of the rival have on jealousy. Subjects were presented with a series of rivals for their partner's attention. The descriptions of the rivals were designed to vary along dimensions thought to be important to subjects' self-definition. Results showed that greater jealousy was reported when the domain of a rival's achievements was also a domain of high relevance to the subject.

Who are the people who most elicit your jealousy? Try to imagine how much jealousy you would experience if you found out that your mate has been having an affair with:

- someone you don't know personally and of whom you have a low opinion.
- someone you don't know personally and know nothing about.
- someone you don't know personally and of whom you think very highly.
- someone you know personally and distrust.
- someone you know personally and find very similar to yourself.
- someone you know personally, trust, and consider a friend.
- a family member.
- your best friend and confidant.
- someone you know personally and are envious of.

Most people who answered this question said that a person they had a low opinion of and didn't know personally triggered the least amount of jealousy. The "slut on the coats" is one example. A "hostess" in a hotel bar with whom a woman's husband had a one-night stand is another example. Having a low opinion about these kinds of people as well as not knowing them personally are two elements that help reduce the threat that involvement with them implies. It's important to note, however, that even this kind of "low-life," unknown person elicits some jealousy.

The most jealousy-provoking "third person" was someone the respondents knew personally and whom they envied: someone they found brighter or more attractive than themselves, or else more successful in exactly the ways they would have liked to be. As DeSteno and Salovey (1996b) demonstrated, the greatest jealousy is triggered when the area in which the rival excels (the domain of a rival's achievements) is a domain of high relevance to the betrayed person. A partner's affair with this type of a rival produces the greatest perceived threat. The reason is obvious; if you think the person is better than you, why shouldn't your partner?

How Jealous Are You?

After people have had a chance to consider their responses to these different situations and rivals, it is possible to ask them directly: How jealous do you think you are? Not at all? Moderately? Extremely? As expected, the majority of respondents described themselves as moderately jealous. Very few described themselves as either extremely jealous or not jealous at all.

Going back to the memory of the most intense experience of jealousy, How long did the experience last? Minutes? Days? Months? Years? Most people report that extreme jealousy lasts for days. In a few cases, when the experience is especially traumatic or the person is especially prone to jealousy, it can last for months and even years.

Jane, an attractive and elegant woman, was happily married for 35 years until she discovered that her husband had had an affair with a younger woman he knew through his job. Seven months after she discovered the affair—long after her husband had ended it—Jane was still unable to get over her intense jealousy. She couldn't stop thinking about the other woman and eventually started spying on her. The first time she was able to "check her out" was at an opera matinee. Seeing her rival in an outrageous backless dress sent Jane into a decline for weeks.

Finding out that your husband of thirty-five years, a man you considered your best and most trusted friend, has betrayed you is no doubt a justifiable cause for extreme jealousy.[4] "Abnormally jealous" people, however, experience extreme jealousy in response to far milder triggers, and far more often. "Abnormal jealousy" may stem from choosing a mate who is likely to make you jealous—because of the mate's personality, the person's lack of confidence, or the dynamic of the relationship. It can be caused by imagining threats even where there are none: "Every attractive woman I see walking down the street is a threat. Thinking about the women he is meeting in his work can make me insane with jealousy."

How often do you experience extreme jealousy? Never? Rarely? Occasionally? Often? All the time? For most people, intense jealousy is a very rare experience. People who are "abnormally nonjealous" never experience intense jealousy. Some manage to protect themselves by avoiding involvement with anyone they are intensely attracted to. Others do it simply by "not seeing," or consciously ignoring, the threat.

Jealousy can be an extremely painful experience, but making it stop is not easy. Question: Can you make yourself stop being (feeling, thinking, acting) jealous? Definitely? To a certain degree? Definitely not? Most people are able to stop themselves from being jealous, but only to a certain degree. When one is in the midst of a jealousy crisis it is especially hard.

Jane said she couldn't stop herself from being jealous. No matter how hard she tried, she couldn't stop thinking about the other woman—the way she looked at the theater in her backless dress, the way her voice sounded on her answering machine ("so unnaturally cheerful"), the way she must have behaved with Jane's husband (free, daring). Jane couldn't stop going over every detail of the affair again and again in her mind.

Through therapy Jane came to recognize the role she had played in enabling the affair—by being away with her daughter and unavailable to her husband when he desperately needed support and assurance of his manhood. She also realized that her husband's affair was only part of the reason for her obsession with the other woman. Her thoughts and feelings were related to her own sense of disappointment with the choices she made in her life. The other woman had a successful career and had achieved many of the things Jane herself would have wanted. As a free and independent woman, her rival could afford to come to the theater dressed in an outrageously sexy outfit. She could also do other things (such as have affairs) that Jane herself, as a married woman and a homemaker with many responsibilities, could never afford to do. Jane's own life was devoted to her husband and children. She never had time for her own interests, but her devotion seemed to go unappreciated. Once Jane was able to understand the underlying causes of her obsession, she could direct the energy that fueled her jealousy into discovering ways to find meaning in her own life.

The Jealous Person and the Jealousy-Producing Relationship

Until her husband's affair, Jane had never considered herself a jealous person. The affair made her change her self-perception. She "discovered" she was jealous. Question: Has your partner ever been unfaithful to you? People who answer yes are more likely to describe themselves as jealous. Actually, the more unfaithful people's mates are—in other words, the more they experience jealousy–provoking situations—the more likely they are to describe themselves as jealous. Unfaithfulness damages one's sense of security in a relationship. It makes one realize that even a good marriage can be threatened. And security, it turns out, buffers against jealousy. The more insecure you feel in a relationship, the more likely you are to be jealous. Of course, the level of security people feel in their relationships is not only a function of their adult attachment history but also (and probably even more so) of their childhood attachment history and style (Sharpsteen & Kirkpatrick, 1997).

A person's sense of security in a relationship is also related to general self–esteem. Yet, as Tuvia Melamed (1991) has pointed out, the level of security a relationship provides moderates the correlation between self–esteem and jealousy: The correlation is less evident in stable and well–established relationships and more evident in people who had experienced jealousy in previous relationships.

Question: How long do you expect the relationship to last? The longer one expects the relationship to last, the less likely one is to be jealous. It is revealing that the length of the relationship in and of itself was not at all related to jealousy—both young and old couples (in terms of the time they had been together) described themselves as jealous, and both young and old couples described themselves as nonjealous. The length that the relationship was expected to last, which is a measure of security and commitment, did correlate with jealousy—the more commitment, the less jealousy.

Commitment to a relationship doesn't develop in a vacuum. It's a reflection of the way a couple feels about each other and about the relationship. The more satisfied people are with their mate and the relationship, the data show, the less jealous they tend to be.

Does the jealousy cause the dissatisfaction, or does the dissatisfaction cause the jealousy? It can be argued that jealousy, with its ensuing drama, conflict, and unhappiness, is the cause of the insecurity and the dissatisfaction. On the other hand, it can also be argued that unstable, insecure, and unsatisfactory relationships make people more sensitive to threats and consequently more likely to experience jealousy. One interpretation focuses on the jealous person, the other on the jealous relationship. Which is correct? In the next two chapters both perspectives are elaborated, with the assumption that both are correct.

As noted before, people don't just fall into a certain kind of a relationship. They play an active role in shaping their relationships as well as problems. Some create relationships in which jealousy is not likely to be triggered. Others choose mates and help build relationships in which jealousy is likely to be triggered often. Once a jealous relationship is established, both mates have to collude to keep the jealousy problem alive.

Do you believe in monogamy? Most people, it turns out, believe that monogamy is the best type of relationship. This is true even for those who don't practice it (Pittman, 1989). While people who insist on sexual exclusivity in their intimate relationships tend to be more jealous than people for whom exclusivity is not that important, monogamous people tend to seek like–minded mates and consequently have relationships in which their jealousy is not likely to be triggered.[5]

If the connection between belief in monogamy and jealousy doesn't seem obvious, let me point to a more obvious connection, between what we do to others and what we fear they might do to us. Have you ever been unfaithful to your mate sexually (Never? Once? Very few times? Many times? All the time?)? The more unfaithful people themselves have been, the more jealous they are likely to be. The more lies one has told, the more attuned one's ear becomes to lies, at times hearing them even when they have not been spoken. The more schemes one has pulled off to get together with one's lover, the more suspicious one become of situations that might be such schemes.

"Projected jealousy" derives either from one's own actual unfaithfulness or from repressed impulses toward it (Freud, 1922/1955). Have you ever fantasized about sexual involvement with someone other than your mate? Most people have at times had such sexual fantasies. What is revealing is that those who fantasize most often about being with someone else are also those who describe themselves as most jealous.[6] Since they themselves are attracted to other people and possibly have thoughts about wild love affairs, they naturally assume that their mate has such thoughts too. Just as they think at times about eloping with a passionate lover, they are sure that their mate has such thoughts too. Projecting their own impulses onto their mate makes them jealous.

Jealousy can be projected onto other people besides one's mate. Indeed, individuals who describe themselves as jealous tend to think that more people in the general population are jealous than do people who describe themselves as not jealous.

Furthermore, people who describe themselves as jealous prefer their mates to be jealous and in general tend to see jealousy as a more positive personality characteristic. They are likely, for example, to see jealousy as a normal reaction that accompanies love, or as an instinctive reaction to a threat. They are less likely to see it as a defect.

It is possible that people who see themselves as less likely to control their jealous response need to believe that jealousy is not such a negative trait. The need to justify their own jealousy is so great that it keeps them from seeing the negative effect jealousy can have on intimate relationships. In fact, the more people described themselves as jealous, the more likely they were to have intimate relationships end because of their jealousy.

Is There a "Jealous Personality"?

People who have several intimate relationships end because of their jealousy usually describe themselves as having been jealous from a very young age. This has made some personality psychologists argue that such a thing as a "jealous personality" actually exists. Differences between people in the propensity to respond with jealousy, they claim, are not only valid and reliable over time—they even run in families.[7]

My own experience leads me to believe that labeling certain individuals as having "jealous personalities" doesn't do them much good, and can even be damaging. It is more helpful to look at people as having different predispositions to jealousy. As we saw in chapter one, jealousy originates very early in life. It is triggered again whenever there is a threat of losing a valued love relationship. People whom personality psychologists label "jealous personalities" tend to have had more traumatic experiences related to unfaithfulness, jealousy, or loss of love in their childhood, and consequently have greater predisposition to respond with jealousy later in life.

How jealous were you during the earlier stages of your life?

- during childhood?
- during adolescence?

- during young adulthood?
- during adulthood?

Of the people surveyed, the majority reported being most jealous during adolescence. It is possible that during this stormy period all experiences, including jealousy, are more intense. It is also possible that adolescents are most likely to fear losing their beloved because a lack of mutual commitment characterizes relationships at that stage of life. Both these reasons help explain the findings of a study of adolescents' love relationships. The study, which involved boys and girls aged 14–17, suggests that jealousy was the main cause of both physical and emotional violence among these adolescent couples (Gagne & Levoie, 1993).

Most people report decreasing levels of jealousy after adolescence (less during young adulthood than during adolescence and less during advanced adulthood than during young adulthood). There are several ways to interpret these findings. It is possible that over time, people develop better coping strategies for dealing with their jealousy. It is possible that, with experience, people avoid relationships in which their jealousy is likely to be triggered often. It is possible that with age most people become more sure of themselves and thus are less likely to be threatened by certain jealousy triggers.[8] It is possible that over time most couples develop a sense of security in their relationship and thus are less likely to view jealousy-triggering incidents as serious threats. And it is possible that the growing openness of society in general and the institution of marriage in particular has caused a general decline in jealousy.[9]

The fact that people who were more jealous than others in childhood also tend to be more jealous later in life supports the notion that people have stable predispositions for jealousy. Such a predisposition is influenced, among other things, by one's family constellation. Developmental psychologists see the roots of adult jealousy in sibling rivalry. The psychological pattern of reacting to jealousy triggers in later life, they argue, is determined by the child's first experience of jealousy when his desire for exclusivity with his mother is threatened by a sibling.[10]

In my research, the more older brothers people had, the more jealous they were likely to be. The more younger brothers they had, the less jealous they were likely to be. The number of sisters was not related to jealousy. This suggests that it's not the presence of a sibling in and of itself that triggers jealousy. The trigger has to be a sibling who is in a position of advantage (an older brother has an age and a sex advantage in our patriarchal society). Adult jealousy is influenced by childhood envy of the older sibling's advantage and by the childhood jealousy triangle with one's sibling and mother.[11]

People who have a predisposition to jealousy can expect those around them to notice it at some point. And they do. The more jealous people are (or consider themselves to be), the more likely it is that people who know them well will consider them jealous. It's not easy to hide the torment of jealousy.

If jealousy is hard to hide from people who know you, it is doubly hard to hide from intimate partners. They are the ones most likely both to trigger and to witness our jealousy. People are less likely to exhibit jealous behavior in public or in casual relationships and more likely to exhibit it in intimate relationships. One obvious reason is that jealousy is more likely to be triggered in an intimate relationship than in a less valued casual relationship. Another reason is that jealous behavior is generally considered socially unacceptable in our culture.[12]

Do people with whom you've had an intimate relationship consider you jealous? The more jealous people feel, the more likely it is that their romantic partners will consider them jealous (far more so than other people who know them well). The reason seems simple enough: When a person is jealous, their mate can't help but notice it and "tell it like it is." Right? Not necessarily. It is also possible that the more a mate considers one jealous, the more likely one will be to consider him or herself jealous. The mate may call one jealous for different reasons, only one of which is that one truly is jealous. Another reason, as we saw, is that the mate either has fantasies about sexual involvements with other people or has real affairs and makes one think one is excessively jealous to excuse his or her own behavior.

When I asked people what they thought caused jealousy, one of the two most common responses was "personal insecurity." Some people, and as we saw earlier some researchers, believe that jealousy is part of a person's personality, that those who are insecure in general are also insecure about their intimate relationships, and that insecurity manifests itself in jealousy.[13] Sounds straightforward enough, doesn't it? Yet the second top-rated explanation was, "Jealousy is the result of being afraid of losing face." Third in the ranking was, "Jealousy is the result of weakness in the relationship." Fourth was, "Jealousy results from feeling excluded and left out."

Being afraid of losing face, feeling excluded, and having problems in the relationship are not stable parts of a person's personality. Rather, they are related to the dynamics of a particular relationship or a particular situation.

This brings us back to the notion that jealousy always results from an interaction between a certain predisposition and a certain triggering event. The predisposition for jealousy is related to other personality characteristics such as insecurity and self-esteem. Whether or not the predisposition will actually reveal itself depends on the relationship—the nature of problems the couple experiences, involvement with other people, as well as the trust and sense of security that both partners have in the relationship.

Whether or not the predisposition to jealousy will reveal itself also depends on people's current mental state, which may have nothing to do with jealousy. The better one's mental state, the less likely one is to suffer from jealousy. Of course, being in the midst of a jealousy crisis doesn't have the best effect on one's mental state.[14]

Poor physical condition, to a lesser degree than poor mental condition, is also associated with a greater tendency to experience jealousy. The better one's physical condition in general, the less likely one is to suffer from jealousy.

Unlike the findings concerning the antecedents of jealousy in people's early childhood experiences—about which they can do little—the findings about the correlation between mental and physical condition on the one hand, and jealousy on the other hand, can be translated to specific recommendations.

People who are frequently tormented by jealousy can prepare themselves to deal with the problem by improving their general mental and physical health. (Mental health can be improved by therapy, by relaxation exercises, or by doing things that make one feel good.) When people feel better psychologically, they are likely to suffer less from jealousy, even if other factors contributing to the situation haven't changed. Similarly, getting into better physical shape improves one's ability to cope with all of life's stresses, including jealousy. People who enjoy dancing, for example, can put on music with a good beat and dance for fifteen minutes each day, especially when depressed, and it will have a positive effect both on their mood and their physical condition—which is likely to help them handle their jealousy more effectively.

A Word about Mild Jealousy

Thus far the focus has been extreme jealousy, the kind that causes tremendous pain and rage. Jealousy is not always that extreme; it comes in milder forms, too. Most people experience mild jealousy far more often than extreme jealousy ("every time I see him flirting with an attractive woman"; "every time she expresses admiration of another man"). The experience lasts a far shorter time (seconds as compared to days or months) and is much less painful and traumatic. In fact, some people even say that this type of jealousy adds spice to their relationships. A woman who describes herself as very happily married explains:

> When I see him flirting with an attractive woman, his eyes shining and his whole face radiating, it reminds me of what a handsome man he is. I feel a twinge of jealousy, but it's not an unpleasant feeling. I can even say that I rather like it. It brings excitement into our relationship, a tease. It assumes I don't take him for granted. What makes me so cool about it is the fact that I feel secure in his love, and know that when we go home we are going to talk about that other woman, and laugh about it all.

Jealousy is like a hot pepper. Use it mildly, and you add spice to the relationship. Use too much of it and it can burn. Indeed, in one of my studies of marriage burnout I discovered that the more people experienced intense jealousy in their relationship, the more likely they were to burn out.[15] The reverse seems true of mild jealousy.

The "Jealous Person" and the "Nonjealous Person"

People who describe themselves as "jealous" also describe themselves as suffering from jealousy more intensely and more frequently than people who describe themselves as "not jealous." For the former group, jealousy is more easily triggered and it lasts longer. They consider their jealousy more of a problem and report experiencing more jealousy during all stages of their life. Other people help validate their perception of themselves as jealous. People who know them well, and people with whom they have had intimate relationships, consider them jealous.

Yet, as we have seen throughout this chapter, people who describe themselves as not jealous also experience jealousy when an important relationship is threatened. Furthermore, they experience it with the same physical, emotional, and cognitive symptoms as people who define themselves as jealous. They experience it in response to similar triggers and in a similar rank order: An affair with someone they know and envy triggers the most jealousy, and an affair with someone they don't know and of whom they have a low opinion triggers the least jealousy.

While the triggers and the actual experience of jealousy are similar in both groups, there are a number of differences between the relationships of self-described jealous and nonjealous people. Nonjealous people feel more secure in their relationships, expect them to last longer, and are more certain that their partners have never been unfaithful. By contrast, it appears that even when self-described jealous people have good reasons to feel insecure in their relationships and experience jealousy, many view their jealousy as a personality trait. They don't say, "I feel jealous because my husband of thirty-five years has had an affair." They say instead, "I feel this intense jealousy because I am a jealous person." One response implies that the problem is a result of the situation and thus can be changed. The other implies that the problem is built into the individual's personality and thus is hard to change.

Given the great agreement among people about what triggers jealousy and how it is experienced, it's amazing that some choose to explain it as a personality trait about which there is little they can do, while others explain it in the context of a particular situation about which they can do quite a lot.

It is possible, of course, that some people view their jealousy as a personality trait because it explains behaviors that would otherwise be unacceptable. Sexual jealousy is widely accepted as grounds for moral indignation in our culture. "Feeling jealous" serves as an explanation or excuse for a wide range of hostile, bitter, and even violent actions. Without the legitimizing context of jealousy, these actions would be taken as symptoms of severe pathology and derangement (Wagner, 1976).

Not surprisingly, people who describe themselves as jealous also tend to attribute more positive effects to jealousy and see it more positively overall than do people who view themselves as not jealous. For example, jealous people tend to believe that jealousy teaches us not to take each other for granted, makes relationships last longer, induces commitment, brings excitement to listless relationships, makes one's mate look more desirable, and makes one examine one's relationship.

But although being "a jealous person" can be effective in excusing certain unacceptable behaviors ("That's why I don't want you to dance with anyone else"; "That's why I had a temper tantrum"), in the long run it causes more problems than it solves. The reason: It greatly reduces people's freedom to act and their ability to cope directly with jealousy triggers.

Having said that, let me return to the question presented at the beginning of this chapter: Are you a jealous person? Whatever people's answer to this question is, they are usually very interested in learning about the unconscious roots of their jealousy—the subject of the next chapter.

A Note to Therapists

The Romantic Jealousy Questionnaire can be used as a diagnostic tool prior to individual therapy, couple therapy, or a jealousy workshop. It can also be used during therapy (starting with the most extreme experience of jealousy). At times, this is what brought the person or couple in to begin with. In these cases, the jealousy is likely related to the discovery of an affair.

The discovery of an affair is a very traumatic experience for a couple. The betrayed spouse is likely to be experiencing posttraumatic stress disorder symptoms. Often, just naming the symptoms seems to help. It suggests that the jealous person is not crazy, just suffering from a known trauma. The treatment of this trauma can be done using cognitive, behavioral, systemic, or psychodynamic techniques suggested throughout the book.

3
The Unconscious Roots of Romantic Jealousy

ॐ ॐ ॐ

No one who ... conjures up the most evil of those half-tamed demons that inhibit the human breast, and seeks to wrestle with them, can expect to come through the struggle unscathed.

–Sigmund Freud, "Dora"

ॐ ॐ ॐ

Jealousy Is Normal and Universal

According to Freud (1922/1955), jealousy is universal not because it is innate, but because it is inevitable. No one can escape it because it originates in painful childhood experiences we all share. These universal childhood traumas are reexperienced whenever our jealousy is evoked in adulthood.

Because everyone experiences it, jealousy is, by definition, normal. Indeed, Freud describes jealousy as "one of those affective states, like grief, that may be described as normal. If anyone appears to be without it, the inference can be justified that it has undergone severe repression and consequently plays all the greater part in his unconscious mental life."

In Freud's view, if a person does not experience jealousy when an important relationship is threatened, something is not altogether right about him. It is akin to not feeling grief when someone you care deeply about dies. Such a response most probably means that the person is working hard to suppress the feelings of jealousy and hide them from self and others.

In 1979, fifty–six years after the publication of Freud's work on jealousy, a psychiatrist named Emil Pinta published an article entitled "Pathological Tolerance," describing a clinical syndrome in which a person who should be jealous is not. Pinta cites several cases in which a husband or a wife accepted a sexual relationship between his or her mate and a third person (Pinta, 1979).

In one case, John (25 years old) and Sharon (33 years old) were married. Michael (age 17), a high–school dropout who was originally hired to help with chores on the farm, lived with them and had become Sharon's lover. Sharon insisted that she loved both men and was unwilling to make a choice between them. John resented having another man in his home making love to his wife, yet was reluctant to leave or to pressure Sharon to decide between himself and Michael.

In another case, Lana (26 years old) was married to Jack (32 years old). During the year prior to her starting therapy, another woman, Marilyn (32 years old) lived with them in their home and shared Jack sexually. Marilyn and Jack worked during the day, leaving Lana at home to babysit Marilyn's two children from a previous marriage. Lana described herself as feeling "unappreciated and misunderstood" by Jack, Marilyn, and the children. Her primary reason for entering therapy was to "have the children obey me." She was aware that her relationship with Jack and Marilyn was emotionally destructive, but refused to consider leaving or insisting that Marilyn leave. Pinta suggests that the dynamics of pathological tolerance are identical to those of pathological jealousy. We will return to the dynamics of pathological tolerance (and to the two triangles) after we examine the dynamics of pathological jealousy. For now, suffice it to say that most people would probably agree with Pinta that in both John's and Lana's case, something is not quite "normal" about their lack of jealousy and their entire relationship.

A clinical syndrome similar to pathological tolerance is "psychological scotoma" (blindness), the inability to notice or to correctly interpret situations that are obvious jealousy triggers to virtually everyone else. An example of psychological scotoma that was first mentioned in chapter one is the husband whose wife flirts with every man around and sleeps with anyone willing and able; the husband is the only one who doesn't know and doesn't suspect. A woman who became sexually involved with a man whose wife seemed to be suffering from psychological scotoma describes the strange experience:

> We were dancing so provocatively, practically making out, that I don't think there was anyone at the party who didn't notice that something was going on. Anyone besides his wife, that is. She was chatting with her friends, smiling at us from time to time. I know she doesn't like to dance and her husband says she doesn't like sex either, so she simply doesn't see when he is mak–ing out with other women. Since he insists that he has to have sex every single day, and for her once every three months is more than enough, there's a lot for her not to see. Who knows, maybe she is relieved that someone else is doing her "dirty work."

The Psychodynamic Approach to Jealousy

The psychodynamic approach emphasizes the unconscious forces operating in jealousy. It assumes that deep in their psyches all peo-ple carry drives, desires, fears, and traumatic memories of which they are not consciously aware. Every conscious feeling and thought is accompanied by its unconscious counterpart, which is often its opposite: One may be consciously disgusted by things to which one is unconsciously attracted; one may consciously love people one unconsciously hates.

The emphasis on innate drives and unconscious motives explains behaviors that are otherwise difficult to understand, such as why some people stay with a mate who is continuously unfaithful to them and why some people drive away a mate they love dearly with groundless jealousy. The psychodynamic approach assumes that people play an active (even if unconscious) role in creating their life circumstances as well as their intimate relationships. It wasn't peo-ple's bad luck that landed them in a relationship with a "pathologi-cally unfaithful" or a "pathologically jealous" mate. They chose their mate very carefully to fill that role.

People's earliest childhood memories, traumas, and deprivations, most of them unconscious, have a powerful influence on the way people experience and respond to the world. Childhood experiences also have a great influence on their choice of a mate. That choice is never arbitrary. Most often people choose a person who is best suited to fulfill emotional needs that were not fulfilled in their childhood.

When one finds such a person, one projects onto him or her the internal image that was shaped during one's childhood. A man who saw his mother cheating on his father may, for example, project his internalized image of an unfaithful wife, which was shaped by the childhood trauma, onto his chaste and faithful wife. Couples have complementary needs. Each mate chooses someone who represents a repressed part of himself or herself. A man who had to repress the emotional part of himself, for example, marries an emotional woman who had to repress the logical part of herself. Their internal conflict becomes externalized as a marital conflict ("Why isn't he more emotional?" "Why isn't she more logical?"). Conflicts between mates, around issues of jealousy as well as all other issues, are a reenactment of inner conflicts. If, for example, infidelity is a recurring issue in a certain couple's conflicts, chances are that both partners have some internal conflict about it.

Childhood experiences of jealousy do not "cause" the adult jealousy. They are reevoked in similar situations and determine how easily and how intensely people will respond to jealousy triggers. The goal of therapy is to bring the unconscious into consciousness. A therapist can help the person suffering from a jealousy problem gain insight into the "true" causes of their jealousy by making the connection between past experiences and present problems. Once people come to understand the roots of their jealousy—that is, which past events are replayed in their current jealousy—and what they are gaining by holding on to it, they are considered cured.

The Roots of Jealousy According to Freud

Freud believed that it is "easy to see" that jealousy is composed of:

- grief, the pain caused by the thought of losing someone we love
- the painful realization that we can't have everything we want, even if we want it very badly and feel we deserve to have it
- feelings of enmity against the successful rival
- greater or lesser amount of self-criticism that hold us accountable for our loss

"Although we may call it normal," Freud added, "this jealousy is by no means completely rational, that is, derived from the actual situation, proportionate to the real circumstances and under the complete control of the conscious ego." In other words, even in normal jealousy—the kind we all experience—there are always some irrational components. The reason is that jealousy "is rooted deep in the unconscious, and is a continuation of the earliest stirrings of the child's affective life" (Freud, 1922/1955, p. 223).

As noted in chapter one, during the discussion of jealousy and envy, Freud believed that jealousy is rooted primarily in childhood events associated with the Oedipal conflict. This takes place during the phallic stage, when the sex organ is becoming the child's center of interest and enjoyment.

Since boys' and girls' sex organs are different, the issues they have to work through are different. Freud acknowledged the importance of this fact for boys' and girls' psychosexual development in his famous dictum: "Anatomy is destiny."

Children spend most of their time with family members. Consequently, family members are their most accessible objects of love and identification. It is only natural for them to direct their first sexual feelings toward someone in the family. For a boy, most often, that someone is Mother; for a girl, it is Father. The sexual feelings are accompanied by enmity against the person whom the child perceives as a rival. This rivalry is the root of the Oedipal complex in boys and the Electra complex in girls.[1]

Oedipus and Electra are tragic heroes of Greek mythology. Oedipus, unbeknown to himself, killed his father and married his mother. Electra loved her father and hated her mother, who betrayed him and caused his death. To avenge her father's death, Electra persuaded her brother to kill their mother. According to Freud, every child experiences some of Oedipus and Electra's pain. The boy is "in love" with his mother; the girl is "in love" with her father. But both have a formidable rival—for the boy, his father; for the girl, her mother. The boy is afraid of his father's anger at discovering that his son covets his wife. He escapes this anxiety by identifying with his father and becoming a man like him. The girl envies her mother's advantage, and overcomes it by identifying with the mother. The grief, the pain of loss, the powerlessness, the realization that they can't have everything they want, the enmity against a successful rival that children experience when they "lose" in this original triangle are all engraved on their psyches and reemerge in adulthood when they find themselves in a similar love triangle.

Projected and Delusional Jealousy

Freud distinguished "normal" jealousy from "projected" and "delusional" jealousy—both of which he viewed as pathological.

Projected jealousy, according to Freud, is derived either from actual infidelity or from impulses toward infidelity that have been repressed. A man who has been unfaithful, or desired another woman but didn't act on it, may "project" that infidelity onto his innocent wife—blaming her for the things he did or wanted to do, and then responding to the projected threat with jealousy.

"It is a matter of everyday experience," Freud wrote, "that fidelity, especially that degree of it required in marriage, is only maintained in the face of continual temptations." Even a person who denies these temptations in himself experiences them. How can such a person relieve his guilt over the impulse or the actual infidelity? One way is to "project his own impulses to faithlessness on to the partner to whom he owes faith. He can then justify himself with the thought that the other is not much better than himself" (Freud, 1922/1955, p. 224).

The jealousy that arises from such projection, says Freud, has an almost delusional character. (Delusion is a belief that persists even with no basis in reality.) Projected jealousy, however, unlike delusional jealousy, often responds well to therapy.

When the jealous person realizes that his jealousy is a result of his own suppressed impulses toward infidelity and that his or her partner has been faithful, the insight is usually enough to solve the jealousy problem. In the case of delusional jealousy, the solution is not so easy.

Delusional jealousy is a form of paranoia. It too has its origin in suppressed impulses toward infidelity, but according to Freud, the object in these cases is of the same sex as the jealous person. (As we will see later, modern psychoanalysts tend to disagree with Freud on this point.) Freud believed that babies and young children are bisexual. Only with maturity and the pressures of socialization, sexual preference (most often heterosexuality) develops. Young children, prior to the Oedipal stage, are attracted to the same sex parent as well as the opposite sex parent. These feelings are repressed, but may emerge again in the form of conscious or unconscious attraction toward one's rival in adult jealousy. This kind of homosexual attraction, according to Freud, is the primary cause and feature of delusional jealousy. In an attempt to defend himself against his unduly strong homosexual impulse, the jealous man says, in effect, "I don't love him, she loves him." Since the homosexual impulse produces much more anxiety than the heterosexual impulse the defense against it is more likely to involve a serious distortion of reality.

Freud presents as an example of delusional jealousy a young man whose object of jealousy was his impeccably faithful wife. The jealousy came in attacks that lasted several days and appeared regularly on the day after he had had sex with his wife. Freud's inference was that after satisfying the heterosexual drive, the homosexual drive that was also stimulated by the sexual act "forced an outlet for itself in the attack of jealousy."

The jealous attacks were focused on minute gestures in which his wife's "quite unconscious coquetry, unnoticed to anyone else, has betrayed itself to him." She had unintentionally touched the man sitting next to her; she had turned too much toward him, or had smiled more pleasantly than when at home with her husband. The husband was unusually sensitive to all these manifestations of her unconscious and knew how to interpret them. In this he was similar to people suffering from paranoia, who cannot regard anything other people do as indifferent. They too interpret every minute gesture—a person laughed to himself, looked with indifference, even spit on the ground—as directed at them personally.

The jealous husband perceived his wife's unfaithfulness instead of his own. By paying careful attention to hers and magnifying it enormously, he was able to keep his own unfaithfulness unconscious. Similarly, the hatred that the persecuted paranoid sees in others is a reflection of his own hostile impulses toward them.

As expected, Freud finds the reasons for the husband's delusional jealousy in his early childhood history. The husband's youth was dominated by a strong attachment to his mother. Of her many sons he was her declared favorite and developed a marked "normal" jealousy toward her. When he got engaged, his desire for a virgin mother expressed itself in obsessive doubts about his fiancee's virginity. These doubts disappeared after their marriage. The first years of his marriage were free of jealousy. Then he became involved in a long-term affair with another woman. When the affair was over, his jealousy attacks started again. This time it was projected jealousy, which enabled him to relieve his guilt about his own infidelity. The fact that his father had little influence in the family combined with a "humiliating homosexual trauma in early boyhood" are described by Freud as the roots of a strong sexual attraction he felt toward his father-in-law, which eventually became a "fully formed jealous paranoia."

Most clinicians working with people who have a jealousy problem agree with Freud that jealousy can vary in degree of pathology all the way from normal to delusional jealousy. They also agree with Freud that delusional jealousy is a form of paranoia and is the hardest to treat and cure. Many do not agree, however, that delusional jealousy is primarily the result of repressed impulses toward homosexuality.

An example of a modern psychoanalytic use of Freud's ideas about jealousy is provided in Dr. Emil Pinta's analysis of the dynamics of pathological tolerance (Pinta, 1979).

Pathological Tolerance

Like pathological jealousy, pathological tolerance (those rare cases described as "abnormally nonjealous") has its origin in the Oedipal conflict. In both, the individual recreates an early family situation and unconscious Oedipal wishes. In the triangle involving John, Sharon, and Michael, John felt, at the birth of his younger brother, that he had been replaced in his mother's love. A similar relationship has been reenacted in his marriage, with Sharon representing his mother and Michael his brother. In the triangle involving Lana, Jack, and Marilyn, the similarities to Lana's family history are even more striking. Jack and Marilyn work and take on the role of surrogate parents while Lana assumes a "big sister" role to Marilyn's children. In therapy, Lana said she felt just the way she used to feel with her siblings. Also, Jack was openly unfaithful to Lana, just as her father was openly unfaithful to her mother.

Another mechanism seen in pathological tolerance that Freud noted in delusional jealousy is the projection of unconscious homosexual impulses. In the first triangle, John's physical attraction to Michael was quite evident. They established a considerable intimacy, sometimes to the exclusion of Sharon. In the second triangle, Lana had a history of homosexuality, and her attraction to Marilyn was evident. The close proximity in which sexual relations occurred in the triad strongly implies the gratification of unconscious homosexual impulses.

Diagnosing Delusional Jealousy

In the official Diagnostic and Statistical Manual of Mental Disorders of the American Psychiatric Association (the DSM–IV) delusional jealousy is described as a subtype of a delusional disorder. The "jealous type" applies

> when the central theme of the person's delusion is that his or her spouse or lover is unfaithful. This belief is arrived at without due cause and is based on incorrect inference supported by small bits of "evidence" (e.g. disarrayed clothing or spots on the sheets), which are collected and used to justify the delusion. The individual with the delusion usually confronts the spouse or lover and attempts to intervene in the imagined infidelity (e.g. restricting the spouse's autonomy, secretly following the spouse, investigating the imagined lover, attacking the spouse) (American Psychiatric Association, 1994, p. 297).

Pathological jealousy is also mentioned as one of the seven criteria for a diagnosis of Paranoid Personality Disorder. People with this disorder "may be pathologically jealous, often suspecting that their spouse or sexual partner is unfaithful without any adequate justification (Criterion A7). They may gather trivial and circumstantial 'evidence' to support their jealous beliefs. They want to maintain complete control of intimate relationships to avoid being betrayed and may constantly question and challenge the whereabouts, actions, intentions, and fidelity of their spouse or partner" (p. 635).

While some clinicians restrict the term delusional jealousy to those cases in which delusions of jealousy are demonstrable and dominate the case, others consider jealousy pathological even in the absence of delusions, where an individual exhibits jealousy with undue haste or intensity in response to events that question, even remotely, the partner's fidelity (Enoch, 1991). Sam is an example.

Sam and Amalya

Amalya describes the problem:

> Sam's jealousy is most likely to flare up when we are making love. It happens often. All of a sudden I feel him withdrawing. The first time it happened I didn't know what hit me. We were in Paris having the most wonderful time. Suddenly, in the middle of lovemaking, he stopped and pushed me away.... By now I've learned what it means. He is disgusted by me. He can't touch me. My body repulses him. He imagines me having sex with other men I was involved with in the past. He can imagine me playing with another man's penis, or the man kissing my nipple, things like that. He thinks my sex with other men was dirty, and it makes him see me as dirty, cheap, despicable, not worthy of someone as pure and wholesome as he is. Once, during a jealousy attack he blared, "All women are whores, except Mary." Mary is his ex-wife. He tells me he didn't love her. They rarely had sex. Mary was dependent on him for everything—she never put gas in their car (which she was the only one to drive) because she didn't know how. When she went shopping, he would follow her on his motorcycle, pay, and carry the bags. Why did he stay with her ten years? Because he was sure she was faithful. Mary couldn't manage without a man around her. She couldn't manage without him.

Sam's parents had a very unusual marriage. His mother—an exceptionally beautiful woman—had an illicit affair with another man for many years. His father, whom Sam describes as passive, weak, impotent, and jealous, also had many affairs throughout their marriage.

When Sam was 15 years old, he and his brother went to get his mother a present for Mother's Day. At the bus stop they saw his mother waiting. She didn't notice them. As they watched, a big blue car rolled by and stopped next to her. The door opened. His mother went in. Sam could see her kissing the man in the car. Afterward, he saw the same big car parked next to the house many times when his father was away. He knew not to go in.

In the mornings, after his father left the house, the man used to call. His mother would take the telephone into the bathroom and have long erotic conversations with her lover while Sam listened outside the door.

Sam's father must have discovered the affair, because one day he appeared with a gun, while his mother had her women friends over for coffee. He started screaming, "I'm going to kill you, you whore!" Sam was in the house at the time and had to rescue his mother from his father's rage.

After the jealousy scene, his father collapsed and had to be hospitalized for what appeared to be a heart attack. Sam, forever the family rescuer, was the one who took him to the hospital.

When Sam was 16 years old, he fell in love with a beautiful young woman, whom he describes as "the cheap type." He never went to bed with her, yet he suffered tremendous jealousy. His first sexual experience was with a married woman neighbor much older than himself. He didn't love this older woman and wasn't jealous of her. He also didn't love Mary, whom he met when he was 17 years old. But Mary seemed to love and need him and she wasn't the type to provoke his jealousy, so he married her.

It may be worth noting that Sam's sister, who is ten years older than him, is unhappily married to an abusive man who has frequent jealousy attacks during which he beats her. She has many affairs, but still remains with him—thus replicating her mother's infidelity and reliving her father's jealousy tantrums.

When Sam met Amalya, he had been separated from his wife but had not yet gone through the divorce. While he was certain that he was unhappy in his marriage, he loved his two young boys and was reluctant to give up completely the security the family gave him. But Amalya is an attractive and charming woman (eight years older than he is), and he fell in love with her in a way he never allowed himself before.

When Amalya met Sam, she said right away that he was the man she wanted to marry. She had never said that about another man, and she had dated many. Before Sam, Amalya wasn't exactly discriminating in her choice of men. The only thing these men seemed to have in common was their unavailability—whether because they were married or because they were emotionally unavailable. That was just fine with Amalya. Having grown up with a father and mother who had had a suffocating symbiotic relationship, she valued her freedom and independence. Things started changing after her 35th birthday. Amalya decided she wanted a family. She was ready, and Sam was the man she had been waiting for.

Their affair was passionate. Sam came to Amalya's house every day after work and they made wild, sweet, passionate love for hours. Sex had never been that exciting for Sam, never that sweet for Amalya.

Their trip to Paris was the climax of the affair. Sam had always wanted to visit Paris, and for him it was a dream come true. For Amalya, the chance to be together twenty-four hours a day was the most important thing; Paris was just a wonderful addition. Spending all their time together made her realize that this was what she wanted. She told Sam she wanted to get married and have a child. This was the backdrop of Sam's first jealousy attack. As Amalya recounts the event:

> He tells me he can never marry me until he trusts me completely. He is troubled by those dark corners in me that are responsible for my past, that might emerge again in the future. Since I was unfaithful in the past, by going to bed with ex-lovers while I dated other men, what guarantee does he have that I'm not going to be unfaithful in the future? After every jealousy attack he feels guilty and remorseful, and apologizes profusely. He tells me he hopes I have the strength and the patience to cope with his jealousy. He asks for my help in dealing with it himself. He knows that it's his own problem and I have nothing to do with it, but when his jealousy flares up, he has no control.
>
> I try to reassure him in every conceivable way. I tell him that I never had such wonderful sex with anyone else. I tell him that my vast experience with other men should make him feel secure—because I have chosen him, and I love him in a way I never loved before. Since I had all those casual sexual experiences, I know what they are like and I have no desire whatsoever to go back to them. Actually, I say to him, I'm the one who should be concerned, because he has had so few sexual relationships that he may still be curious and at some point want to experiment. For me, all that is finished.

But nothing I say seems to matter. He knows I love him, but he can't understand my past. How could I have done the things I've done? They seem so unlike the person he thinks he knows. The fact that I did them makes him distrust me. The threat he feels is so immense that nothing I say calms it.

The Roots of Delusional Jealousy

When Sam was an adolescent, he discovered that his mother was having an illicit affair. Adolescence is considered the second Oedipal period. What goes on in the mind of a boy like Sam, in this period of heightened sexuality, when he discovers that his mother is unfaithful to his father? Psychotherapists John Docherty and Jean Ellis describe one possible consequence. Docherty and Ellis (1976) treated three couples whose chief complaint was "obsessive–delusional jealousy" in the husbands. A striking coincidental finding emerged in these couples during the course of treatment. In all three cases the husband had witnessed his mother engaged in extramarital sexual relations during his early adolescence.

The jealous husbands' accusations diverged noticeably from a realistic picture of their wives. In fact, the accusations more appropriately fitted their mothers. In one case, the husband claimed his wife of twenty-seven years was drinking excessively and having sex with undesirable characters. He monitored her telephone calls, examined her purse, and berated her until she knelt at his feet and begged him to trust her. During the course of treatment it became apparent that the man's accusations didn't fit his wife—but did fit his mother.

The mother was an alcoholic; as an adolescent he had to bring her home on several occasions because she was too drunk to get home on her own. She had worked as a waitress and fraternized with various unsavory customers.

Having noticed these discrepancies, the therapists pursued the matter further until the man recalled a memory that carried a great emotional charge. When he was 12 years old he had returned home unexpectedly early one day and found his mother having sex with a strange man. He had not said a thing about it, even though his mother's affairs became the subject of violent arguments between his parents. It had left him feeling bitter resentment toward his mother and guilty disloyalty toward his father.

In the second case, a couple who had been married for two years sought treatment after the husband became enraged by his wife's suspected infidelities. He had been drinking heavily and had become physically abusive. The husband's suspiciousness had plagued the couple's relationship almost from the start. The wife had learned to be extremely cautious in her interactions with other men. At parties she could only be with her husband or with other women, never with other men. He needed to know her whereabouts at all times.

In the course of treatment the therapists noticed again that the man accused his wife of things that were not true of her, but were true of his mother, such as gross negligence in her household duties. This led them to pursue the question of the mother's sexual activities. The husband remembered that when he was a young teenager, he had seen his mother at a neighborhood tavern with other men. On one occasion he had come home and seen her having sex with one of those men. He had not told his father, but from that time on had tried to cut himself off emotionally from his mother.

In the third case, too, the husband was convinced that his faithful wife was having affairs. Once again it came out that when he was 14 years old, he had returned home one day after having been sent shopping by his mother, and had found her having sex with a strange man.

From Freud's perspective (1922/1955), it's obvious why a mother's sexual infidelity would have such a traumatic effect, especially when it happens in early adolescence—a period characterized by an Oedipal resurgence. As the mother has demonstrated that she can be sexually available to someone other than the father, the adolescent experiences a marked intensification of Oedipal fantasies and drive toward their fulfillment. However, while the mother appears to be more sexually available to the boy, she is not. Her promiscuity constitutes, in effect, a tease.

The trauma can also explain the aggression that at times accompanies jealousy in these cases. Docherty and Ellis (1976) explain:

> The rage that the son feels for being second best in the Oedipal situation is exacerbated in a more serious, profound, and damaging way. Now he is not only second best to his father but to a strange man who has no valid claim on his mother at all.

By cuckolding the father, the mother makes him second best. Thus the son is unable to use identification with the father to achieve preeminence. He is doomed unalterably to second-rate status" (p. 681).

It is significant that all three men described their fathers as hard-working, long-suffering, and passive. We can add to the list Sam's description of his father as passive, weak, and impotent.

It is not necessary for the adolescent boy actually to witness his mother engaged in sexual intercourse for the trauma to occur. Finding out about her infidelity (the way Sam did) or seeing her acting openly flirtatious with other men can be enough.

The rage the boy experiences upon discovering his mother's infidelity is enormous, and so is his need to undo the trauma. How does he accomplish this? One way is to marry someone who will never be unfaithful, and then continuously harass her with groundless accusations of infidelity. For these men, the faithful wife represents Mother, the way she should have been in their childhood fantasies. He accuses the wife of being unfaithful, the way his mother was in reality. The accusations enable him to replay his childhood trauma, but with a different ending. His wife's repeated assurances of her fidelity are supposed to help undo the terrible reality of his mother's betrayal. Yet no reassurance is quite enough because the trauma was enormous, the wife is not the mother, and the situation is not really the same.

This helps explain why people with delusional jealousy avoid situations that might provide positive proof of their suspicions. They don't really want to believe that their mates have been unfaithful. On the contrary, they want to be convinced that unlike their fathers, and unlike the childhood situation, this time they are "number one" with their faithful mates.

Choosing a faithful wife and harassing her with groundless accusations is one way a man tries to overcome a trauma of his mother's betrayal. Another way is to choose an unfaithful mate who will provide ample opportunities to master the childhood trauma. In this case the jealousy is not delusional; it derives from an actual situation. Yet it is still not under complete control of the conscious ego. It represents a "repetition compulsion," an irrational need to replicate a traumatic experience. In such a case the adult seeks situations in which he or she seems to master repressed conflicts and traumas of childhood, even while the true conflicts remain repressed.

Not all people suffering from delusional jealousy have a parent who was sexually unfaithful during their adolescence. Another cause, in my experience, is a perceived threat to the relationship that is projected on the partner, but has other causes. An example is a woman who was convinced that her loving husband had an affair with his secretary. Her jealousy was groundless. It started after a series of terrible losses that included the death of one of her twin boys from cancer, followed by the death of her mother and of an older sister who raised her. (The mother, who had twelve kids, did not have much time for her.) What seemed to have triggered the jealousy was another sister's painful discovery that her husband had been unfaithful. The woman's childhood experiences as the tenth child in a poor family with an overworked and overburdened mother did not give her enough security in her own loveability. The losses she experienced made her feel even more dependent on her husband's love. The thought that she could loose him was terrifying. No assurance of his love was enough to calm her anxiety. She felt that if she were to loose him (like she lost her child, her mother, her sister) she would die. With the influence of her sister's painful experience of betrayal, her fear of abandonment took the shape of delusional jealousy.

Another antecedent of delusional jealousy reported in the literature is either undergratification or overgratification by parents during the earliest stages of life—both of which leave the person in chronic need of self-aggrandizing love from others and suspicious of rivals. In clinical terms: narcissism. Such people enter relationships to bolster their self-esteem. When doing so they unconsciously relive their childhoods.[2]

In men, another cause of delusional jealousy is real or imagined smallness of the penis. Clinical work with men who suffer from this problem suggests that they feel at a disadvantage to other men in the struggle to obtain and hold a mate. Their feelings of inadequacy—which are also common among impotent husbands, elderly husbands married to young wives, and plain spouses wedded to handsome ones—pave the way for the advent of delusional jealousy (Todd et al., 1971).

Similarly, delusional jealousy in elderly individuals was found to be related to such things as organic disease that rendered the older person housebound, disparity in age and health between the older person and the spouse, and previous infidelity (Breitner & Anderson, 1994).

In addition to psychological antecedents of delusional jealousy, studies found it to be related to a variety of organic causes including brain damage, organic psychoses, alcoholism, and alcohol psychosis, as well as such seemingly unrelated problems as hyperthyroidism and carcinoma.[3] Interestingly, in women, the ovulatory phase of the menstrual cycle was found to increase sensitivity to jealousy (Krug et al., 1996).

However, delusional jealousy is best known for its relationship to a variety of severe mental disorders, especially schizophrenia and paranoia. It was also found in people diagnosed as suffering from borderline personality disorder and mental handicap.[4]

It should be noted that when researchers are talking about the prevalence of delusional jealousy in those psychiatric disorders, they are not talking about very high percentages. In one much-quoted study by Michael Soyka et al. (1991), case histories of 8,134 psychiatric inpatients were reviewed. The prevalence of delusional jealousy overall was only 1.1%. It was most frequent in organic psychoses (7%), paranoid disorders (6.7%), alcohol psychoses (5.6%), and schizophrenia (2.5%).

Since delusional jealousy in these psychiatric disorders is organic, caused at least in part by chemical changes in the brain, the treatment of choice for most psychiatrists and many clinical psychologists is pharmacological, which is to say, drug therapy.[5] Cognitive-behavioral therapists, many of whom oppose such chemical intervention, suggest instead cognitive techniques for the treatment of delusional jealousy.[6] System oriented therapists believe that it is the couple, not the individual, that should be treated in the case of delusional jealousy.[7] The majority of psychodynamic therapists agree with Freud that delusional jealousy is a defense, or the result of a defense, against repressed memories, and thus it is best treated by individual psychotherapy.[8]

Having explored the psychodynamic explanation of delusional jealousy, and some of the approaches that have been used in treating it, we can return to Sam and Amalya.

Back to Sam and Amalya

After falling in love with a woman like his mother (both promiscuous and attractive) and suffering the painful jealousy such a relationship can generate, Sam chose to marry a woman he did not love and who, because of her dependence on him, was sure to be faithful. It worked. Throughout the years of his marriage Sam never felt the pangs of jealousy. The price was that he didn't feel the ecstasy of love, either—just a comforting sense of security. For a while this was enough.

Things were sure to be different with Amalya, an attractive woman who had had many sexual liaisons with other men, just as his mother had done. A relationship with her had to be both more passionate and more emotionally risky.

Sam's jealousy of Amalya was not entirely delusional—he was not harassing her about imaginary affairs with other men. His jealousy was of men she had indeed had affairs with and, for all he knew, could have affairs with again. Yet Sam's jealousy wasn't rational, either; it wasn't congruent with reality. Sam knew Amalya loved him and was faithful, yet he couldn't stop imagining her with other men, men she no longer cared about.

Why would anyone imagine things that cause him pain? One of the factors contributing to Sam's jealousy was an unconscious mechanism called "split-off projection." The "split-off" part is a disavowed part of themselves that people project onto another person. They do this because it is easier to deal with negative features in another person than it is to deal with them in oneself. If one believes oneself to be lascivious and immoral, one can try to cope with and control these difficult feelings. One can also do something that turns out to be much easier: choose someone appropriate and project these qualities onto that person. This makes it possible for a person to deal with the feelings in interactions with the spouse, without having to acknowledge that they are within themselves.

In Sam's case, the "split-off" was the part of him that was like his mother: immoral, lascivious, unfaithful. Sam could not accept that he was like his mother. He could not accept that maybe, just maybe, he too did the unthinkable (for example, desired his own mother). Once he split off that part of himself and suppressed it, he could convince himself that he was pure and moral. But the split-off part

pushed to be expressed, and it was finally expressed in Sam's relationship with Amalya. Sam projected on Amalya his forbidden
desires and the internalized image of his unfaithful mother.

While Sam was helpless to do anything when he witnessed his
mother's unfaithfulness as a child, as an adult he had some control
over the situation he perceived as similar. He could punish Amalya
(who represented his mother) for her involvement with other men
by withdrawing from her sexually and by refusing to marry her. It
is telling, however, that Sam started doing this only after he was sure
that Amalya loved him and would not be unfaithful.

In addition to reenacting the childhood trauma of his mother's
betrayal, the jealousy served two important functions for Sam. First,
it gave him a "legitimate" excuse to postpone his divorce from his
wife and his marriage to Amalya. Second, it enabled him to enter-
tain sexual fantasies that, given his self-perception as pure, moral,
and innocent, he had difficulty admitting even to himself. The jealousy gave him an excuse to both imagine and interrogate Amalya
about the details of her sexual relations with other men. This could
have stimulated both voyeuristic and homosexual fantasies for him.

And there was something else. As I mentioned before, most modern day clinicians tend to disagree with Freud about the role played
by repressed homosexuality in delusional jealousy. Yet it is interesting to note the role played by just such repressed homosexuality in
Sam's jealousy. Amalya described Sam's never-ending interrogation
of her earlier sexual relationships with men. He wanted to know in
detail everything they did to her and everything she did to them.
Why? According to Freud, this gave Sam an excuse to satisfy a suppressed homosexual drive. In other words, he could imagine her
having sex with those other men, without a threat of having his own
interest in men discovered.

An Evaluation of the Psychodynamic Approach

The psychodynamic approach contributes to our understanding of
delusional jealousy by making us aware of the unconscious forces
underlying it. These forces explain behaviors that are otherwise difficult to understand, such as jealous people's choice of an unfaithful
mate, their relentless efforts to seek out confirmation of their worst
fears, their drive to push their mate toward their rival, or their ten-

dency to become obsessed with painful images of the mate in a passionate embrace with the rival. Such thoughts and behaviors
increase the jealous person's pain but, according to the psychodynamic approach, they provide a defense against even more troubling
feelings and thoughts.

Another contribution of the psychodynamic approach is its view
that the roots of adult jealousy are in early childhood experiences.
According to Freud, these experiences occur in the Oedipal stage.
Since Freud saw these experiences as universal, he was convinced
that reexperiencing them as romantic jealousy in adulthood was
both inevitable and universal.

Other psychodynamic writers believe that the origin of some feelings associated with jealousy may be even earlier than the Oedipal
stage. When a hungry baby cries and Mother doesn't appear, the
baby experiences tremendous anxiety and fear of abandonment.
These fears are universal. Consequently jealousy, which is their manifestation in adult life, is universal.[9]

In every adult there is a child that at some point felt abandoned
and scared, a child that cried in pain and raged with frustration. In
most adults there is a longing for the complete security felt in the
first weeks of life. Many felt resentment for the love they had to share
with a sibling or a parent. As adults they may not remember those
feelings, but they carry them nonetheless. These are the feelings that
cause them to respond in exaggerated and inappropriate ways to
jealousy triggers.

Because psychodynamically oriented therapists believe that jealousy both expresses and disguises some of our deepest fears and
desires, they treat jealousy as a psychological problem in the mind
of the jealous individual that is best treated in long–term psychotherapy. Other approaches question both psychodynamic
approach's assumptions and methods.

One of the major criticisms of the psychodynamic approach is
directed against its tendency not to consider the reality that may
have prompted the jealousy and to assume that all jealousy is to
some extent delusional—a product of a person's mind, unrelated to
reality. Little attention is paid to literal infidelity, except sometimes
to show how the person provoked, or in some sense desired, the very
betrayal that aroused his or her jealousy (Downing, 1986).

A related criticism is directed at the tendency to blame the individual for choosing or creating the circumstances that give rise to the jealousy problem. Psychodynamically oriented therapists tend to ignore what the jealousy suggests about anyone other than the jealous individual.

The psychodynamic approach is also criticized for putting too much emphasis on the role of the unconscious and not enough emphasis on conscious expectations and real events that create a jealousy problem and help maintain it.

Yet another criticism is directed at the tendency to put too much emphasis on the role of early childhood experiences in creating a jealousy problem and not enough emphasis on present forces, especially the dynamics of the relationship. The approval that is most closely associated with this criticism is the systems approach, which will be discussed in the next chaopter.

A Note to Therapists

When working with individuals who are concerned about the intensity of their jealousy—the "crazy" things they feel, think, and do when jealous—it is important to examine two questions. First, is it possible that the jealousy is not only a response to a spouse's jealousy-provoking behavior, but also a reenactment of an early childhood trauma? In other words, what are the roots of the jealousy? Have either Mother or Father been unfaithful? Has either parent been unusually jealous? Has the person ever witnessed a violent jealous outburst between the parents?

The second question is, What hidden payoffs does the person get from being jealous? What function does the jealousy serve? Does it provide affirmation of the partner's love and loyalty? Does it force the partner to behave in a more considerate way? Does it make it possible for the jealous person to project impulses toward infidelity onto the partner? Is it a way to punish oneself for having unacceptable fantasies or desires? Is it a way to indulge in sexual fantasies?

4
Treating the Couple, Not the Jealous Mate

&? &? &?

Quarrels would not last if the fault were only on one side.
—La Rochefoucauld, *Reflections*, 1675

&? &? &?

The Systems Approach to Jealousy

According to the systems approach, jealousy is a result of dynamics within a particular relationship and is best treated as a problem the couple shares.[1]

In psychological terms, a system constitutes "a complex of interacting elements and the relationships which organize them."[2] Emotions, actions, and thoughts are interacting elements of a system we call a person. The person is a subsystem of a more complex system involving an intimate relationship, which at times is called marriage. This relationship is a subsystem of a more complex system of an extended family, which itself is a subsystem of a particular society.[3]

Unlike the psychodynamic emphasis on events in our past, the systems approach considers the past mostly irrelevant to the treatment of jealousy. The unconscious roots of the jealousy problem also do not matter. What matters instead are the forces that elicit and maintain the problem. The focus is no longer the mind of the jealous individual, but the higher-order system, the whole, of which the individual is a part. The whole involves first and foremost the couple, but can also include the jealousy triangle, the couple's family of origin, and even the community and the culture in which the couple lives.

Higher-order systems (such as the couple) both influence and are influenced by lower-order systems (such as the actions, thoughts, and emotions of the jealous person). This reciprocal influence can cause negative-feedback loops that maintain the jealousy problem or positive-feedback loops that promote change. Disrupting a negative feedback loop in a higher-order system (a relationship) may involve or lead to change in a lower-order system (the jealous person).

With the passage of time, patterns of behavior become rules, or habits that are difficult to change. A couple's relationship functions according to these rules. (One of the most important rules dictates who makes the rules.) Once rules are established, the couple system tends to resist change. Yet a healthy system can exhibit both stability and change at one and the same time.

Instead of asking "Why?" (i.e., why is the individual jealous?) systems therapists ask "What?" What is the cause of the jealousy problem? And, more important, what can be done to bring about change? Psychodynamically oriented therapists give interpretations aimed at helping the troubled individuals gain new insights into their jealousy problem. By contrast, systems therapists give couples concrete recommendations designed to disrupt the destructive patterns that cause the jealousy problem and to help maintain the positive change. Disrupting those destructive patterns, instead of unearthing their cause, is the primary goal of systems therapy.

To bring about change in the person suffering from jealousy, that person's marital system must change. The focus of the therapeutic intervention is on behaviors in both mates that help maintain the jealousy problem. Because the goal is to disrupt a destructive feedback loop, the therapist tries to find the point that is easiest to change. This can involve a change in behavior that produces a change in the rules of the system or a change of rules that produces a change in behavior. The case of Dave and Lillian, which will be presented shortly, provides an example of such a system change.

While the focus of the specific intervention can vary, the general focus of systems therapy is always the system and the circular processes (feedback loops) that take place in it. Systems therapists assume that a change in one part of the system (for example, one mate) always causes change in the other parts of the system (for example, the other mate), and therefore changes the whole system. When the husband withdraws, the wife responds with an attempt to get closer. When the wife tries to get closer, the husband responds by withdrawing. The response of one mate provides the stimulus to the other: Does he withdraw because she gets too close, or does she get closer because he withdraws?

In a marital system, according to systems approach, it is impossible for one mate to be totally passive. Even when one does not respond to something one's partner did, such as blaming one unjustly for being unfaithful, the lack of response gives the partner a powerful message.

Roles such as victim and victimizer are seen as a result of an arbitrary decision in which both mates take part. If the husband plays the role of the unfaithful villain, a systems therapist is likely to assume that the wife is contributing to or getting something from the role of the betrayed victim. One goal of therapy is to change such arbitrary definitions. A change in the way a couple perceives a chain of events (for example, what preceded the affair that can help explain it) can change the couple's dynamic.

Systems therapists see jealousy as caused by destructive, self-reinforcing patterns of interaction and not by events in the individual's past. When a couple comes to therapy and the husband describes the "crazy things" his wife does because of her "pathological jealousy," the therapist is likely to ask what in the husband's behavior caused her to behave in this way. Another question the therapist might ask concerns the husband's response, which may reinforce the wife's jealous behavior. When the wife identifies the husband's affair as the central problem, the therapist is likely to ask her what she might have done to cause her husband to have an affair, or else what she did in response to the affair.

Even though only one person in the couple may experience jealousy, systems therapists believe that jealousy serves a function in the couple system. Symptoms such as affairs or jealousy are viewed as forms of communication. Dave and Lillian demonstrate how an affair can be a form of communication.[4]

Dave and Lillian: An Affair as a Form of Communication

When Dave and Lillian first met, Lillian was insecure and impoverished. She was attracted to Dave's stability and quiet self-confidence. Dave, for his part, was attracted to Lillian's high energy and intense emotionality. During the first years of their marriage Dave was a stable breadwinner, which enabled Lillian to go back to school and get a degree. Both were happy in their marriage.

After about six years, however, Dave decided he needed a change and took a job in real estate, a field that Lillian considered "gambling" instead of a "real job." Dave's income in this new job was unstable; in addition, the real-estate field went into a slump shortly after he entered it, making even his unstable income rather meager. During that time they had to rely on Lillian's salary, which she said was "all right," but in fact was not all right with her. Lillian explains:

> Dave's career has not been successful. For the past four years I have been the steady breadwinner while Dave has tried to break into commercial real estate. Although he did have one fairly good year, he brought in a total of about $40,000 during a four-year period. Even when he made some money, neither of us felt it could be freely spent because there was no way to know when or if he would make the next deal and another commission. Sales, especially during these hard times for real estate, can be very stressful work. Dave has put out a lot of effort, undergone a lot of stress, and gotten very little back for it.

Lillian understood that what she saw as Dave's "failure" was the result of bad luck rather than "a symptom of inherent failure tendencies or inadequacies" in Dave. Still, she felt "emotionally impacted by a sense of his 'failure.'" It triggered childhood fears and insecurities that were related in part to the fact that she viewed her father as "a total and complete failure in the business world." Dave's problems and lack of success threatened her sense of security in Dave and in the marriage, and the experience affected her sexual feelings:

> The sexist woman in me expects a man to be stronger and steadier and more financially successful than I am. Someone inside me wants to be a delicate, charming little girl ... with a big, powerful, successful man to take care of me and overwhelm me with his forcefulness, his sureness, his surefooted success. I must admit that I expect a husband to be successful, and Dave is not successful. Although I don't consciously make his career success a condition of my love, I am sure that on an emotional level I

am experiencing deep disappointment in him. I have wondered
if this disappointment is behind my lack of sexual attraction....
Dave's financial dependency is the crux of my anger and disappointment.... The whole failure issue—men should succeed; my
father was a failure—has a lot of emotional energy around it and
generates its own dynamic.

The effect of Dave's perceived career failure on Lillian's sexual feelings had a concrete manifestation:

Dave is relatively short for a man. He is also very slender. I am
fairly slender but more solid than he is. I never used to think
about it at all, but lately I have been craving largeness in a man.
Dave is wonderfully endowed sexually, and fills me up as no
other man has ever done quite so well. But in terms of body size
and weight I have lately found him lacking. I crave bigness and
power on top of me when we make love these days. I feel
cheated because my arms wrap so easily around his slender
body. I feel like a protecting mother/companion/comfort-giver
... when I want to feel like a nymphet overwhelmed by a large,
powerful, passionate man who is driven to frenzy by my love-
liness.

Lillian has not always been disappointed with Dave's size. As a
matter of fact, the opposite is true.

Is this body-disappointment based upon the failure disappointment that I feel on an emotional level? Have I got his
smallness of body mixed up with his smallness of income? Will
this body-disappointment go away when Dave gets a new career
under way and has success? And will sexual excitement ignite
between us then?

Despite the intensity of her disappointment and rage, Lillian was
unable to discuss her feelings openly with Dave. She valued the security her marriage provided, and was afraid that if she expressed her
true feelings openly, Dave might get so upset and angry that he would
leave her. So she blocked out her negative feelings. It is impossible,
however, to block emotions selectively; once you put on an emotional

shield, it inhibits all emotions. Consequently, when Lillian repressed her anger she also repressed her feelings of love and passion.

Although he did not admit his failure in real estate, Dave was worried about his financial future. He wanted to protect Lillian from his fears and his feelings of insecurity and inadequacy, feelings that were caused by his "unmasculine" dependency on Lillian's earnings. Dave couldn't admit those feelings even to himself. So he blocked them out, blocking with them his passion. Lillian describes the results:

> As must be typical, the symptoms of the problem come up most glaringly in the bedroom. I no longer feel sexually attracted to or excited by Dave. Dave says he is still attracted to me—and that the lack of enthusiasm comes from me rather than from him. But the predictability and low-key style of his lovemaking cause me to think that perhaps our lack of enthusiasm is shared. I have no complaints about his willingness, frequency, sweetness, or consideration and giving during lovemaking. It is the lack of creativity, of genuine excitement, of passion that I refer to. And I do nothing to introduce these elements myself, since I no longer feel any passion or strong attraction. I do not find myself motivated to exhibit feelings I am not having although some pretense on my part might get the ball rolling, perhaps. It's just not something I want to force myself to do.

Just then passionate sex became very important to Lillian:

> Maybe I am no longer the same person who fell in love more than ten years ago? Certainly I have very different needs today than I did when I met Dave a decade ago. As a thirty-five-year-old woman (no children, successful career) I find that passionate sex (or the lack of it) is far more important to me than ever before. I am no longer working to build a career. I enjoy my work and feel successful. I think this is the age when a woman is supposed to reach her sexual peak ... perhaps that is why I crave passionate sex in a way that I did not use to.

According to Lillian, it was boredom with marital sex that precipitated her illicit affair. But, clearly, boredom was only a small part of the story. It all started during a party at which Dave pointed out to Lillian a grubby-looking bearded man wearing a dirty, torn T-shirt, and said, "Isn't that the most disgusting-looking man you have ever seen?" Earlier, Dave had heard the man talk about his teenage daughter in lascivious terms that just added to the negative impression made by his appearance. Soon afterward, Lillian chose to have an affair with this very man:

> About six months ago I became involved with a man who elicited passion in me that I did not know I was capable of feeling. For years I had just figured that I was not a very sexually oriented person. Though Dave and I had much more exciting sex before we were married and during the early years, we had not had passionate sex for at least three years prior to my affair with this other man.
>
> Although my affair was with a strange and crazy man whom I no longer have any interest in or desire to see, it elicited some powerful feelings at the time so much so that it was impossible for me to hide the fact that I was having an affair.

Lillian's behavior could have made it easy for Dave, who claimed to be "not the slightest bit jealous," to discover the affair. But he simply refused to notice the hints she was dropping all around him. So she started to make those hints bigger and more obvious until he finally understood and responded, for the first time ever in their relationship, with tremendous jealousy. His interrogations enabled Lillian to tell him about the affair—something she secretly wanted very much to do. In fact, letting him know and making him jealous were the main reasons she had started the affair in the first place:

> Indiscretions on my part aroused Dave's suspicions, and I ended up telling him (in stages) the full extent of my extramarital involvement.
>
> Dave was wounded to the core. His infinite trust in me dissolved, and he said he lost the capacity to trust completely. It would do him no good to divorce me and try to find another woman he could trust, since he had lost the capacity for complete trust in another person. If I—whom he loved and trusted so completely—could betray him that way, then anyone could,

at any time. He had never felt such jealousy before, and never wanted to feel it again.

Once Dave discovered the affair and was appropriately jealous, Lillian suddenly lost interest in the other man:

> When I came so close to losing Dave, my emotions swung back powerfully toward him. I no longer cared about the other man or the affair, but only about repairing the damage I had done to the man I love—my husband. I felt that I would kiss his feet for the next ten years if that were necessary to win back his love and trust ... to restore the bond and comfort that I had ruptured.
>
> It was mostly my intense desire to right the wrong and stay on the good-wife path in the future (as well as his love and need for me, and his perception of my love for him) that convinced Dave to give me another chance.

Coming to therapy was part of Lillian and Dave's attempt to "right the wrong" and give their marriage another chance. Their work as a couple was fueled by Lillian's "passionate desire to heal Dave's jealousy and pain, and repair the damage I had done ... and not lose the man I had loved all these years and still love so much."

As is often the case when an affair is explored openly and nondefensively, Lillian and Dave realized that the affair was, more than anything else, a communication. The affair enabled Lillian to communicate feelings toward Dave that she was too embarrassed to admit even to herself, and too scared to communicate directly to Dave:

> Clearly the affair had more to do with what I was feeling toward Dave than what I was feeling toward the other man, especially given that the other man is of absolutely no interest to me anymore. Now that I am not acting out affair-type behavior, feelings about Dave are surfacing that I was not allowing myself to experience before.
>
> Perhaps the affair was a way of doing something to prevent myself from knowing what I was feeling toward Dave, since these are threatening feelings. I experienced anger, resentment, disappointment, concern, fear. I am beginning to see the affair as a way of not having to experience these feelings.

In a tearful and highly emotional session, after much encouragement and with great effort, Lillian and Dave were finally able to open up to each other. They discussed all their feelings, negative and embarrassing as they were. The result was a tremendous relief. Lillian was able to tell Dave about her anger and resentment. She said she was afraid that if she expressed her anger and disappointment (she envisioned these emotions as a monster she was keeping in the closet), something terrible would happen and her whole world would collapse. Dave was able to admit his jealousy, despite his belief that it was a negative and shameful response.

Lillian discovered that despite her "terrible feelings" Dave still loved her, and actually was delighted to find out what had been troubling her all along. After learning that jealousy is a protective response to a perceived threat to a valued relationship, Dave was able to share his jealousy and his financial insecurities with Lillian and discover that her feelings toward him were not altered because of this. With the emotional relief they experienced during this mutual exploration came a powerful surge of the old passion. And, as both reported, "sex has never been better."

Open discussion also enabled Dave and Lillian to confront directly the sensitive issue of money and to come up with a solution that suited them both. Dave continued in real estate while training for a new career with a much better potential for providing a stable and secure income. In the meantime they decided to rent a part of the house, which helped ease some of their financial stress.

Lillian and Dave's case demonstrates that an affair can be a form of communication to the mate. As Lillian said:

> The affair needed to be looked at as communication to Dave, rather than as an inability to restrain my impulses. I needed to look at what I was feeling toward Dave, and trying to communicate to him by having an affair—and by being so obvious about it.

This case demonstrates several key points of the systems approach. Dave and Lillian, in their years of marriage, created a system in which the unspoken rule was that Dave was the stable provider. When Dave changed this established pattern he broke the rule. Lillian punished him by having the affair, thus breaking the fidelity rule. Dave's jealousy, an unusual experience for him, and Lillian's fear that he might leave, brought them to therapy.

The focus of the therapy was not the unconscious roots of Dave's jealousy or Lillian's infidelity, but instead on the rules governing the marriage. As a result of this exploration, Lillian and Dave were able to compromise and accept a change of rules with which they both felt comfortable.

Throughout therapy, the affair as well as the jealousy it triggered were treated as a couple issue. The therapy made it clear that Dave and Lillian each played an active role in the process that led to the affair, and each played an equally active role in trying to save their marriage when they perceived a threat to it. Treating the affair and the jealousy it triggered as a couple issue enabled Lillian and Dave to reestablish trust and turn the traumatic event into a growth experience.

Jane and Dan: An Affair as a Form of Escape

The most common trigger of extreme jealousy is an illicit affair. As noted earlier, virtually all the people who were asked about it said they would feel "very jealous" if they discovered their mate was having an illicit affair. How should such jealousy be treated in a constructive and growth–enhancing way? While the jealous response seems justified, it not only causes excruciating pain for the individual (as noted earlier, PTSD which has been used to describe the reaction to acute jealousy triggered by an affair, was first used to describe the response of soldiers to a battle trauma), but also can be destructive to the relationship and, in extreme cases, lead to violence.

Systems therapists look at the affair in the context of the relationship as a whole. The affair is not "something that just happened" to the unfaithful partner, but a statement about something important that happened to and involves both mates. In a book dealing with treatment of marital conflict, Philip Guerin and his colleagues note that affairs "almost always represent externalization of a dysfunctional process going on within the family."[5] Their approach to the treatment of affairs, which is shared by many systems therapists, focuses on three goals:

1. bringing out the part each spouse played in the process
2. changing the behavior of both spouses
3. reestablishing trust in the marital relationship

The following case illustrates this systems approach. The case involves a woman called Jane, who found out that her husband of thirty-five years, Dan, had had an affair.

The discovery of an affair is painful for both mates. It sets off a crisis in which ordinary daily functioning suffers severely. The first thing Jane needed to do was learn to take one day at a time and make priorities in her daily responsibilities so she could manage what was most essential. Then, to minimize the emotional impact of the affair, both Jane and Dan needed to understand the parts each of them had played in the affair, the function the affair served in the marriage, and the process that had led up to it. Understanding these things does not mean that people are not accountable for their behavior. Dan had an affair, Jane did not. Yet both were responsible for the state of their marriage. Since an affair often is seen as an unforgivable sin, it is important for both mates to place the affair in the larger context of their marriage.

Many times an affair is a refuge from relationship problems or from pain in one's personal life. To understand the function of Dan's affair, it is necessary to understand the state of things prior to the affair. Two problems seem particularly relevant: an operation for cancer of the prostate that Dan had before the affair and Jane's over-involvement in their daughter's divorce.

The prostate cancer operation was traumatic for Dan. Not only did it make him confront his own mortality, it made him question his sexual adequacy—something he had never questioned before. He desperately needed Jane's support, but Jane was too involved with their daughter's recent divorce to notice. She stayed with their daughter for weeks at a time, and when she was home they spent hours on the phone. In fact, when Jane first sought therapy it was to discuss her daughter's marital problems and how she could best help her resolve them.

Over the course of the months following the operation, an emotional distance grew between Jane and Dan. Each felt distressed, yet was unable to share these feelings with the other. Dan's affair with an attractive woman, ten years younger than himself, helped him get the emotional and sexual reassurance he needed. It started when Jane was out of town. Dan had a business dinner to attend and didn't like the thought of going alone. It was natural for him to invite a woman who was working in a nearby office to join him.

After dinner she invited him for a drink at her apartment, and Dan rediscovered how wonderful it was to talk to someone who was totally attentive and focused on him, the way Jane had been during most of their married life. The fact that a young, sexy woman still found him attractive and desirable was exhilarating. With her he felt more alive sexually than he had in a long time—more manly, more interesting.

As long as the affair remained secret, Dan had his sexual and emotional needs met, and Jane was free to continue her intense involvement with their daughter. When an anonymous phone call from a watchful secretary in Dan's office informed Jane of the affair, Dan stopped it right away. He told Jane he was sorry for what he had done and for the pain he had caused her. What he wanted more than anything else was to forget the whole thing. But Jane was inconsolable in her jealousy and couldn't let go. She barraged Dan with questions about the affair, searched through his drawers and office files, couldn't stop thinking about it, and vacillated between humiliation, rage, and despair. Her jealousy brought her back to therapy.

At the beginning of my work with Dan and Jane, I encouraged Jane to talk about the feelings she had experienced since the discovery of the affair. It was important to validate the emotional turmoil she was in, without making Dan the villain. Pursuing Dan for details added to her emotional turmoil, and it was important that she stop the interrogations. She was able to do that by focusing on her role in the marriage and the affair.

Once both Jane and Dan understood the function the affair had in their marriage and the roles both of them played in making it happen, and once they were able to talk about the affair openly, the arduous task of reestablishing trust in the marriage began. Many couples, relieved that the crisis is over, hope time will take care of old wounds and drop out of therapy before achieving this difficult and important goal.[6]

Jealousy Serves a Function

Whether an affair is a form of communication or a form of escape, the jealousy it triggers is always a relationship issue. It focuses attention on a threat to the relationship. According to the systems approach, jealousy always serves a function in the relationship. While it is experienced and expressed by one mate, it is part of a particular couple's relationship and reflects a particular family disturbance. A nice example of this appears in Robert Barker's book *The Green-Eyed Marriage*. Barker is not a systems therapist, but rather a psychodynamic therapist who views jealousy as "the result of long-standing and deep-seated psychological and behavioral problems within the jealous person."[7] Despite this clear allocation of blame, the case is a wonderful example of the systems notion of the function that jealousy plays for both mates—exactly the opposite conclusion from the one Dr. Barker drew.

Darryl and Lucy were married ten years and fought constantly throughout this time. In a typical interaction leading to a fight, Darryl would start making overtures signaling that he wanted to have sex, and Lucy would appear enthusiastic. Then she would casually mention something that would arouse his jealousy. The argument would culminate with one of them sleeping on the living room couch.

While Darryl may have been the jealous mate, it is clear that Lucy played an equal part in having the jealous scenes continue. Dr. Barker notes correctly that "both had something important to gain by keeping it going." Both Darryl and Lucy had long histories of sexual problems. Darryl was often troubled by premature ejaculation and was anxious about his sexual performance. Lucy suffered from a chronic, painful sensitivity to touch and pressure in the genital area, which caused an aversion to sexual intercourse.

Lucy used Darryl's jealousy to minimize sexual contact with him. When he made overtures, she simply stirred his jealousy. His typical response made the outcome predictable: They would fight and forget about sex. "Guilt-free absolution from sex" was Lucy's payoff: She didn't refuse him. She was willing until he started acting jealous again. Darryl, too, wanted an excuse to avoid sex and the performance anxiety associated with it. The jealousy-related arguments provided an acceptable way to avoid it.

Darryl and Lucy illustrate the degree to which jealousy is a couple issue. Even when one mate appears "abnormally jealous," it is legitimate to ask what benefits the nonjealous mate is gaining from the jealousy problem. The question is especially relevant when jealousy has been a problem in the relationship for a long time.

One of the most common discoveries in working with couples with an "abnormally jealous" spouse is that the "nonjealous" spouse has a good reason, psychologically speaking, to stay in the relationship. As Darryl and Lucy's case demonstrates, at times that reason is so important that the "nonjealous" mate actually fuels the jealousy.

Lucy provoked Darryl's jealousy in an attempt to conceal a sexual problem. In other cases, jealousy-based arguments may be used to divert attention from other problems in the spouses, in the relationship, or in both.

In addition to concealing other problems, jealousy can serve a positive function as well; in small amounts it can add excitement to the relationship. As we will see in the chapter on jealousy in open relationships, for example, swingers like to watch their mates having sex with someone else. The jealous flash they feel fuels their sexual interest in their mate.

Other couples enjoy the drama jealousy produces. Both mates identify drama with passion, and they keep passion alive in the relationship by coproducing the jealousy scenes. In one such case, the jealous lover is a successful businessman who makes frequent trips abroad. Since he can't stand the thought of his girlfriend staying home alone, he takes her along on most of his trips. On those rare occasions when that's impossible, he makes frequent overseas calls to her house, to friends, and even to restaurants to check on her.

The girlfriend, who is a plain-looking woman, grew up in a poor family. She loves the trips abroad and the attention her lover's jealousy produces. To fuel his jealousy, she drops little hints about men she saw during his absence. Yet when he makes surprise visits to check on her, he always finds her chatting innocently with a group of friends or a woman friend. When that happens, and it happens often, she accuses him of being pathologically jealous. They have a "terrible fight" and then make passionate love. This pattern has been going on for eight years, with no end in sight for either the jealousy or the passion. A couple like this may appear furious at each other, but they actually love the drama their jealousy creates. They rarely seek therapy for the jealousy, and when they find themselves with a mate who is not jealous or unfaithful, they find that mate "boring." Jealousy keeps the sexual spark in their relationship alive.

Jealousy indeed produces excitement and can make life more interesting. It can also make one's mate look more desirable. If the businessman I just described saw his girlfriend not through his jealousy-struck eyes but the way the rest of the world saw her, she would doubtless lose much of her appeal.

Some people fuel their mate's jealousy when they feel taken for granted. Some do it because it gives them a sense of power over their jealous mate. Others do it as a form of revenge, using their jealous mate to heal an ego that was injured by this relationship or a previous one. It may be worth mentioning in this regard the findings of a study conducted by Edwin Brainerd and his colleagues (1996) that show that the use and approval of jealousy-inducing behaviors were predictors of high need for interpersonal control and use of psychological aggression. The use of jealousy-inducing behaviors combined with disproval of them was a strong predictor of physical aggression toward one's partner.

It is not enough for one mate to want to create a jealousy problem. Both partners have to collude in keeping a jealousy problem alive in the relationship. This is why, according to the systems approach, jealousy is best treated as the couple's joint problem, even when one mate is "abnormally" jealous.

Working on jealousy as a couple issue tends to bring about faster change, because it involves both mates. In Lucy and Darryl's case, for example, what would have happened if Darryl went for individual therapy to deal with his "abnormal jealousy"? The focus of therapy would undoubtedly have been on Darryl's feelings of sexual inadequacy, which were the cause of his jealousy. Changing those is a long and slow process. Changing destructive patterns in the relationship that contribute to a jealousy problem can alleviate the problem much faster.

A person in a relationship with a mate who is "abnormally" jealous would probably have trouble accepting the idea that he or she, too, plays an active role in keeping the jealousy problem alive. It is much easier to blame the jealous partner than to take responsibility for one's part in shaping the relationship one shares. Yet, in the long run, blaming the partner is not the best approach. Taking responsibility—which is not the same as taking blame—means that one has some control over the problem. People who accept the fact that they played a part in creating a problem can draw comfort from the knowledge that they can also play an active part in solving it.

The Systems Approach to the Treatment of "Abnormal Jealousy"

Mark suffered from what was described by his psychoanalyst as "delusional jealousy."[8] This diagnosis was based on a whole set of symptoms: Mark could not stop tormenting himself about affairs his wife might be having. He said his jealousy was "like a poisonous gas that permeated everything." Every time he came home from work, Mark checked the mileage on his wife's car to make sure she hadn't taken trips out of town to see her imagined lovers. He checked her underpants for stains that would indicate she had had sex with those "lovers." He checked the contents of her wallet for any clues she might have left to an illicit affair. To find out whether she talked to her "lovers" on the phone while he was out of the house, he would put a hair on the receiver. If the hair was not there when he returned, it would be a clear sign that she had talked with some lover. But whenever he returned and the hair wasn't on the receiver, he could never be sure whether it was his wife or the wind that had blown it away.

Most significant in the diagnosis of delusional jealousy, however, was that Mark's jealousy was groundless. His wife has always been faithful to him. Since Mark's therapist was psychodynamically oriented, his therapy centered on the function that the jealousy served in the dynamics of Mark's inner life.

Although this was a case of "abnormal" jealousy, Mark already had a jealousy problem when his wife first met him, fell in love with him, and decided to marry him. What was it that attracted her to him at the early stages of their relationship? Could it have had something to do with his jealousy?

In similar cases I have worked with, I have discovered that nonjealous mates actually enjoy the jealousy at the beginning. The reason, in most cases, is that they perceive the jealousy as a sign of love and commitment to the relationship.

Unfortunately, we don't know what attracted Mark's wife at the beginning of the relationship, because Mark's wife was never seen in therapy. Since Mark and his therapist defined the problem as "Mark's pathological jealousy," this was also the focus of his individual psychotherapy.

As noted earlier, the traits and behaviors that attract couples most when they first meet often cause the most distress later in the relationship. This is also true for jealousy. For a person with an abnormally jealous partner, one of the most important and interesting questions to explore is what attracted him or her to that partner at the beginning of the relationship. Understanding the attraction helps understand the jealousy. Ann and Leonard are an example.

Ann and Leonard met when Ann was 17 years old. Leonard, 24 years old at the time, seemed not only older but wiser and more impressive than the boys her age. She loved the way he made her the center of his world and took care of her needs. But now, after twenty–seven years of marriage, she wants a divorce. The reason: "Leonard's pathological jealousy." "I feel suffocated," says Ann. "Leonard is so jealous, he doesn't let me breathe. I feel imprisoned. He can't stand the fact that I have my own interests. He doesn't let me go out on my own. He follows me everywhere I go. I've had it with him." Leonard, on the other hand, says he still loves Ann as much as he did when they were first married. "I am worried about her going out on her own at night," he says. "That's the only reason I follow her and why I want to know where she's going and with whom. I think my concern is normal and perfectly justified. Every man you'll ask will agree with me."

From the time they met through the first years of their marriage, Ann loved being the center of Leonard's world. She saw a sign of love in his protectiveness and concern. It made her feel secure. He was the loving father she never had. Now she sees his protectiveness as possessiveness, and his concern as pathological jealousy. Being the center of his world no longer makes her feel secure, because that world has shrunk into a cage. Ann and Leonard created a destructive cycle in which Ann responded to Leonard's jealousy by withdrawing, and he responded to her growing withdrawal with increasing jealousy, which makes her withdraw love further, which makes him even more jealous.

Shifting from the Jealous Mate to the Couple

Dean and Melanie came to therapy because of what Dean called Melanie's "pathological jealousy." He said that I had to "fix" her because he simply "can't take it anymore." Melanie agreed with the label and appreciated Dean's support in coming to therapy with her.

During our exploration of the problem, it became evident that Melanie had a reason to be jealous. When they first met, Dean was engaged to marry another woman while at the same time having an affair with that woman's sister. He told Melanie about all of his wheelings and dealings in trying to manage these two relationships—while starting a third one with her. One may ask, of course, why Melanie would get involved with a man she knew was engaged and cheating on his fiancee. But as I noted earlier, such a question is irrelevant for a systems therapist.

Sometime after they became involved, Dean and Melanie had a fight and separated for a brief time. Melanie later discovered that during the separation Dean had had an affair with his secretary. Dean used all his "old cover-up tricks" to keep Melanie from finding out about the affair. This affair, on top of Dean's "history of deceit," made Melanie suspect anything that could possibly be a clue to a new affair. Her suspicions made Dean, who according to his own testimony was now "innocent as a lamb," furious. He didn't understand why Melanie needed to drag out things that were "old history." She was, he concluded, "pathologically jealous."

While Melanie agreed with Dean that she had a problem with jealousy, she observed, in her own defense, that she had never before been jealous, neither with any of her boyfriends nor with her former husband.

As is almost always the case, Dean and Melanie's jealousy problem was related to what they found most attractive about each other when they first met. Melanie was attracted to Dean's masculine charm and charisma: "He was then, and still is now, a very attractive man." Dean was attracted to Melanie's sensitivity and attentiveness: "I felt from the very beginning that she was someone who could create a home for me." Now Dean's attractiveness to other women has become a major source of stress for Melanie, while Melanie's excessive sensitivity has become equally stressful for Dean.

Dean was convinced that every interaction he had with another woman was a jealousy-trigger for Melanie. He argued fervently that all the things he had done in the past were "insignificant and trivial" compared to his "complete honesty and truthfulness in the relationship now." To Melanie, however, it seemed that her suspicions were quite adequately justified by Dean's behavior in the past. The triggers of her jealousy were well defined; they included all situations involving women when there was even a slight chance that Dean was dishonest with her. Seeing Dean interact with an attractive woman and thinking that he might be attracted to the woman or even have an affair with her and lie about it were enough to make Melanie wild with jealousy.

When Dean and Melanie walked together, Dean occasionally

would bump into a woman he knew and exchange a few words with her. He knew that this was enough to raise Melanie's suspicions. She would start asking questions about the woman and his acquaintance with her. Her interrogations made Dean more and more angry. Finally he refused to answer her questions. "I know the way her mind works," he said, "and it drives me nuts."

The "scratches incident" was the final straw. Melanie noticed that Dean had scratches on his back, which he didn't remember getting; Melanie felt he couldn't possibly have caused the scratches himself. When she started to question him about the scratches, Dean felt "something explode" in his head. He says he didn't know what he was doing. He started to hit Melanie. The violence shocked and scared both of them and was the real reason they came for therapy.

In trying to figure out how both of them contributed to the dynamic of their jealousy problem, Melanie claimed that her main problem was lack of trust in Dean. If Dean would swear to tell her the truth—even if he was attracted to another woman, even if he had a fling—she was sure she could handle it. But Dean refused to give his word. He saw Melanie's suspicions as groundless and found her interrogations intolerable. "I've had enough of this madness," he said. "Melanie has a problem, and she is the one who has to solve it." Since Dean and Melanie seemed stuck in their positions, I asked them to reverse roles, and explain to me each other's positions.[9]

Both had difficulty with the task. Melanie had a great deal of trouble expressing the extent of Dean's resentment and anger at her suspicion. Dean had problems expressing the extent of Melanie's hurt and distrust of him. It was as though Dean and Melanie had supersensitive antennae, he to signs of her jealousy, she to signs of his possible unfaithfulness. Once they both realized the extent of each other's sensitivity, they were able to focus their effort on "reducing the volume" of their respective responses.

Dean agreed to tell Melanie the truth about his romantic involvements, actual or possible, with other women. In exchange, Melanie promised to trust him, to stop being suspicious of every woman he interacted with, and to cease her interrogations of him. Though this solution may sound too simple to work, in this particular case it did. Melanie stopped being "a jealous person." When I last spoke to Dean and Melanie, two years after they made their agreement, they no longer had problems with jealousy. One reason the agreement worked was that they attempted to solve the problem together. Another reason was Melanie's willingness to put complete faith in Dean's word. Once he gave it, she was convinced he'd never lie to her.

This does not mean that every "jealous person" will stop being jealous the minute his or her mate promises to be honest about involvement with others. Other couples may need different solutions. The challenge in each case is to discover the solution that works.

Leading systems theorists Paul Watzlawick, John Weakland, and Richard Fisch (1974) give an example of the way a jealousy system is activated, maintained, and perpetuated: A wife feels excluded from her husband's life, so she starts questioning him. The husband feels that her questioning is an intrusion, so he withdraws. His withdrawal increases her anxiety and suspiciousness, so her efforts to "find out" become more persistent and more desperate. Her jealousy and suspicion increase his resentment and cause him to withdraw and withhold even more. The husband and wife are caught in a no-win situation. The wife (in this case the jealous mate) realizes that questioning her husband will probably lead to angry withholding or forced reassurance that ultimately does not reassure her. The husband (in this case the nonjealous mate) realizes that withholding leads to further distrust and jealousy, yet is afraid that disclosing any information may exacerbate the problem (Watzlawick et al., 1974).

In other cases the husband may be the jealous mate and the wife the nonjealous mate. In gay couples, the less committed partner and the partner who has more outside options tend to be nonjealous. Mary and Sharon, whom I mentioned before, are an example.

In addition to the fact that Mary was more attractive and more elegant than Sharon, Mary was also very attached to her family of origin and her many male and female friends. Sharon was cut off from her family of origin, and did not have close friends. As a result, Sharon was more dependent on Mary than the other way around. This created a dynamic that systems theorists call "pursuer—distancer" with Sharon pursuing and Mary distancing. As is typically the case, Sharon expressed a great deal of jealousy toward the people in Mary's life whom she perceived as posing a threat to their relationship. Her jealousy angered Mary and made her withdraw even further. The pains of her jealousy and the realization that all she succeeds in doing when expressing it is push Mary away brought Sharon into therapy.

The goal of therapy was to change the pursuer–distancer dynamic by helping Sharon stop pursuing. This was accomplished by helping Sharon make some contact with her family of origin (since she was very close to her mother in the past, that proved possible); by encouraging her to visit old friends and to make new ones (the place where she lived had an active gay community that she has never contacted); and most of all, stop calling Mary. When Sharon stopped pursuing Mary, she discovered to her great joy and dismay that now Mary was pursuing her. This change, which is predictable from a systems perspective, helped increase Sharon's security and decreased her jealousy.

Systems Approach Techniques for Treating Jealousy

The role–reversal technique used with Dean and Melanie, in which each mate takes turn describing the other's point of view, is an example of a systems approach technique. It helps couples understand each other better and realize how both contribute to the creation and maintenance of the jealousy problem.

Systems therapists Won Gi Im, Stephanie Wilner, and Miranda Breit suggest a variation of this technique called "Turning the Tables." The nonjealous partner is instructed to act the part of the jealous one. The attentiveness and new–found interest enable the jealous mate to regain lost self-confidence, and allows the nonjealous mate to re-discover the partner's more positive qualities.[10] Another technique they suggest is "Scrupulous Honesty." The nonjealous mate is instructed to be unwaveringly honest about every detail of the day's experiences and to flood the jealous mate with information. The flood of information helps dispel anxiety in the jealous mate, who felt excluded and suspicious about clandestine events supposedly taking place.

Yet another technique, used throughout this book, is called re-framing.[11] Reframing involves changing the perception of a symptom, a problem, or an action by casting it in a new light. This may be accomplished by reframing the meaning or function of the behavior. Rather than viewing Lillian's affair as a terrible betrayal, the couple learned to see it as a form of communication. Similarly, Darryl's jealousy was described as serving a function in the marriage. This kind of reframing casts the problem, be it unfaithfulness or jealousy, in a less problematic light. Pejorative language used to describe jealousy often prolongs the problem. Instead of using words such as "pathological" or "irrational," one can describe jealousy as a protective response to a perceived threat to a valued relationship. One can further reframe the jealousy problem by describing it as a relationship issue, rather than as the jealous mate's problem. The next step is to figure what function the jealousy serves for both mates and what they are doing to keep the problem alive.

A shared awareness of what both mates are doing to foster the jealousy problem, and what is likely to trigger the jealous response, often helps to break the circular pattern. As family therapist Gayla Margolin notes, "In general, the more spouses know about how their own problems escalate, the more capable they are of handling them. All it takes is for one spouse to refrain from engaging in his or her prescribed role, and the cycle cannot proceed."[12]

Margolin cautions, however, that just because the couple has succeeded in disrupting a pattern does not mean the pattern will not reappear. She recommends the establishment of rituals that serve as cues for the new, preferred behavioral sequence, such as weekly "dates" to assess how the marriage is doing. The development of new communication skills can also help circumvent the old patterns. The language of the systems approach, which emphasizes interpersonal processes rather than individual pathology, offers new ways of communicating.

Carlos E. Sluzki, one of the leading systems theorists, notes that jealousy is "an interpersonal scenario directed and acted by two players." "Characters involved in the scenarios of jealousy usually experience themselves as totally trapped by the plot, though they are, without knowing it, also its coauthors," Sluzki says. The goal of systems therapy is "to help them discover alternative plots, different scenarios that make them aware that they are the owners of their own lives."[13]

An Evaluation of the Systems Approach

The systems approach makes a major contribution to our understanding of jealousy in viewing jealousy as a problem that is best treated at the relationship level. Although the focus is on the relationship, the assumption is that treating the couple involves or leads to individual change as well. As people view their mates and relationships in a more positive and realistic way, they also begin to feel better about themselves. When both partners try to disrupt the destructive pattern in a relationship, positive change happens faster, is more visible for both mates, and is more likely to endure the test of time.

One of the major criticisms of the systems approach is directed at its disregard of the contributions of childhood experiences and unconscious processes to the origin of jealousy. According to critics (most of them psychodynamically oriented), a jealousy problem can never be cured entirely unless these "deeper" issues in the jealous individual are treated.

Question: Is jealousy a result of a particular dynamic in the relationship, or is it a product of unconscious forces in the mind of the jealous individual? My strong belief is that jealousy is both—and much more.

A Note to Therapists

From a systems perspective, the most important task facing a therapist who is asked to help an individual or a couple deal with a jealousy problem is to help the person or the couple understand:

1. the parts each mate played in creating the jealousy problem
2. the function the jealousy serves in the relationship
3. the process that maintains and perpetuates the jealousy

5

Men Get Angry, Women Get Depressed

Jealousy is the rage of man: therefore he will not spare
in the day of vengeance.
—*Proverbs*

The jealous are readiest of all to forgive, and all women know it.
—Dostoevsky, *The Brothers Karamazov*

Ron and Carol

When Carol met Ron, he had been divorced and a swinger for several years, "trying to make up for all the good times" he had lost being married for twenty-six years. Soon after they started dating, it became clear to both of them that there was something special about their relationship. Carol told Ron that she was not interested in being just another member of his harem. "If he wanted a relationship with me," she said, "it had to be with me alone." Ron agreed, and has remained sexually faithful to Carol. This, however, did not prevent him from keeping in touch with former girlfriends. Carol describes the growing problems it caused:

> His girlfriends call him day and night, paying absolutely no attention to the fact that Ron is living with me now. When I dare say anything about their phone calls or about his going to visit one of them, he attacks me for being jealous, demanding, and un-

reasonable. He has promised not to have sex with anyone else but me, and he says he has kept his promise. What else do I want? The main reason we decided to come to this workshop was that we both felt a need to work on this problem—which Ron keeps referring to as my jealousy problem. The other reason was to spend a week together at Esalen. [The Esalen Institute at Big Sur, California, became famous during the early days of the encounter movement, and is still active as a site for a variety of workshops.] Ron has been here before and told me it was one of the most beautiful places he has ever seen. With that, at least, I can agree.

When we arrived here yesterday, the first thing we did was go down to the office to register. All of a sudden, a woman called Wendy, whom Ron knew from one of his previous visits here, leaped on him and gave him this very big welcome hug. Then she proceeded to massage his chest with a circular motion and I saw the circles growing bigger and bigger, and her hand getting lower and lower down his chest, and I was standing there wondering just how low her hand would get.

While all this touchy-feely stuff was going on, I continued standing there like a fool. He never even bothered to introduce me. I don't think he necessarily had to say, "Wendy, this is Carol, the woman I love and am living with now." He could have just put his arm around me to indicate that we are a couple, that he is no longer the swinging bachelor he was when they first met. But he just stood there, clearly enjoying himself, letting her give him a sensuous chest massage.

When we were alone in our room, I told him how I felt, but I said it calmly. He said he was so excited about seeing Wendy, whom he hadn't seen for a long time, and whom he liked very much, that he behaved rudely, and he was sorry. I accepted his apology and thought this would be the end of it. I should have known better.

This afternoon, right after lunch, he disappeared. I looked for him everywhere. Finally, after about two hours, he appeared in our room and told me that he'd had "an interview" with Wendy. I felt the blood rush to my head. What, exactly, is "an interview"? Why not call it "a date," which is what it was? And why is he having a date with Wendy on the week we took to be together and work on our relationship?"

As can be expected, Ron had a different perspective on these events:

I'd been married for many years, in a very unhappy marriage. My wife and I were high-school sweethearts, so neither of us had experience with anyone else before our marriage. Even though we had practically no sex life for the last years of our marriage, I was always faithful to my wife. I guess I'm just not the cheating type. After the divorce, which, by the way, wasn't initiated by me, I discovered women. I also discovered that I love women. I had several girlfriends. Every one of them knew I was seeing others too, and accepted it. They understood that I wasn't ready for a monogamous relationship. Besides, each one of them knew that when I was with her I was with her totally. I know how to give to a woman, and I love giving. So they accepted what I had to give. We all had a great time.

Then Carol came into my life. Soon after we started dating, it became clear to me that this was going to be a very different story. When Carol demanded that I stop seeing other women, I agreed. It was a tremendous sacrifice for me. I was willing to do it for Carol, only because I care about her a great deal. But there were all these women that during my years as a bachelor had become close, intimate friends. Was I supposed to just dump them because I was now living with someone? I've explained this to Carol a hundred times, but she refuses to understand. I've given her no reason to be jealous, but it makes no difference. She's simply a jealous person, and nothing I say or do can change that.

I feel that I have made a far greater sacrifice for the relationship than Carol has made, and I've proved to her that I care. I think her demand that I not see other women at all is unfair and unreasonable. Wendy is a dear friend of mine, whom I haven't seen for a long time. There was nothing wrong in my seeing her. We sat in her room talking, and the door was open the whole time. I feel that I did nothing wrong. So I called it an "interview"—does that justify the scene Carol is making?

It was clear that this discussion was familiar to Ron and Carol—so familiar, in fact, that they weren't really listening to each other. "I think we understand the way both of you are seeing the situation,"

I said. "But I'm not sure you two see each other's perspective that clearly. Maybe hearing it from someone else might help." I turned to the group and asked whether anyone felt familiar enough with the issue Ron and Carol were discussing to be able to present it.

Jim and Susan, who are not a couple, volunteered. I asked them to sit in the middle of the room facing each other, and to present Ron and Carol's positions to the best of their ability.

Without a moment's hesitation, Jim and Susan continued the heated discussion. For the rest of us it seemed as though Ron and Carol's argument was never interrupted. "If you cared about me and about the relationship, you wouldn't go and spend time with another woman. Especially not here and not this week. The fact that you didn't go to bed with her on this particular occasion doesn't change that fact," Susan said.

"I've given you more than I've given any other woman in my life, but it's not enough. Nothing is enough for you. You are jealous, demanding, and unreasonable. Next you'll ask me to get rid of my bicycle, because it makes me spend time away from you," Jim responded.

Ron and Carol were listening, dumbfounded. "Does that sound like something you two could have said to each other?" I asked. "This is unbelievable," said Ron. "It's as if Jim were talking straight from my head." "Susan is saying it even better than I can," added Carol. "It's because I am speaking from my own experience," said Jim. "I can't tell you how many times I've had this very conversation myself," agreed Susan.

"Let's see if anyone else in the group has had a similar experience. If you feel that you can speak for either Carol or Ron, please come and join Jim and Susan," I said. In a few minutes every one of the twenty-two participants in the jealousy workshop was sitting in the middle of the room. The women sat next to Susan. The men (except for one who kept changing his place and position during the argument) sat next to Jim. The argument continued with raised voices and emotions. The women: "If you want to have a truly intimate relationship, you give up a little freedom. It's more than worth it!" The men: "Who are you to say that it's worth it? If you give up your freedom, you are a prisoner. In a good relationship, you trust each other. You don't imprison each other. You women are simply jealous!" The women: "You think we are jealous because we want to protect the relationship. Let's see you guys when you think there is a threat to the relationship. You'd be as jealous as we are, if not more. All we ask is for some safeguards. If we let you guys have your way, there'd be no relationship, or else there'd be a relationship not worth having!"

It became clear to Ron and Carol that they were not alone in their "jealousy problem." Like so many of us, Carol and Ron falsely assumed that their problem was caused by some innate personality deficiency—in the other. Ron blamed Carol's jealousy. Carol blamed Ron's womanizing. Hearing the men and the women in the group helped break Ron and Carol's "fallacy of uniqueness"—the false assumption that whatever is happening to us is unique, that no one else experiences it in quite the same way. The issue no longer was "You are not being considerate," but rather, "Men and women look at relationships differently and that can cause problems."

Men's and Women's Different Approaches to Intimate Relationships

What became clear to the group was that the problem had less to do with Carol's or any other woman's jealousy than with a basic difference in the way men and women approach intimate relationships.

Meta-analysis of hundreds of studies that investigated psychological differences between men and women suggests that the difference in the meaning attached to sex may be one of the strongest of all gender differences (Hyde, 1993). This difference can be summarized this way: Women generally connect sex with affection, closeness, intimacy. Men generally connect sex with achievement, adventure, control, or pure physical release (Basow, 1992). In addition, leading feminist psychoanalysts argue that women's sense of self and of self-worth is grounded in their intimate relationships.[1]

A study by David DeSteno and Peter Salovey (1996b) shows how the importance of intimate relationships for women impacts their jealousy. In the study, characteristics of the rival were studied in terms of their impact on jealousy. Results showed that women, more so than men, consider the desires of their partner in identifying rivals who evoked jealousy. In other words, when women know that their partner is attracted to a particular feature in a woman, and the rival has this feature, they respond with jealousy. Men, on the other hand, consider as rivals those who excel in areas important to their own

definition of themselves. They do not consider their partner's preference. This suggests that intimate partners have a greater impact on
women's self definition and, because of that, on what they will consider a threat in a rival.

Because of the great importance of intimate relationships to
women's sense of self, there is a difference between men and women
in "mate selection criteria." This observation received research support in a much quoted study by Douglas Kenrick and his colleagues
(1993). In the study, young men and women specified their minimum
criteria for a date, sexual partner, exclusive dating partner, marriage
partner, and a one-night sexual liaison. Sex differences were greatest for casual sexual liaisons, with men's criteria being consistently
lower than women's. In other words, while for men a casual one-
night stand may mean nothing, for a woman any sexual liaison is
likely significant and therefore approached with caution.

In my clinical work I have discovered again and again the value
of telling couples that their jealousy problem is shared by most men
and women. Like Ron and Carol, when couples discover that their
problem is commonly experienced by others, they stop looking for
defects in each other. When it becomes clear that like most men and
women they too have different ways of being intimate, much of the
energy that was spent in blaming the other and protecting themselves from attack is freed and can be used for better coping.

Another interaction between Carol and Ron in the workshop
demonstrated another important point: the connection between
couples' original attraction to each other and the primary cause of
their subsequent stress or jealousy.

"What attracted you to Carol when you met?" I asked Ron.

"Well, she's obviously a very beautiful, sexy woman," answered
Ron. "She's also warm and intelligent. But what was most important
to me was that she's a strong, independent woman who has a mind
of her own. I don't like weak, dependent women."

"And what attracted you to Ron when you first met?" I asked Carol.

"First, I was attracted to his looks. I love thin, tall men and I love
gray hair; Ron is skinny, very tall, and has wonderful gray hair. But
I was attracted to his warmth and gentleness even more than to his
looks. He really knows how to make a woman feel special like no
other man I've ever known."

"So you were attracted to Ron because he is a good-looking man and knows how to relate to a woman, and now you are upset because he is attractive to other women and knows how to relate to women. A bit unfair, isn't it? And you, Ron, were attracted to Carol because she is strong and independent and has a mind of her own, but now you are upset because she wants the relationship to be the way she believes a good relationship ought to be. Strong women who have a mind of their own tend to have their own ideas about relationships, too."

When I first noted that people tend to be most distressed by an aspect of their mate's character or behavior that they initially found most attractive, I related it to the notion of our romantic image. The person we are attracted to—the person we choose to fall in love with and make a commitment to—fits our internalized romantic image in some significant way. That romantic image is most influenced by our parents, who are our first models of love. It is also influenced, albeit to a lesser degree, by evolutionary and cultural definitions of who is an attractive man or woman.

According to the evolutionary (sociobiological) approach, this definition of attractiveness is related to our evolutionary history, in which the men and women considered attractive were the ones who had a better chance to breed and provide for their offspring, and thus had a better chance to pass on their genes to future generations. In other words, cultural stereotypes for attractiveness are based on qualifications for breeding.[2]

Examples are big (but not too big) breasts in women and a tall, muscular (but not too tall or too muscular) body in men. Indeed, Ron described Carol, who is big-breasted, as "a very sexy woman"; Carol, like many other women, said she liked tall, lean men. Why are big breasts attractive in a woman? Because, argue sociobiologists, it suggests the woman has the attributes needed to nurse a baby. Why are height and a muscular body attractive in a man? Because, say the sociobiologists, they suggest that the man has the attributes needed to be a good provider and protector.

Which Is the More Jealous Sex?

The answer to this question depends on our definition of jealousy. If we compare the frequency of the experience of jealousy, its symptoms, and its intensity, men and women are very similar. Actually, a consistent finding in my research has been the relative lack of differences between the sexes.[3] Similar findings were reported in other studies that examined gender differences in jealousy.[4]

When asked how jealous they were, and how jealous they had been during earlier periods of their life, again there was no difference between men and women. There was no differences in either frequency or duration of the most intense experience of jealousy, and no difference in either the emotional or the physical components of jealousy. There was also no difference between men and women in the number of other people who consider them jealous, either among people who knew them well, or among people with whom they had an intimate relationship. There were few gender differences concerning people or situations that elicit jealousy, all of them related to women's greater belief in monogamy.

Women and men showed no differences in the components of the experience of jealousy, its intensity or its frequency, and showed few differences in the triggers of jealousy. There were major differences, however, in the ways men and women responded to jealousy. (See Tables 11–19 in Appendix C.)

How Do Men and Women Respond to Jealousy?

When you are jealous, how do you usually respond? Do you:

- talk about it with your partner?
- try to ignore the whole thing?
- let your partner understand that you are hurt?
- scream and shout?
- get away?
- respond with violence?
- respond in some other way?

When this question was presented to 285 men and 283 women, there were several differences between the responses of men and women, but there were many more similarities than differences.[5] For both men and women, the most frequent response to jealousy was to "talk about it." Talking is obviously the best response (and "right answer"). The finding that men talk more often than women contradicts the stereotype of the silent man and the talkative woman.

Yet it confirms the findings of many studies that show that men do indeed talk more than women.[6]

For women, the second most frequent response was to "try to ignore the whole thing." This was a far less frequent response for men. These findings seem to suggest that when her partner is triggering her jealousy, a woman is able, or willing, to ignore it more than a man does. As we will see shortly, evolutionary approach has an explanation as to why this is so. Nevertheless, it should be noted that a study by Paul Mullen and Judy Martin shows that men tend to cope with jealousy by using denial and avoidance, whereas women are more likely to express their distress (Mullen & Martin, 1994).

While men and women are similar in their likelihood of letting their mate know that they are hurt, they tend to do it in different ways. For women, responses tend to include crying, sulking, and looking hurt, while men are more likely to express their feelings by lashing out in anger.

For most men and women, these three responses—talking, ignoring, and expressing hurt—accounted for the majority of the total responses mentioned (81% for men and 80% for women). Only a small percentage of men and women described themselves as either shouting, getting away, or resorting to violence because of jealousy. Despite the small percentages, it's worth noting that women reported using more verbal abuse than men did, while men reported responding with physical violence three times more than women did. This too confirms the findings of others' studies.[7]

While the findings of men's greater tendency to respond to jealousy with aggression seem to fit gender stereotypes and other data about men's greater violence, the results of a recent study seem to suggest that things may be changing. The study asked male and female undergraduates whether a male victim of a partner's infidelity should react more aggressively than a female victim, and how the respondents themselves would react to a partner's infidelity. Contrary to their expectations, the researchers discovered that the subjects, particularly females, expected females more than males to react aggressively and revengefully when confronted with infidelity. Females were also more likely than males to declare that they themselves would verbally and physically abuse their partner. Other than this role reversal, females anticipated behaving in a more typical feminine way—cry, feign indifference, and try to look cool and attractive (deWeerth & Kalma, 1993).

Despite the findings of this study—of what women and men think men and women should do when confronted with infidelity—it seems that men and women respond differently to the actual discovery that their mates have had an illicit affair. Men tend to lash out in anger, which in extreme cases can be expressed violently, and to leave the situation or the relationship. Women tend to respond with depression, disappointment, self-blame, self-doubt, and attempts to bring the man back by making themselves more attractive or by making the man jealous.[8]

One interpretation of the differences between men's and women's responses to jealousy is that men are more likely to protect and maintain their self-esteem, while women make a greater effort to maintain the relationship.[9]

When discussing affairs their mates have had, men and women have different concerns. Most men seem interested in the sexual and more "technical" details of the experience and in comparing themselves to their rival: "How big was his penis?" "How many times did he make you come?" "Was he better or worse than me in bed?" Women, on the other hand, tend to be more interested in the significance of the experience for the quality and future of the relationship: "Do you love her?" "Do you feel closer to her?" Women also tend to be more concerned with the damage the affair might have caused to the intimacy of the relationship. They are often obsessed with such questions as, "What did you tell her about me?" "Did you share with her any intimate details about me or us?" Women feel tremendous betrayal in discovering that a mate has disclosed such intimate information.

During the reconciliation talk after the discovery of an affair, a man is likely to say—in an attempt to belittle the threat it posed to the relationship—"It was only a physical thing, I didn't feel anything toward her." (In other words, "I didn't make a commitment.") The woman, on the other hand, is likely to say, "It was a platonic friendship. He never touched me." These explanations (chosen consciously or unconsciously) reflect the different anxiety the affair raises for men and for women. The opposite explanation—a man excusing an affair as being a platonic friendship, and a woman excusing it as being only a physical thing—is far less common.

One possible explanation of these different reactions to jealousy has to do with men's and women's different sex roles. Women are more likely than men to view an intimate relationship as central to their identity and look to find a sense of meaning in it for their life. Because women tend to identify with their relationships more than men do and to have better interpersonal skills, they are more likely to take on the roles of a relationship monitor (the guardian of the relationship), and of an emotional specialist who understands feelings and helps take care of them.[10]

Women's greater involvement helps explain why they are more likely to try to improve the relationship after an affair, while men are more likely to use denial or leave. A man may choose to deny or refuse to acknowledge the threat instead of consciously ignoring and minimizing it, which women are more likely to do. The reason: If he notices, he will have to do something about it, and he may be simply too busy for that.

Another difference between men and women, related to their different levels of involvement in their relationships, is women's greater likelihood to induce jealousy. Psychologist Greg White (1980) discovered five motives for inducing jealousy: to get a specific reward, such as attention; to test the strength of the relationship; to inflict revenge because the partner was unfaithful; to bolster self-esteem; and to punish the partner. The most popular method of inducing jealousy was to discuss or exaggerate attraction to someone else, followed by flirting, dating others, fabricating rivals, and talking about former romantic partners. Women were more likely to report inducing jealousy than were men, and were more likely to do it if they were more involved in the relationship than their partner. White believes that the reason for these differences lies in women's tendency to use power that is indirect (manipulative) and personal (based on interaction rather than on concrete resources, such as money).

White's explanation focuses on the power difference between men and women. It assumes that women induce jealousy because they have less power than men in our patriarchal society. The evolutionary approach, on the other hand, assumes that all the differences between men and women, including the differences in their response to jealousy, are innate—the results of a lengthy process of evolution and natural selection. While the differences between men and women are a secondary issue in the psychodynamic and systems approaches, they are a primary issue in sociobiology.

The Evolutionary (Sociobiological) Approach

The evolution of sex differences was one of the central themes in Charles Darwin's theory.[11] According to Darwin, as males and females ascend the evolutionary ladder, differences between them become more distinct in both biology and behavior. Males become larger, more aggressive, and more intelligent. Females become more nurturing. The growing differences between the sexes are the result of a process of "natural selection."

An organism able to survive and to out-reproduce others is in evolutionary terms a "superior" organism. In fighting against each other for possession of the females, the most powerful, most intelligent, and most aggressive males (those who were the best hunters) won and thus passed on these characteristics to the next generation. Because these men were the better hunters, they were better able to protect and provide for their women and offspring. For similar reasons, children of nurturing mothers had a better chance of surviving, and passed on these women's characteristics to the next generation.

Darwin also saw an evolutionary reason for jealousy. He believed that jealousy was an instinctual defense (or, according to the definition of jealousy offered earlier, "a protective response") of the pair bond. Feelings and behaviors associated with jealousy served to increase the likelihood that the pair would stay together, reproduce, and raise the offspring to maturity, thus replicating their genes. The fact that jealousy appears among animals, too, was seen by Darwin as a proof that jealousy is innate.

Modern sociobiologists also describe jealousy as having an important function for genetic survival.[12] Since all males confront the problem of "uncertain paternity," jealous males who guard at all times against sexual rivals are more likely to raise their own offspring rather than their rivals'.

A man whose wife has committed adultery is called a "cuckold." The term is derived from cuckoo—the bird that lays its egg in another's nest. It is never used to describe a woman whose husband has committed adultery. Why? Because a woman cannot be cheated the way a man can in wasting her "parental investment" on a parasite. Parental investment is a key concept in sociobiology; it refers to the energy expended by parents to produce and raise offspring.

The evolutionary risk men face of being cuckolded explains why, in the majority of human societies, there is an asymmetry in chastity laws: While adultery is forbidden for both sexes, commonly the woman is more severely penalized for it than the man. A prereservation Apache husband, for example, could beat his adulterous wife, kill her and her lover, or cut off the end of her nose so that she was too ugly for anyone to want her again. An Apache wife whose husband committed adultery, on the other hand, could only withdraw from the relationship, attempt to get her husband back, or, in the most extreme circumstance, divorce him.[13] In most known cultures a husband can punish his wife more severely and dissolve the marriage more easily than a wife can.

In a survey of types of marriage around the world it was discovered that out of 554 societies in which some kind of marriage exists, only 135 practice monogamy. The majority of societies practice polygamy. The husbands in these societies can have two or more wives. Polyandry, the practice of a wife having two or more husbands, exists only in 4 of the 554 societies.[14]

In addition to anthropological reports about different forms of marriage around the world, sociobiologists use evidence from a variety of other sources, including analogies to the animal world (with the assumption that if animals' jealousy is genetically controlled, so is human jealousy); the existence of differences between men and women in response to jealousy; the fact that male jealousy often leads to conflict and violence; anthropological evidence of the nearly universal male constraint of female sexuality; and both anthropological and psychological reports of men's concerns about their paternity.[15]

From everything said so far, it must seem obvious why sociobiologists think men and women respond differently to the discovery of an affair. For a man, such responses as rage, lashing out, revenge, or leaving are all perfectly reasonable from an evolutionary perspective. The betrayal affects not only the situation at hand but also future generations. A cuckolded man who doesn't leave may be providing for another's offspring and genes. From an evolutionary perspective, the woman who has been betrayed faces a far less serious threat. The fact that her husband is spreading his sperm around is not a threat to her own offspring and genes as long as he stays and continues to provide for them. Thus her motivation is to get him away from the other woman and keep him attached to her.

Clearly, sociobiologists view jealousy as an understandable response that may appear irrational only when attention is focused on the individual who experiences and expresses it. From the perspective of that individual's genes, jealousy is extremely rational. Consider, for example, why a man should care about sharing his wife with others if he is convinced that it will in no way affect the satisfaction of his own needs. From this purely "rational" perspective there is absolutely no logical reason for jealousy scenes and violence. But when one views the situation from the perspective of the man's genetic survival, there is a perfectly good reason for his jealousy. It is a response to the threat that his genes may not be passed on to future generations. For a woman, who is always sure that the baby she carries has her genes, the focus of jealousy is on another kind of threat—that she won't have a man to provide for her and her offspring.

In summary, from a sociobiological perspective, gender differences in jealousy result from an essential male–female asymmetry in parental confidence. While females cannot easily misidentify their young and misdirect their parental care, males can only be confident of their paternity if they are the exclusive sexual partners of their mate. Therefore, the main reproductive threat associated with male infidelity is the risk of lost resources, whereas the main threat associated with female infidelity is the risk of alien insemination. Because of the different risks they face, females can be expected to be less jealous than males, and less concerned with the sexual infidelity of their partner than with the potential loss of attention and resources needed for the raising of offspring.

To prove this point, David Buss and his colleagues (1992) asked students which would distress them more upon discovering that the person with whom they were seriously involved was becoming interested in someone else: "Imagining your partner forming a deep emotional attachment to that person," or "Imagining your partner enjoying passionate sexual intercourse with that other person." Results indicated that more men were upset by the possibility of sexual infidelity, whereas more women were upset by a potential emotional infidelity.

These findings together with Buss's evolutionary perspective on jealousy generated a heated debate and made the study of gender differences in jealousy a hot topic. Among the studies supporting his findings and interpretation was a study by Bram Buunk and his colleagues (among them David Buss) who studied sex differences in jealousy in the Netherlands, Germany, and the United States. In all three counties men showed greater psychological and physiological distress to sexual infidelity, while women showed greater distress to emotional infidelity. However, the magnitude of these sex differences varied somewhat across cultures. It was large for the United States, medium for Germany and the Netherlands (Buunk et al., 1996).

Very similar findings were reported by David Geary and his colleagues in a study that examined sex differences in jealousy in China and the United States. Once again, findings supported David Buss's evolutionary prediction: A higher proportion of men reported distress to a partner's imagined sexual infidelity and a higher proportion of women reported distress to imagined emotional infidelity. However, a much higher proportion of American men and women reported more distress in response to sexual infidelity compared to their same-sex Chinese peers. This seems to suggest that the predisposition to romantic jealousy is influenced by sexual permissiveness in the general culture (Geary et al., 1995).

Other scholars accepted the findings reported by David Buss and his colleagues, but took issue with their interpretation. Christine Harris and Nicholas Christenfeld (1996a), for example, argued that the fact that men are especially bothered by evidence of their partner's sexual infidelity, whereas women are troubled more by evidence of emotional infidelity, can be the result of what they call "reasonable" differences between the sexes in how they interpret evidence of infidelity. A man, thinking that women have sex only when in love, has reason to believe that if his mate has sex with another man, she is in love with that man. A woman, thinking that a man can have sex without love, should still be bothered by sexual infidelity, but less so, because it does not imply that her mate has fallen in love as well.

Other scholars challenge Buss's overreliance on the theory of evolution. David DeSteno and Peter Salovey (1996a), for example, agree with Buss that evolution may play a role in determining human behaviors such as jealousy, but they argue that one should not forget that human behavior is also influenced by cultural variables to a much greater degree than the behavior of other species.

In a similar vein, Ralph Hupka and Adam Bank (1996) argue that the findings reported by Buss and his colleagues were due to ascribed gender norms rather than to differences in innate propensities for jealousy between men and women. They support this argument with the findings of a study as well as numerous ethnographic reports that call into question the evolutionary view on jealousy and support a sociocultural perspective. In the study, which involved 745 students, it was found that over 50% of both men and women reported greater upset over imagined emotional infidelity.

In one of my studies of sex differences in jealousy, it was found that while there was no sex difference in the jealousy triggered by the thought of a sexual infidelity (both men and women reacted very strongly to this) there was a sex difference in response to an emotional infidelity (women responded more strongly than men) (Pines & Friedman, 1998).

In light of these and other studies, it seemed appropriate for Christine Harris and Nicholas Christenfeld (1996b) to suggest that, instead of proposing a specific innate mechanism to explain sex differences in jealousy, it might be more useful to focus on the fact that both men and women are bothered by both emotional and sexual infidelity.

What did Buss and his colleagues (1996) have to say in response to all this criticism? Their response was simply that by all scientific standards the evolutionary account of sex differences in jealousy "appears to be in good standing."

A Power Perspective on Jealousy

According to social psychologists, and other critics of the evolutionary perspective, the differences in jealousy between men and women do not result from an evolutionary process; they are primarily the result of social processes and existing conditions in the society that affect all couples and all individuals. One such social condition with special relevance for jealousy is the power difference between men and women. Power, for the purpose of this discussion, is the difference in dependency on each other within a couple—the partner who is more dependent has less power. The dependency can be emotional, financial, social.

The more powerful person in the relationship, whether a man or a woman, tends to respond to the jealousy-trigger in the "masculine" way—lashing out in anger, leaving, and so on. The weaker person typically behaves in the "feminine" way: crying, sulking, trying to become more attractive, trying to make the mate jealous, etc. Sadly, the person who cares less or has more outside alternatives has more power in the relationship.[16]

Many women tend to respond to jealousy in the typically "feminine" way, not because they are women but because they have less power in their relationships. A woman in her fifties who has spent most of her adult life rearing children and supporting her husband's career has far fewer alternatives outside the marriage than does her successful husband. When she discovers that her husband is having an affair with his young secretary, her jealousy is not only a response to a perceived threat to a valued love relationship; it is also a response to a threat to a marriage that defines her entire life.

A nice demonstration of the impact women's vulnerability has on their jealousy was provided in a study by Ada Lumpart. Vulnerability was defined in the study as the fear of being abandoned and willingness to accept hurtful behavior from one's partner. Lumpart asked men and women: What would you do if you discovered that your mate is unfaithful? She found that women who had the highest scores of vulnerability said such things as, "I would accept it. What other choice do I have?" Women who had an average vulnerability score said such things as, "I would give him an ultimatum—it's either me or her." Women who had low vulnerability scores said, "I would leave."

Women's vulnerability was not an innate characteristic, but a result of their life circumstances. Vulnerability was low when the woman had no children, highest when she had young children, and low again after the children left home. Men's vulnerability was similar to women's before the children were born, but went down with the birth of the children, and up again after investing time and energy in them. After the children left home, the vulnerability of men and women became similar again (Lumpert & Friedman, 1992).

This brings us back to the difference between men's and women's involvement in relationships. Women are socialized to care more about relationships and to desire commitment more than men. The result is their loss of power to men. These power differences are not innate. They are primarily a result of power differences in the society, which are reflected in power differences within the couple. A wife who creates alternatives for herself outside the marriage and is less dependent on her husband emotionally, socially, and financially is less likely to take on the role of the jealous mate. One couple, both in their early fifties, is an example of this kind of role reversal.

The wife, Laura, had been a homemaker from the time her oldest child was born until the youngest finished high school. At that time she felt that she could afford to do something for herself, so she went back to school and got a business degree. With the help of high grades and excellent recommendations from her teachers, she was able to get a job in a large pharmaceutical company. There, her enthusiasm and hard work earned Laura one promotion after another. Soon she was managing the state office of the company, traveling often, meeting interesting people, and coming home late.

Her husband, Adam, was an engineering manager in a small industrial company, and hadn't advanced much in his career during those years. At about the time Laura started flying up the career ladder, he started feeling bored with his work, frustrated, and angry. Just when she was finding success and great significance in everything she was doing, he started asking himself, "What's the meaning of it all?" While neither one of them acknowledged the change, Adam was now more needy of Laura than she was of him, and felt very threatened by the people she interacted with at work. Whenever Laura came home late, which was often, Adam demanded to know where she had been, with whom, what they had done, and what they had talked about.

At first Laura tried to be patient and understanding. Whenever possible, she called Adam if she was going to be late, and explained in detail what she did during her absence. She also tried hard to ignore his hostile tone when he interrogated her. But after a while she started to lose her patience and resent his jealousy. She was having a wonderful time at work and was doing nothing to justify his jealousy and rudeness.

The happier Laura was with her world outside the marriage, and the more unhappy Adam was with his own world, the more jealous he became. He didn't trust Laura's explanations, and continued to feel hurt and excluded even when he knew she had spent an evening with her women friends. Indeed, he was excluded from her world, just when he needed her most.

According to sociobiology, there was absolutely no reason for Adam to be jealous. First, Laura was spending time with women friends, so there was no chance of his being cuckolded. Second, Laura had already gone through menopause, so there was no chance she could become pregnant and carry someone else's genes. Furthermore, they had finished rearing their children, and he was as assured of his genetic survival as anyone can be.

From the power perspective, however, there was a good reason for Adam to be jealous. Throughout their life together he had been "the man" in the family and, as such, had more power than Laura. Now suddenly their roles were reversed and he was the one with less power in the relationship.

Adam, who is a handsome, masculine, and successful man, responded to the perceived threat to the quality of his marriage in a traditionally "feminine" way. He became depressed, sulked, bought himself new clothes (hoping Laura would notice), and tried to make her jealous by seeing friends without her. The problem was that Laura didn't mind at all. She even encouraged him to see his friends more often.

Adam had to realize that as long as he was doing things to get a response from Laura, he was still dependent on her. He also had to come to terms with the fact that at the core of his jealousy were feelings of powerlessness and dependency.

In order to overcome his dependency, Adam renewed contacts with people he liked but with whom he hadn't kept in touch. Since Laura had been responsible for maintaining social contacts in their marriage, when she didn't like some of Adam's friends and colleagues she had arranged to avoid seeing them socially. Now that Laura had her own social world, Adam could choose the people he wanted to have as friends, independent of those he and Laura were seeing as a couple. The task was not an easy one for Adam, who had relied on Laura throughout their marriage to do the social talking for him. In fact, Laura's social skills and high energy were the things Adam had found most attractive when they first met. Each time he called someone, he was afraid he would discover that the person was surprised and not happy to hear from him after all this time. This never happened.

When Adam became involved with his own friends, interests, and activities—he loved hiking, for example, so he joined the Sierra Club and started mountain hiking regularly—he stopped perceiving Laura's work as a threat. His increased satisfaction with his life and an increased sense of power in the marriage led to a decrease in jealousy.

We've seen that men can respond to jealousy in a way that is typ-ically female, and women can respond in a way that is typically male. Yet research shows that couples like Adam and Laura are the excep-tion, especially during the child–rearing years. Most men and women tend to respond to jealousy in the way that is characteristic of their sex. As Ron and Carol's case demonstrated, knowing about these dif-ferences can help couples break their own fallacy of uniqueness and work toward resolving their jealousy problem.

The fact that there are exceptions, however, suggests that the dif-ferences between "male" and "female" jealousy are not innate, as the sociobiologists claim. Genetic programming is not all–powerful, especially in a creature as sophisticated as a human being. Instead, these differences result from the working of evolutionary forces in combination with a variety of other forces in the society.

This brings us back to the notion of jealousy as a result of an inter-action between a certain disposition and a certain trigger. Genetic programming and power differences prescribed by society each influence men's and women's predispositions to jealousy. Whether or not these predispositions will manifest themselves depends on the dynamics of the relationship on and internal processes in the mind of the individual.

An Evaluation of the Evolutionary Approach

The sociobiological approach helps focus attention on the different ways men and women express jealousy. When couples are told that other men and women experience jealousy conflicts in a similar way, they are vastly relieved. As a result, they are often able to con-front their own and their mate's jealousy with more understanding and less blame.

Unlike the sociobiological focus on the differences between men and women in jealousy, the psychodynamic, the systems, and the behavioral approaches view sex differences as mostly irrelevant in treating jealousy. The psychodynamic approach recognizes that the childhood experiences of boys and girls are different, but the process of unearthing the unconscious trauma at the base of a jealousy prob-lem is the same for men and for women. In the systems approach, though men and women may play different roles in a romantic rela-tionship, the goal of disrupting negative interaction patterns does not depend on who plays what role. In the behavioral approach, it doesn't matter whether a man or a woman responds inappropriately to a jealousy trigger; the goal of therapy is to unlearn that inappropriate response and replace it with a more appropriate one.

The sociobiological approach has received a great deal of criticism for using circular reasoning and explanations that can never be empirically substantiated or refuted. It looks at existing phenomena, such as sex differences in jealousy, and argues that there must be an evolutionary reason for their existence. Sociobiologists are convinced that if there were no evolutionary reason for the survival of a certain trait, it would not have existed today. But proving a phenomenon by its existence is not a valid proof.

Another criticism has been directed at sociobiologists' attempts to link human jealousy to animal jealousy—both supposedly a result of genetic programming. In fact, critics argue that there is no empirical research that directly links jealousy with a particular gene.[17]

Furthermore, the sociobiological notion that jealousy is "natural" and reflects some kind of biological imperative is dangerous. It can justify unacceptable responses to jealousy, such as violence. There is a long tradition of tolerance toward men who kill their lovers and rivals because of the belief that these men cannot help themselves. This biological imperative is far less likely to be evoked in defense of jealous women.[18]

The notion that men and women are genetically "wired" to respond to jealousy in particular ways can also be used as an excuse not to work on a jealousy problem.

Integrating the Sociobiological and Power Perspectives

After reviewing the two explanations for sex differences in jealousy—the evolutionary and the power perspectives—one may be left wondering which explanation is the "correct" one. Are gender differences in jealousy the result of evolutionary or social forces? Scholars in each of these fields believe that they have the only possible answer to this question. It is possible, however, to integrate the two perspectives. Jealousy is a result of an interaction between evolutionary forces and current social forces. It is also the result of processes in the mind of the jealous individual and of destructive patterns within the couple relationship. Jealousy is best described as a circle within a circle within a circle. The first circle is the individual. The second is the couple. The third is the culture in which the couple lives. It is experienced by the individual, played out in the couple relationship, and shaped by evolution and social forces. Now we can move on to examine the social forces that define how jealousy is experienced and expressed.

A Note for Therapists

Evolutionary theory can provide a powerful educational tool in the context of therapy by helping to break the fallacy of uniqueness—the false assumption that every jealousy problem is unique. One of the workshop exercises I use to illustrate this point is a "jealousy sociodrama."

I start by drawing an imaginary line across the room. On one end is the position that an intimate relationship has to be monogamous: "You can't truly love more than one person. Jealousy is normal and natural when your mate shows an interest in another person." On the other end is the position that loving more than one person is not only possible, but also natural: "Jealousy is not natural, but learned, and thus can be unlearned. If you truly love someone, you want to see him or her happy, even when it is with someone else." I ask two volunteers from the group to argue for each of these two extreme positions. After that I invite the rest of the group to join in and find a spot that fits each of their positions along the continuum.

What inevitably happens is similar to what happened to Ron and Carol in the role play described earlier. Most of the women in the group cluster around the "monogamy" side of the jealousy line, while most men cluster around the "love should be free" side—demonstrating the basic sociobiological argument. When couples discover that their conflict about jealousy is shared by most other men and women, and that it actually makes sense from an evolutionary perspective, they are able to stop blaming each other, stop feeling guilty, and devote their energy to coping.

6

Romantic Jealousy in Different Cultures

From the moment of his birth, the customs into which [an individual] is born shape his experience and behavior. By the time he can talk, he is the little creature of his culture.

—Ruth Benedict, "Patterns of Culture"

Jealousy [has] a human face.

—William Blake, *Songs of Experience*

A comparison of the ways people in different cultures experience and express jealousy shows that social forces exert a major influence on people's responses to it.[1] A situation that provokes jealousy in one culture at a particular time in history does not necessarily provoke jealousy in another culture or time. A response considered normal and acceptable in one culture may be considered abnormal and unacceptable in another. The comforting conclusion is that everything one has done or imagined doing, no matter how strange one's own culture would consider it, is probably normal somewhere else. The subject in this chapter is the social–psychological approach, which views jealousy as a social phenomenon rooted in the culture in which we live.

Let us start with an example of the ways men in different cultures respond to being cuckolded. A turn–of–the–century Bakongo African husband who discovered that his wife had an affair demanded a large sum of money from her lover.[2] A Samoan husband cut out the eyes of the lover or bit off his nose and ears.[3] A "liberated" American husband, living at the end of the twentieth century, has been taught that jealousy is evidence of low self-esteem and tries hard to overcome it.[4]

Can you imagine a situation in which a newlywed bridegroom would actually ask another man to have sexual intercourse with his bride? This, too, happened at times among the Bakongo. Upon completion of the marriage ceremony, it was customary for the village elders to enter the house of the newlywed couple to make sure that everything was in order and, most important, that the bridegroom was able to consummate the marriage. If he was unable to do it, the marriage was dissolved. Sometimes, to avoid shame and humiliation, an impotent husband would find a suitable young man and permit him to have sex with his wife. If a child was born out of their union, the husband treated it as his own. A similar custom was practiced by the Plateau tribes of northern Zimbabwe. A sterile or impotent husband would at times ask his brother to have sex in secret with his wife, so the couple could have a child.[5] Similar choices are being made today in our modern Western society; infertile women have eggs donated by their sisters or mothers rather than have a surrogate ovum donor.

According to cross-cultural psychologist Ralph Hupka, cultures affect our response to jealousy in two primary ways:

1. By defining or not defining a particular event as a threat, which includes (a) designating the events that make us jealous; (b) specifying when are we allowed to perceive a threat; and (c) creating the conditions that dispose us to jealousy.
2. By giving us certain options for responding when an event is defined as a threat.[6]

Events That Make Us Jealous

The culture defines for people the events that will make them perceive a threat to their marriage. These events vary widely, and don't always include an interloper having sex with their mate. For example, a husband among the Yurok tribe of California or the Pawnee of the American plains saw another man's request for a cup of water from his wife as a clear signal that the other man was after her.[7]

An Eskimo husband, on the other hand, offered his wife to a guest in a ceremony of "putting out the lamp." A good host was expected, after turning out the lamp at night, to invite the guest to have sexual intercourse with his wife. A husband who did not give his wife to his guest was considered stingy, mean, and inhospitable. Therefore, a husband upbraided his wife if she was slow to respond to the guest. Yet the same husband would become intensely jealous if his wife had sexual intercourse with that same guest in circumstances other than the lamp ceremony. An Eskimo husband could even kill such an interloper.[8]

The examples of the Yurok and the Eskimo demonstrate that the culture, more than the individual, determines when it is appropriate to perceive a threat to the marriage. Anthropologist Margaret Mead describes another example of this in the marriage customs of the Banaro of New Guinea. These customs are full of occasions that in modern Western culture would give rise to tremendous jealousy.[9]

A young Banaro man who eloped with the woman he loved did not approach her sexually during the elopement. Instead of submitting to their mutual passion, he brought her, a virgin, to his father's house where he knew she would be submitted to a cruel public defloration ceremony. Then the young bridegroom had to allow another man to enjoy his wife sexually for a whole year after their marriage, before he himself could approach her.

Each Banaro man had a ceremonial friend. It was the duty of this friend to initiate his friend's son's future wife into sex. This was done very formally in the "Goblin House," in front of the sacred pipes upon which no woman was allowed to look. After the ceremony the young bride was returned to her father-in-law's care. The ceremonial friend had sex with her, always ritually, until a child was born. The child was known as the "goblin child." Only then was the husband allowed to take his wife.

Meanwhile, the young bridegroom was initiated sexually by the wife of his father's ceremonial friend. The initiation started with the young man being sent to look for the older woman in the forest. Later, on ceremonial occasions, the young bridegroom and his ceremonial friend would exchange wives. Their wives could even bear children to their husband's friends, instead of their husbands. Clearly, what would be an obvious jealousy trigger for us had a different meaning for the Banaro.

When Are We Allowed to Perceive a Threat?

Cultures vary widely in what is considered acceptable evidence for people to conclude that there is a serious threat to their marriage. The Saora of India required the husband to see his wife in the act of sexual intercourse with her lover before he could accuse her of adultery.[10] For the Dobu of equatorial Africa, personal suspicion was legitimate enough cause to make an individual perceive a threat to the marriage.[11] Among the Plateau tribes of northern Zimbabwe, the proof of the wife's infidelity was the birth of a stillborn child or her own death in childbirth. The woman who lay dying or mourning the death of her baby was asked to name her lover, whether or not she actually had one. The man she named was considered guilty without a need for further proof.[12]

In chapter two, I mentioned that for the 728 Americans I questioned, the most serious perceived threat was a sexual liaison their mate had with someone else.[13] A Zuni wife, on the other hand, did not perceive her husband's sexual liaisons as a threat to her marriage; instead, it was the gossip of the village people about her husband that caused her to perceive a threat and confront him.[14]

Another example of what in our culture would be considered a legitimate reason for jealousy can be found in polygamous societies. In such societies, marrying several women is the rule for rich and influential men, and women don't perceive their husbands' marriage to other women as a threat.[15]

Actually, it seems that when a woman is the first wife, she may even favor this arrangement for the help with household chores, female friendship, and prestige that it provides for her husband and for herself. Margaret Mead describes a case of a woman in a polygamous culture who hauled her husband into court on the charge that she had been married to him three years and borne him two children, yet he had not taken another wife. The native court allowed the husband six months in which to take a second wife. A second wife would add to this woman's prestige by conferring upon her the rank of "first wife." In addition, the second wife would provide the household with another laborer and childbearer. Because the addition of other women to the household enhanced the first wife's status and self-esteem there was no occasion for jealousy—unless one of those secondary wives became the favorite. The usurpation of the first wife's dignities provided both the occasion and the justification for jealousy.[16]

Similarly, in most polyandrous societies, the multiple husbands tend to show little jealousy as long as the appropriate status differences are observed.

All of these examples demonstrate how cultures define the rules for verifying the existence of a threat to a marriage. Members of a culture will not support someone's jealous behavior unless that person provides the appropriate justification.

How Cultures Create the Conditions That Dispose Jealousy

According to the social-psychological approach, jealousy is not simply a psychological phenomenon that takes place in the mind of an individual. It's a social phenomenon as well—a product of growing up in a certain culture, anchored in the basic decisions made in that culture about such fundamental issues as physical survival and mating. These decisions become integrated into the customs, morals, and laws of the culture. They define for the individual what is valued and must therefore be protected from possible loss. In this way the culture also defines for the individual the situations that trigger jealousy. If we consider what is valued in our society, we discover that it is related to the most common triggers of jealousy.

Societies differ greatly in the conditions that make people susceptible to jealousy. The more members of a society depend on their mate to fulfill different needs or help face threats to survival, the greater the potential for jealousy.[17]

The Ammasalik Eskimo, for example, was dependent on a competent mate to survive the long, harsh winter. Consequently an interloper presented not only a threat to the marriage, but to actual survival. One cultural solution was a custom of wife-stealing. A man who lost his mate to another was allowed, among other solutions, to steal the wife of another husband. A man who dared to carry away the wife in the presence of her husband was considered a powerful person, and his status in the community increased.[18]

The Dobuan of the D'Entrecastreaux Islands, east of New Guinea, lived in tiny hostile kin groups on very limited and unfruitful lands. A Dobuan man would stay up half the night uttering magic spells and incantations to protect his crop of yams and seduce the yams of his neighbor's field into his own. But no amount of spells and hard work produced a really fine and bountiful crop. The Samoans, on the other hand, lived in large villages united by formal ceremonies on abundant and fertile land. This difference is one of the conditions that, according to Margaret Mead, help explain why jealousy was a widespread phenomenon among the Dobuan, while among the Samoans jealousy was rare.[19]

Marriage happened at a young age for the Dobuan, and not always by mutual consent. It came after a period of great sexual freedom, and imposed strict fidelity on both mates. As a result, during the engagement both mates were tortured by the suspicion that the other was returning to those just recently abandoned sexual adventures. The suspicions only increased after marriage. A Dobuan husband followed his wife everywhere. He sat nearby, watching while she did her work, and counted her footsteps if she left for the bush. A Dobuan wife was never allowed to go to another village alone.

The punishment for adultery among the Dobuan was as harsh as their jealousy. A man who was discovered having sex with another man's wife was likely to have a spear thrust in his back. When that option was not available, the betrayed spouse could try to commit suicide by taking fish poison.

Options for Responding to Jealousy

Culturally sanctioned responses to jealousy are as varied as the cultures on earth. They range from doing nothing to killing both the unfaithful mate and the interloper. The first option is most often given to women, the latter to men. As noted during the discussion of the evolutionary perspective, the difference between men and women in "paternity confidence"—the fact that while women always know that their offspring are theirs, men have no such assurance—explains why the majority of human societies penalize women more severely than men for adultery.

As an example of a woman's comparatively mild response to jealousy, we can look again at the Zuni wife, who at first said nothing to her unfaithful husband. But when his sexual liaison became the source of tribal gossip, forcing her to respond, she refused to wash his laundry. This made it clear to him that the affair was common knowledge, and that he'd better stop it. Among the Murngin of Australia, a wife had only one culturally sanctioned way to respond to her husband's infidelity: assault him verbally in public. If she ran away, her father and brothers would search for her and return her to her husband, who would then beat her as punishment and warning.[20] Physical aggression is allowed among women only when directed toward a rival. Among the Toba Indians of Bolivia, a wife was allowed either to leave her unfaithful husband or fight her rival. Fights could go on for hours, the two women beating each other with their hands and scratching each other with fingernails or cactus thorns.[21]

Culturally acceptable responses to a wife's unfaithfulness tend to be far more severe. In cases of jealousy–related "justifiable homicide," the justified party, almost without exception, is a man.[22] An Antakerrinya husband in South Australia who discovered that his wife had been unfaithful was allowed to cut her across her buttocks and thighs or burn her.[23] A Marquesan husband, under similar circumstances, could punish his wife either by whipping or by killing her.[24] Apache husbands would cut all the hair from the heads of their unfaithful wives, and sometimes cut their noses.[25]

A nineteenth–century husband of an Aboriginal tribe of New Zealand had several culturally accepted options for responding to his wife's unfaithfulness: He could beat, divorce, or kill her. He could also demand either compensation or a duel from her lover. In the duel, both men were armed with spears. At first the husband could try to pierce his rival's chest with his spear while his rival was allowed only to ward off the thrust. After the rival warded off the third thrust, the debt was considered paid and both men continued to fight on even terms.[26]

In all these cases, the options for response available to the jealous individual are related to the culture's evaluation of the offense and the threat it implied. In addition, cultures allow responses according to the assigned responsibility.

Among the Maori of New Zealand, when a wife was unfaithful, her family was required to compensate her husband with a land settlement. But if she ran away with her lover, the husband was held accountable; in the interest of the community, he should have been aware of what was going on and prevented the escape. Because the husband was held responsible, his property was taken away as punishment.[27]

Since the stability of marriage is important to society—it ensures that children will be born and taken care of by both parents—most societies accept jealous behavior as legitimate. According to sociologist Kingsley Davis, a jealousy situation is not a triangle but a quadrangle, because the public or the community at large is always an interested party. By failing to acknowledge the public or community, we fail to grasp the social character of jealousy. To understand jealousy, argues Davis, we must understand the social function it serves.[28]

Most cultures support the betrayed mate and condemn the transgressing mate and the interloper. Yet the punishments prescribed by the social norms of different cultures, and even the person designated to deliver the punishment, can vary greatly. Among the Plateau tribes of northern Zimbabwe, for example, when the adultery was between individuals of equal rank, it was the duty of the tribal chief to flog the male lover. Punishment was much more severe when the husband caught his wife and her lover "in the act." In such cases the husband was expected to kill both wife and lover. If he chose not to punish them, and the wife was caught again, the villagers took on the responsibility for punishment. They impaled the unfaithful wife and her lover on sharp stakes, and then taunted them until they died.[29]

The punishments delivered by the husband, the villagers, and the chief were all prescribed according to a social code and designed to serve as deterrents. They all demonstrate the relationship between the individual's jealousy and the prohibition against adultery that protects the institution of marriage.

Among the Hidatsa Indians of North America, a husband had several options if his wife ran away with another man. One option was to kill his wife and seize the property that belonged to her lover and his friends. This custom encouraged men not to get involved with married women for fear their friends might have to pay for their transgression. But the most praise-worthy alternative was to treat the whole affair as good riddance from the wife by inviting the runaways to his lodge and formally presenting his wife to her new lover.[30]

Everything said so far indicates that the ways in which we experience and express jealousy reflect the norms and social structure of society. What social forces encourage or discourage jealousy? Following Ralph Hupka, this question will be explored through a comparison between the turn-of-the-century Toda of Southern India[31]

and the prereservation Apache Indians of North America.[32] The Toda
tended to minimize expressions of jealousy; the Apache expressed
jealousy frequently.

The Toda and the Apache

For the Toda, jealousy was akin to selfishness, and was considered a
minor sin. According to Toda religion, people who died traveled
across a river on a bridge made of spiderwebs before they reached
the home of their god. Individuals who were jealous during their life
had heavy hearts that tore the thin bridge. They fell into the river,
where they were bitten by leeches. Swamp–dwellers would detain
them for a period of time proportionate to the severity of their jealousy and selfishness. For the Apache Indians, jealousy was a culturally acceptable emotion. One did not need to apologize for
expressing jealousy or repent for experiencing jealousy.

The Toda were primarily polyandrous. When a woman married a
man, she automatically became the wife of his brothers as well, even
of those not yet born. She had sexual relations with the brothers as
well as with the husband who married her. The woman and her
"husbands" lived together as one family. Marriage was not a require-
ment or a reward. Needs for food and shelter were provided by the
joint effort of all the men in the family. Emotional needs for com-
panionship were also easily satisfied.

The Apache, on the other hand, were monogamous. Marriage for
an Apache was the key to recognition as a mature adult and to economic self–sufficiency. Adults without mates were rare and considered abnormal. Both husband and wife were expected to contribute
to the economy of the family. Men hunted; women gathered wild
fruits and vegetables.

For the Apache, marriage was a prerequisite to sexual gratification. Virginity in both sexes was associated with purity, and premarital sex was discouraged. For the Apache, sexual pleasure was a
reward earned after a long period of deprivations—a reward to be
jealously guarded against the threat of an interloper.

The Toda, by contrast, had few sexual restrictions, and sex was easily obtained before and after marriage. Both husbands and wives
were allowed to have lovers. When a man wanted someone else's
wife as a lover, he sought the consent of the wife and her husband

or husbands. If consent was given by all, the men negotiated for an annual fee to be received by the husband(s). The man then visited the woman at the house of her husband(s), or in some cases had her live with him as if she were his wife.

Among the Toda, the clan owned the most valuable property: the sacred buffaloes and the land. Each family had its own nonsacred buffaloes, whose milk was a major source of food, and its own house. Material possessions were few and not highly valued. People had almost no personal property.

The Apache owned most property individually, and such property was not used by anyone else, even a parent, without permission. Handling someone else's belongings implied a special and intimate relationship. A husband's clothes could be washed only by his wife, mother, or daughter. Any other woman who did his laundry was assumed to be having an affair with him.

The Toda were casual not only about personal property, but about personal descendants as well. Men took little interest in knowing whether the child they were rearing was their own; fatherhood was a legal relation established through a ceremony in which the man gave a bow and arrow to the mother. At times that man had no physical contact with the mother prior to the ceremony. The oldest husband in the family usually performed the ceremony when the wife was about seven months pregnant, yet all the husbands were regarded as the father of the child.

To the Apache, children were a great asset that provided not only status and prestige, but also a form of social security since children fed and cared for their parents in old age. Daughters attracted sizable marriage gifts and after their marriage, their parents had access to their husbands' labor and to portions of the game the husbands brought home. In addition, family and children were the major vehicle for attaining high status in the tribe, because family size was a reflection of wealth. The ability to support a large family indicated that a man was a good hunter. Because the Apache placed such great importance on personal lineage, "paternity confidence" was extremely important to them. When an Apache husband was away, he had a close blood relative spy on his wife to make sure she was not seeing other men.

Another difference between the Toda and the Apache had to do with the importance of women's economic contribution. Toda women contributed little; the men did virtually everything, including the cooking. Women fetched water, embroidered clothes, pounded grain, and cleaned the house. They were not allowed to approach the buffaloes or handle the milk. They were also excluded from all political and religious activities. Apache husband and wife were economically self-sufficient and both contributed significantly to the economy of the family, men by hunting, women by gathering and preparing food.

The Toda and the Apache had different response options for unfaithfulness. As noted earlier, an Apache man whose wife had been unfaithful could kill her and her lover, or else mutilate her face. For the Toda man, the discovery that his wife had sex with another man implied a far less serious threat. In fact, there was a positive side, in that an appropriate fee would be arranged for the borrowing of his wife. Thus, the husband was not expected to show any jealousy at all.

Differences in the social organization of the Toda and the Apache can explain, far better than individual characteristics of a particular Apache or Toda, why the Apache were so much more likely than the Toda to respond with jealousy.

We can now move on to consider the question: Is the social organization of North American society the kind that encourages or discourages jealousy?

Jealousy in American Culture

In a survey of popular magazine articles on jealousy over a forty-five-year period, sociologist Gordon Clanton discovered that the experience, expression, interpretation, and treatment of jealousy in the United States have changed substantially. From the end of World War II and until the late 1960s, almost all articles said that a certain amount of jealousy was natural, a proof of love, and good for the marriage. The reader (most often a woman) was advised to keep her jealous feelings under control and to avoid unreasonable jealousy marked by suspicion, hostility, accusations, and threats. The woman was told to avoid situations that might make her husband jealous, but to interpret his expressions of jealousy as evidence of love.

Around 1970, a new view of jealousy started to take root. Magazine articles began to question the appropriateness of jealous feelings in intimate relationships. They no longer assumed that jealousy was evidence of love. For the first time, guilt about jealousy became a problem for large numbers of people. According to this emerging view, jealousy was not natural; it was learned. "Jealousy was no longer seen as a proof of love," Clanton observed, "It was, rather, evidence of a defect such as low self-esteem or the inability to trust. Thus, jealousy was no longer seen as good for relationships; it was bad for them. From this it followed that one could and should seek to eradicate every trace of jealousy from one's personality. Various prescriptions for achieving this were offered by therapists, gurus, and advice givers."[33]

The main difference between cultures that encourage and those that discourage jealousy lies not in the norms for or against expressing jealousy, but in the social organization that determines the likelihood that jealousy will be provoked.

Americans tend to be monogamous. When a marriage doesn't work, they divorce and remarry, a practice termed by family therapists "serial monogamy." Marriage may not be the key to recognition as a mature adult and to economic self-sufficiency, but it is nonetheless important. The vast majority of Americans marry at some point; remaining single throughout life is rare and considered not altogether normal.

Despite this testimony to the importance of marriage, in recent decades people have been getting married later, and more couples have been living together out of wedlock. According to the 1990 Statistical Abstracts of the United States, there are 2,588,000 heterosexual unmarried couples living together. This is more than three times the number in 1970, and more than four times the number in 1960. According to the famous sociologist Jessie Bernard, the importance of marriage is reflected in the attitudes toward jealousy.[34]

Another change that has taken place since World War II is the growing contribution of married women to the family income. Labor statistics indicate that women's participation in the labor force has increased steadily since 1950. Attitudes toward married women's work have also changed. In the 1990s, more people accept a career as a life choice for women than have ever done so in the past. A nationwide survey discovered that three-quarters of those surveyed approved of employed wives. A similar survey conducted forty years earlier showed that three-quarters of those surveyed disapproved of a wife working if she had a husband who could support her.[35] Work-ing wives are less dependent on their husbands and on the marriage than are housewives. When such career women do not find their marriages fulfilling, they are far more likely than housewives to leave their husbands.[36] Other surveys show that the American view of women's roles has become increasingly more liberated.[37]

Over the last fifty years, American society has also become more permissive, especially toward premarital sex. A Harris poll taken in the mid-1980s found that 70% of the women and 79% of the men aged 18–29 thought it was all right for regularly dating couples to have sex. On the other hand, only 40% of the women and 55% of the men aged 50–64 thought this was acceptable.[38] This change in atti-tude is expressed in behavior as well. A survey among married cou-ples indicates that of the couples 18–24 years of age, 95% of the men and 81% of the women had had premarital sex.[39]

According to Kingsley Davis, jealousy is a culturally sanctioned response to a violation of sexual property rights.[40] As sexual norms regarding such issues as premarital sex and virginity become more liberal, we can expect that the norms supporting the expression of jealousy will weaken.

There has been a change in attitude toward virginity in the United States. The same Harris poll showed that 22% of men and 27% of women aged 18–24 said it was important for a woman to be a vir-gin when she gets married, compared to 41% of men and 64% of women aged 50–64. Clearly, virginity is no longer considered neces-sary for young women, and therefore few feel compelled to retain it or to say that they have. Actually, Lillian Rubin argues that the sex-ual revolution, which freed women to say yes, went too far in mak-ing it difficult for them to say no.[41]

For most Americans, monogamy remains a strongly held moral idea, even when they don't always adhere to it. The results of large surveys of extramarital sex conducted in the 1980s and the 1990s indicate that 50% to 65% of married men and 45% to 55% of married women engaged in intercourse with outside partners.[42] Despite this high rate of infidelity, most people still continue to say that they believe in monogamy.[43] Sociologist Robert Whitehurst argues that the importance of viewing the American society as a paired and family-oriented society cannot be overestimated. Strong pairing norms make for a heightened sense of ownership ("my wife," "my husband") and exclusivity. They encourage overprotectiveness and vigilance and increase our predisposition toward jealousy.[44]

Growing up in America, men and women are socialized to take personal descendants seriously. This can explain the growing popularity of such solutions to infertility as artificially implanting a husband's sperm in his wife's uterus or paying a "surrogate" to be artificially impregnated, carry the husband's baby, and deliver it. Fatherhood is a legal relation that, once established by blood and tissue tests, defines certain financial obligations toward the child.

Despite women's economic contribution in housework, child care, and actual income, they still don't participate equally with men in political and religious leadership. This lack of power influences both their likelihood to perceive threats to their relationships and their likelihood to respond to those threats with jealousy.

The results of a study I did in the early 1990s suggest that attitudes toward jealousy may be changing again. The study involved 120 men and women who were asked to respond to the question, "How jealous are you?" I compared the responses these people gave in 1991 to the responses of 103 American men and women who were asked the same question in 1980. People in 1991 reported significantly higher levels of jealousy. One reason may be that in the 1990s people are more committed to monogamous relationships, either as a result of the threat posed by AIDS and other sexually transmitted diseases, or in backlash against the sexual promiscuity of previous decades. With the greater commitment to monogamy comes a greater acceptance of jealousy.

Paul Mullen (1993), who studied the changes in the social and legal concept of jealousy across cultures and throughout history, suggests that jealousy has been transformed from a socially sanctioned response to infidelity into personal pathology (especially in cases of crimes of passion). In making jealousy a symptom of psychopathology, says Mullen, it ceases to be the responsibility of the individual and allows claims of diminished capacity with respect to crimes of passion.

After this long discussion of jealousy in "the American Society" it should be emphasized that American society is far larger, more complex, and more varied than the primitive cultures described throughout this chapter. Different subcultures relate to jealousy differently. The cultural heritage of men and women growing up in an

Italian, Japanese, or Irish subculture is likely to have a major influence on their predisposition to jealousy. Indeed, marriage therapists Christie Penn and her colleagues (1997) suggest that therapists should understand the significance of infidelity in their work with ethnic minorities in the United States. They give as an example three such ethnic minorities—African Americans, Hispanic Americans, and Asian Americans—whose beliefs about infidelity are influenced by their different religions. In Catholicism chastity is expected before marriage, and fidelity afterwards. In Eastern philosophy, infidelity is traditionally accepted for a man if his wife cannot produce a male descendent. In Islam, fidelity after marriage is demanded—for women. In Protestantism, there is clear ban on infidelity.

As a result of these different religious beliefs, as well as different traditional beliefs about marriage, beliefs about infidelity vary among these minorities. Among African Americans infidelity is tolerated, even if not approved, especially for males. Among Hispanic Americans, open infidelity is frowned upon, yet is acceptable for males. Among Asian Americans, infidelity is acceptable for males, and females are blamed for it (the wife for not giving the man what he needs, the other woman for taking him away).

Is Jealousy Universal?

No known culture, including those in which jealousy is considered shameful and undesirable, is completely free from jealousy. Even among the Toda, despite the societal sanction against jealousy, their belief that they would be punished in the afterlife for being jealous indicates that the sanction did not eliminate it altogether. If there is punishment, there must be offenders. A culture can socialize people against expressing jealousy, but it cannot keep them from feeling jealous when they perceive a threat to a valued relationship.

The conclusion that jealousy is universal is supported by research as well. In one study, Dutch and English children were compared to children in an isolated Himalayan village. Both groups were knowledgeable of situations that provoke various emotions, among them jealousy.[45] In another study, students from Hungary, Ireland, Mexico, the Netherlands, Russia, the United States, and Yugoslavia were asked about situations likely to elicit jealousy. Results indicate that for nearly everyone, kissing, flirting, and sexual involvement between their mate and a third person evoked a jealous response. Far less jealousy was provoked by the partner dancing with others, hugging them, or having sexual fantasies about them. There were, however, some cultural differences related to particular responses.[46] In yet another study comparing jealousy among Chinese and American students, it was found that while both Chinese and American students reported distress in response to sexual infidelity, a higher proportion of American students reported great distress—suggesting that jealousy might be influenced by sexual permissiveness in the general culture (Geary et al., 1995).

Freud also believed jealousy was universal. Unlike cross-cultural psychologists who base their conclusion on evidence gathered in different cultures, Freud based his conclusion on evidence gathered from the unconscious depths of the human psyche. Freud believed that jealousy is universal because it is rooted in childhood experiences all of us share.

It may be worth noting, however, that while Freud believed that jealousy is the product of the individual's mind, he also believed that the culture contributes to it. Jealousy is aggravated in a culture that worships a monotheistic God who proclaims, "Thou shalt have no other gods before me ... for I the Lord thy God am a jealous God."[47] Jealousy is also aggravated in a culture that upholds an ideal of monogamous marriage and of a repressed self. Such a culture encourages people to expect exclusivity in love, which makes it difficult for them to accept infidelity, real or imagined. While some cultures may mitigate the pains of jealousy, Freud could not imagine one in which people are completely free of this "discontent."[48]

Sociobiology also supports the notion that jealousy is universal. Darwin saw jealousy as an innate defense of the pair bond, which evolved through natural selection to increase the likelihood that the pair would stay together and reproduce.

What Does This Have to Do with an Individual's Jealousy Problem?

People suffering from a jealousy problem can take comfort in the knowledge that such widely differing sources as psychoanalysis, sociobiology, and cross-cultural psychology come to the same conclusion: Jealousy is universal. But is this kind of comfort enough to help people cope with jealousy?

As I was writing this chapter, Amalya (whose problems with her boyfriend's jealousy were described earlier) asked me what was I working on. I started telling her about the Apache and the Toda and the Eskimos. "How can knowing about the Eskimos help me deal with Sam's insane jealousy?" she asked. "It can make you realize how much his jealousy is influenced by the culture we live in," I responded. "That doesn't help me," said Amalya. "I need to understand what makes Sam jealous and what I can do about it." Amalya noted a potential problem in the application of the social–psychological approach: Because the focus is on the culture, we may lose sight of the individual.

Although drawing practical advice from the study of other cultures may seem difficult or irrelevant at first, it is far from impossible. In fact, sociologists such as Gordon Clanton believe that a social perspective on jealousy can lead to better self–understanding and more effective therapy. Awareness of social forces, says Clanton, can both enhance our understanding of jealousy and provide a basis for a critique of misleading views. An example of such a misleading position is the view that jealousy is caused by low self–esteem, and that raising self-esteem can reduce or "cure" jealousy. Instead of accepting this assumption uncritically, Clanton believes that we should search for its social roots.

His own search suggests that this view, which is taken for granted both by professionals and lay people, is typical of a wide tendency to attribute a variety of personal failures and problems to low self-esteem. In fact, Clanton argues, one may have high self–esteem in general, but still experience jealousy if a valued relationship is threatened. Furthermore, it is at least as plausible that the jealousy causes the low self–esteem and not the other way around.[49] Clanton's view is supported by cross–cultural surveys that reveal that low self–esteem plays little or no role in explaining jealousy in various cultures.

In Sam and Amalya's case, it is possible that the powerful and disturbing experience of jealousy helped diminish Sam's good feelings about himself. His bad feelings were reinforced by the cultural view of jealousy as a personal defect, a view reflected in Amalya's attitude toward his jealousy problem. Awareness of the culture's influence on our experience of jealousy makes us less likely to adopt erroneous and potentially damaging views.

In addition to making people aware of cultural influences on jealousy, social psychology—which focuses on the interaction between individuals and their social environment—has another important implication for coping with jealousy. It can help individuals and couples see their jealousy problem in a new way.

There are two kinds of explanations or attributions for events: dispositional (related to stable personality traits of the person or people involved in the event), and situational (related to the special circumstances in which the event took place).[50] People who say: "I am a jealous person" explain their jealousy in dispositional terms. When they have feelings, thoughts, and physical symptoms in response to a situation that triggered their jealousy, they say, "I am experiencing these symptoms because I am a jealous person." In other words, "That's the way I am and there's nothing that can be done to change that." Another person experiencing a similar set of symptoms in response to a similar situation may explain things in situational terms: "I am experiencing these symptoms of jealousy because the person I am married to has had an affair."

People who explain their jealousy in situational terms leave open the possibility that in a different situation they may respond in a different way. When they feel excluded because their partner is flirting with someone, they are likely to attribute their jealousy to that particular event and focus their efforts on changing this situation. People who explain jealousy in dispositional terms are far less motivated to change, because for them change means the virtually impossible task of changing a "jealous person" to a "nonjealous person."

When an individual or a couple comes to therapy, most often the dispositional label "jealous person" is already in place. Their typical goal for therapy is to change the jealous person so that he or she will stop being jealous. To challenge this dispositional attribution, I ask the "jealous person" such questions as, "Have you been that jealous in all your intimate relationships?" or, "Have you always been that jealous in this relationship?" The answer to these questions is almost always no. Even if the person can recall only one instance of atypical jealous behavior, it still means that the person is not "a jealous person" but someone whose jealousy is triggered more easily in some situations than in others. The challenge then becomes to identify what it is about a particular relationship or situation that makes the person jealous. As difficult as that task may seem, it is far easier than changing a "jealous person" to a "nonjealous person."

If the person has in fact been extremely jealous in all previous intimate relationships, and during all stages of the current relationship, the label "jealous person" might seem appropriate. It is still unlikely that he or she has felt equal degrees of jealousy in all relationships and at all times. Such a person can try to discover which situations increase the jealousy and which situations reduce it, then make an effort to avoid the former and seek the latter.

An Evaluation of the Social-Psychological Approach

The major contribution of the social-psychological approach is the notion that jealousy is a social phenomenon as well as a psychological one. The different ways that people in different cultures respond to jealousy help to prove that jealousy is related to the values and norms of the culture in which we live. In the discussion of diversity in culture, ethnicity, class and gender, diversity in sexual orientation also has an important place (see, for example, Jacobson & Christensen, 1996).

Major criticism of this approach is that it underestimates the importance of processes operating in the mind of the jealous individual. Ralph Hupka's conclusion is an example of this extreme social position: "Jealousy is a function of a culturally defined event, not the cause of it. It is the situation which sets the occasion for jealousy. It is not the jealousy which creates the situation. Jealousy is a social phenomenon. It is not a product of the mind of an isolated individual."[51]

Instead of this either/or proposition, I would like to suggest that jealousy is both a social phenomenon and a product of an individual's mind. The psychodynamic, the systems, and the behavioral approaches are all part of clinical psychology and, as such, have elaborate recommendations for the treatment of jealousy. Unlike these clinical approaches, social psychology doesn't offer explicit suggestions for coping. Yet an awareness of the cultural influences on jealousy and the ability to shift from dispositional to situational attribution can help people cope with jealousy in a less emotionally loaded way.

A Note for Therapists

The social-psychological approach, while not directly applied to therapy, still has two important implications for the therapist: First, the importance of the normalizing effect that the information about the diversity and the universality of jealousy has, and second, helping individuals and couples make the shift from dispositional to situational attributions.

The task of shifting from a dispositional to a situational attribution of the jealousy problem can be accomplished by addressing at length such questions as, "What is it about this relationship or this particular situation that triggers your jealousy?" "In what other relationship or period of time in this relationship have you been least jealous?" "What was it about that other relationship or period of time that made you feel more secure and less likely to respond with jealousy?" Another line of questions can address the couple's perception of norms related to fidelity, to discover whether the jealousy problem is related to a difference in their understanding of these norms.

These kinds of questions are different from the questions "Why am I a jealous person?" or "How can I stop being a jealous person?" By treating jealousy as a situational issue, the couple is motivated to work together to change the situation so that jealousy is less likely to be triggered.

7

Romantic Jealousy in Open Relationships

Erotic love is exclusive, but it loves in the other person all of mankind,
all that is alive.... In essence, all human beings are identical....
This being so, it should not make any difference whom we love.
—Erich Fromm, *The Art of Loving*

Jealousy is a kind of fear related to a desire to preserve a possession.
—Descartes

Imagine the experience of a person whose spouse admits to having sex "on the side" occasionally, but assures the person that it is the result of a need for variety and is not caused by any lack of love or by a problem in the relationship. The extramarital sex will in no way affect the relationship—but will go on—because the spouse feels there is nothing wrong with it. Imagine further that the marriage has been happy and satisfying up to this point. Should the person agree to this "arrangement?" Consider a divorce? Consider separation? Be jealous?

A study comparing 100 "swingers" (husbands and wives who together engage in sexual mate exchange) and 100 nonswingers indicates that swingers are far less likely to consider extramarital sex (which to them is not the same as an illicit affair) a sufficient reason for divorce or separation. They also said they would be far less jealous in such a situation.[1]

Swingers are an example of people who manage to develop a relative immunity to jealousy.[2] Such people consider sexual variety and freedom important to a relationship. Some also subscribe to an ideology of universal love (of which Erich Fromm's quote is an example), which makes overcoming romantic jealousy an important philosophical issue as well as a practical one.

In their book *Open Marriage*, George and Nena O'Neill devote a whole chapter to love and sex without jealousy.[3] As can be expected, the O'Neills believe that the "dark shadow" cast by jealousy has no place in an "open marriage" and is not necessary in a "closed marriage," either.

The O'Neills view jealousy not as natural, instinctive, and inevitable, but as a learned response, determined by cultural attitudes. And since it is a learned response, they argue, it can be unlearned. As evidence for their claim that jealousy is not "natural" in intimate relationships, the O'Neills mention societies around the world in which jealousy is minimal.

Why is jealousy so prevalent in Western society? The O'Neills blame the "closed marriage" contract, which creates the impression that people "own" their mates. Sexually exclusive monogamy breeds dependency and insecurity. "Jealousy is never a function of love," they argue, "but of insecurities and dependencies. It is the fear of a loss of love and it destroys that very love."

The O'Neills discuss several "misconceptions" that, in their view, cause jealousy to occur in closed marriages. They believe that by doing away with such misconceptions, an open marriage helps disassociate jealousy from love and sex.

One of these "misconceptions" is the idea that there is a limited quantity of love—that you cannot love more than one person at a time. The "truth," they argue, is that we can love different people, each one of them for the unique things that make him or her lovable.

Another "misconception" is the idea that jealousy proves the existence of romantic love. The "truth" is that jealousy proves the existence of insecurities and dependencies, not love. Monogamy, they say, "perverts" jealousy into a "good" (for example, some husbands and wives actually try to make their mates jealous). But jealousy is never good or constructive.

A third "misconception" is the idea that humans (especially women) are sexually monogamous. The "truth" is that humans of both sexes are not sexually monogamous by nature, evolution, or force of habit. The obvious proof, they say, is that most people fail to live up to a standard of monogamy. Indeed, monogamy does not mean having sex only with your partner. It simply means being married to one partner at a time.

The creator of rational–emotive therapy, Albert Ellis (1962/1996), has a similar criticism of monogamy, which, in his opinion, not only "directly encourages the development of intense jealousy, but also by falsely assuming that men and women can love only one member of the other sex at a time, and can only be sexually attracted to that one person, indirectly sows the seeds for even more violent displays of jealousy."

In my own work with people who have had open relationships, I discovered that the practice of nonmonogamy is far more complicated and difficult than the O'Neills and Ellis imply. It is difficult to unlearn the jealous response, especially if you live in a society that encourages possessiveness and jealousy. Because of these and other reasons, overcoming jealousy, while possible, requires tremendous work.

One couple, Kim and Larry, decided to open their marriage after seven years of monogamy. Both felt secure in the marriage and wanted to add variety to their sex life, which had lost some of its passion. They decided that on Tuesday and Thursday nights Larry could go to see his lovers, while Kim could bring her lovers home.

One of Kim's lovers recounted the strange experience to me:

> You wake up in the morning naked under the blankets after spending the night making love. Suddenly her husband comes into the bedroom, says good morning to you, and then starts an argument with her about who was supposed to take out the garbage last night.

Kim described some of her own experiences:

> I was the one who pushed to open the marriage. I thought this would be the ideal arrangement—you get to have your cake and eat it too. At times it really is like that. This happens when I have an exciting lover, with whom I can spend the night on Tuesday and Thursday, without having to deceive Larry. The problem comes up when I don't have an exciting lover, or when I don't

have any lover at all. In those times, the fact that Larry goes out
and spends a night with a woman that he finds exciting (possibly more exciting than me) drives me absolutely nuts.

Studies of swingers suggest that most often swinging is initiated
by the husband out of boredom or desire for sexual variety, with the
wife's reluctant consents.[4] Other couples in open marriages also have
rules that limit the extramarital involvement: One couple is open
only with other couples, another is open only when one of them is
out of town. For one couple, the rule is "you can have sex, but not
spend the night"; for another, sex is allowed "only with strangers
whom we are not likely to meet socially." Contracts differ in degree
of openness and are rewritten whenever the partners see fit to do so.

Despite the rules, many couples discover that the effort to keep a
marriage strong while being open to involvement with other people
requires too much effort: "You have to talk all the time in order to
make sure your marriage doesn't suffer. The time and energy
involved in that are so big that little is left for anything else." Many
of the couples I interviewed or worked with who had tried open marriage decided eventually to go back to monogamy. Studies of
swingers suggest that despite the self-selection that screens out
highly jealous people, jealousy remains a problem for swingers: Up
to a third of swingers soon drop out because of their own or their
spouse's jealousy.[5]

Some people have made unusual attempts to combine the security of a good relationship with the sexual variety offered by being
involved with other people.

A Life without Jealousy?

Is it possible to eliminate jealously from your life? The answer,
according to the members of an urban commune called Kerista, was
"definitely yes!"

The Keristans described themselves as an "egalitarian, nonmonog-
amous, utopian community." Kerista included, at the time I studied
them, fifteen women, seventeen men, and two children living together
in San Francisco. It was founded twenty-five years ago as a "polyfidelitous family." "Polyfidelity," a coined word, is a "group of best
friends, highly compatible, who live together as a family, with sexual

intimacy occurring equally between all members of the opposite sex, no sexual involvement with people outside the group, a current intention of lifetime involvement, and the intention to raise children together in multiple parenting."[6]

A polyfidelitous family resembles a traditional marriage in that family members did not become sexually involved with each other until they had made a mutual commitment to a "current intention of a lifetime involvement," and in that once the commitment was made, they were totally faithful to each other. A polyfidelitous family differs markedly from a traditional family in its basic assumption that one can have many primary relationships simultaneously.

Members of the commune described a high degree of love and tenderness for each other. Each one of the men claimed to be equally "in love" with each one of the women, and the women claimed to love equally each one of the men. Women referred to other women affectionately as "starling sisters"; men referred to other men as "starling brothers." The terms connote the affection experienced and expressed by the commune members toward their same-sex partners. Members had three-letter names (Jud, Eve, Geo, Ram) that were selected after an individual entered the commune.

Sexual relationships within the family were nonpreferential and happened within a rotating sleeping pattern. The sleeping pattern, which followed a set formula, scheduled nighttime to be spent in a twosome. The sleeping pattern did not schedule sexual intercourse; having sex or not having it depended on the feelings of the two partners spending the night together.

The economics in Kerista were managed according to a system of "surplus income sharing." In this system, members put all their surplus income above their own expenses into a common fund and set a personal wealth limitation of one thousand dollars. Policy decisions on how and where to spend this common fund, like all other decisions, were made by a majority vote. Kerista was doing well financially. In 1990, for example, its gross revenues came to $15 million.

Kerista had developed its own religion and is a legally recognized church. Members shared a belief in "Divinity—a higher order of reality." In addition, they had a mythological deity called Sister Kerista, who is "an intermediary between the individual and Divinity, that the mind can more easily reach out to."

Interactions among members, including strong differences or personal problems, were settled through a round–the–clock "communication process." All members were equal participants. The official power structure was one of "absolute equality." All decisions were made democratically by majority vote.

How Polyfidelity Combats Romantic Jealousy

The Keristans approached me some years ago when I was going to lead a jealousy workshop. They volunteered to tell the workshop participants how they had managed to overcome their own jealousy. I found the things they said so fascinating that I asked them to take part in my jealousy research, which they did.

Before joining the commune, the Keristans said, they had all felt jealous at some point in life, but the commune enabled them to rid themselves of their jealousy. Following are some of the elements in their lifestyle that helped them overcome jealousy.

In Kerista, nonpreferentiality was an ideal and a norm. All one-on-one relationships were viewed as unique: "The nonpreferentiality doesn't mean limiting the depth of intimacy and caring for the sake of equality and variety. Because of the strength of each one–to–one bond, no one sees the strength of another relationship as a threat to the uniqueness of their intimacy bonds."

The Keristans extended the limits of the twosome to include fifteen people. Within a family unit of fifteen people jealousy is just as ridiculous as it is within a traditional family structure. Furthermore, in a traditional marriage, all the emotional resources are invested in one person. When that person withdraws or leaves, the result is a serious trauma. In Kerista, the emotional investment was spread among fourteen people. Consequently when one person left, the trauma was much smaller.

The possibility of losing a partner is far less threatening in a polyfidelitous family than it is in a traditional marriage. First, if a person leaves, other members are not likely to see it as a personal rejection and therefore can tolerate the loss more easily. Second, the loss is shared by all members, and therefore is less painful. Since the threat and the pain of loss are small, they are less likely to trigger jealousy.

In Kerista, jealousy was viewed as "a conditioned response that flashes whenever residual emotions from the past are triggered." It was not considered a response to a threat to the relationship's exclusiveness. On those rare occasions when someone felt jealous, all group members talked about it openly, assuring the person feeling jealous of his or her secure place in the commune. Furthermore, there was no exclusive relationship to be guarded or threatened. Every intimate detail about the sexual habits of each member was well known to everyone and was the subject of open discussion. "Everyone knows if one of the men has a problem with premature ejaculation, or if one of the women has a problem reaching coital orgasm, and we all talk about it together," one member explained.

When Eve and Ram went together to an erotic film festival (on their scheduled night for being a twosome), Azo felt a flash of jealousy. At first, he didn't recognize it as jealousy; all he knew was that he felt somewhat depressed. When he entered the kitchen, several people were there. Right away he said he was upset. This was a recognized invitation and the others responded accordingly. They started to question him about his depression. Eventually they discovered that it was triggered by a fear that he might lose a measure of intimacy with Eve because he was not sharing the experience of the erotic film festival with her.

When his feelings were clarified, his partners assured him that both Eve and Ram were solid in their commitment to nonpreferential love and that he was not likely to lose any measure of intimacy with Eve. Azo also had an opportunity, during the discussion, to examine his own wishes to have a preferential relationship with Eve, and to reaffirm his own commitment to a polyfidelitous lifestyle.

At Kerista, the sexual involvement between one's lover and another person, which for most people is the strongest elicitor of jealousy, was expected to increase one's sense of security. Keristans saw sexual involvement between their male and female partners (they were heterosexual) as an affirmation that their polyfidelitous ideology works. They did not see it as a threat to their relationship with those partners or to their egos, so they were not likely to feel jealous.

The Keristans claimed that their total trust in each other (and consequently their lack of jealousy) extended to people outside the community. In other words, outsiders were not viewed as a threat. When Lee stayed out until the early morning hours on a date with an old boyfriend, for example, no one doubted her total fidelity, and therefore no one experienced jealousy.

A major component of jealousy, for many people, is the suspicion or resentment of the rival. In Kerista, on the other hand, the relationship that every man had with the other men and every woman had with the other women elicited what they called "compersion" rather than jealousy. "Compersion is the positive warm feeling you experience when you see two of your partners having fun with each other. It's the antonym of jealousy."

The Keristans disagreed with the sociobiologists who claim that jealousy is a natural, instinctive reaction. They believed instead that "it is natural to be free of jealousy. The natural instinctive reaction is compersion." Like the O'Neills, the Keristans were convinced that because jealousy is culturally learned, it can, and should, be unlearned.

Since the Keristans viewed jealousy as a function of a particular social structure and sex role socialization, they had put a great deal of effort into creating a new social structure and new sex roles within it.

If jealousy is a response to a feeling of powerlessness in the relationship, as some psychologists have argued,[7] then a community like Kerista, in which members share equal power, is likely to minimize it.

If jealousy is a sanctioned response to a violation of sexual property rights, as some sociologists have argued,[8] it is less likely to occur in a social structure where sexual property rights include all the adults in the community rather than a single couple, and where intimacy is shared equally by all members of the family.

Likewise, if jealousy arises from a desire to preserve a possession,[9] a society that discourages possessions is less likely to elicit jealousy, especially in a group for whom sexual involvement of one's partner with others doesn't imply a threat of possible loss.

When I compared the Keristans' responses to *The Romantic Jealousy Questionnaire* (see Appendix B) to the responses of 103 people in conventional relationships, I discovered that all the Keristans described themselves and their partners as "not at all jealous." They also said that they never experience jealousy, dislike jealousy, do not want their partners to be jealous, and do not consider their own jealousy a problem. All this was true only from the time they joined Kerista. During their childhood, adolescence, and young adulthood they were just as jealous as the other people surveyed. The Keristans viewed jealousy as an undesirable personality characteristic and never considered it an appropriate response, even in the most extreme of situations. Unlike most of the other people surveyed, they believed that one can stop oneself from being jealous.[10]

As can be expected, none of the Keristans believed in monogamy. All of them described themselves as being totally open with their partners about other sexual experiences, and all of them believed that their partners were totally open with them as well. They also believed that they were totally faithful to their partners (every single one of them) and that all their partners were totally faithful to them.

Their responses were so similar that I wondered whether they discussed the questions and decided on the "group answer." The Keristans assured me that they did nothing of the kind. They didn't have to. They talked about these issues with each other so often that they knew each other's positions without having to talk about it.

In Kerista, jealousy was an unlikely response because, within a polyfidelitous subculture, events that usually trigger jealousy (one's mate having sex with someone else, for example) were not likely to be appraised as threats. In addition to the way the Keristans appraised jealousy triggers, they also made every attempt to keep such triggers to a minimum. They avoided displays of affection in front of other partners; they were faithful to their partners; and they shared a commitment to a lifelong involvement with each other, thus ensuring that even if some of the group members leave, the "family unit" will remain and the individual will not be left alone.

As a result of all this effort, Keristans were not likely to encounter many situations that trigger jealousy. On those rare occasions when they did encounter such situations, they were not likely to appraise them as threatening. And when a situation was appraised as threatening, social norms that define jealousy as unwholesome and undesirable guaranteed that the response to the threat would take the form of an open discussion.

For those who may have decided by now that the best way to conquer jealousy would have been to join Kerista, or perhaps establish a similar commune in their own neighborhood, a word of caution is in order. Kerista represented a selective group of people who got together from all parts of the country because they believed in a polyfidelitous lifestyle, and because they shared a commitment to a utopian ideology whose ultimate goal is to make the world a better place in which to live. Despite their unusual practice of sleep rotation, the Keristans were quite conservative in their sexual attitudes and practices. Few people nowadays require a lifetime commitment before they get involved sexually, but the Keristans did. The Keristans did not practice open marriage. They were totally faithful, only in their case that meant being faithful to fifteen partners.

It is tempting to conclude that polyfidelity eliminates jealousy. This may be true, but there are problems with relying on what people say about themselves. People may be unaware of their own feelings, or they may be unwilling to be truthful if their responses put them in an "undesirable" light. It may be that since jealousy was not acceptable in the commune, Keristans were reluctant to own up to it.

It also may be that when describing their experiences and filling out the questionnaire, Keristans simply reiterated their ideology, rather than reporting their actual experiences with jealousy. I am reluctant to accept these alternate explanations. In my long acquaintance with the Keristans, I learned to trust their honesty and willingness to explore difficult issues.

On the other hand, self–deception cannot be ruled out. It is possible that because of their huge investment in their alternative lifestyle, Keristans couldn't accept the possibility of failure; therefore they distorted their feelings unwittingly.

Still, the Keristans demonstrated that a selective group of people, living in a secure social milieu where jealousy–triggers were reduced to a minimum, can succeed in overcoming jealousy. This can be seen as proof that jealousy can be conquered.

It can also provide testimony to the power of jealousy—if it requires so much effort to be conquered. After all, only a small and unusual group such as the Keristans, living in an unusual, self–created social structure, were able to overcome it. For those who made the kind of monogamous commitment the Keristans outlawed and who live in a less protected environment, some degree of jealousy seems almost inevitable.

The less protected the environment, the more likely is jealousy. A good example of this is another commune I visited. This was an urban commune like Kerista, comprising about twenty adults who shared living space and expenses. Unlike Kerista, this commune had many children, which meant that members had to put much more effort into parenting. More significant to the issue of jealousy, however, was that the commune's members had constantly shifting preferential relationships. At the time I visited the commune, for example, one of the men was living with two women, one of whom had previously lived with another man in the commune. The man himself had been married to one of the other women members, who was now living with another threesome, and so on. In addition to changing sexual liaisons within the group itself, members were open to outside relationships. The first man, for example, made an obvious pass at me during the interview—something unthinkable for the Keristans. As a result every woman in the group was perceived as a competitor by every other woman, and every man was a potential threat for every other man. This caused a serious problem of jealousy that hours of conversation among members of the commune did little to help.

When I last visited the town where the commune lived, I discovered that internal conflicts—mostly jealousy related—had overwhelmed the commune and caused it to fall apart. While jealousy wasn't the only cause of these internal conflicts, it was definitely a major contributor.

A review of the literature about communes suggests that the role played by jealousy in this second commune is the rule and not the exception. Jealousy, it turns out, is a significant problem in communes in general, especially in group marriages.[11] A survey of thirty group marriages suggests that jealousy was a problem for 80% of the members. This percentage did not vary much as a function of the stability of the marriage or the age of the group members.[12] It seems that without the elaborate social structure that the Keristans had created, jealousy can unleash its destructive power.

When jealousy comes up in a commune or a group marriage, it is most often a result of men comparing themselves to other men.[13] A survey of 280 swingers, for example, indicates that men were far more likely than women to take part in such social comparison and to feel threatened by it.[14] This is especially interesting since, as noted earlier, husbands are most often the ones who initiate swinging.

The comparison between the Keristans and members of other communes and group marriages suggests that low sensitivity to jealousy is an important selection factor for living within a sexually open relationship, but it is not enough. A social organization that minimizes threat, prescribes how to handle threat constructively, and provides members with a sense of security is essential in overcoming jealousy.

Jealousy among Swingers

Most people, especially those with a "jealousy problem," will prob-ably find it inconceivable that people could allow their partners to have casual sex in their own home with a stranger or acquaintance. But to swingers this is considered an acceptable form of social recre-ation, according to family expert Brian Gilmartin.[15]

Gilmartin studied 100 swingers and compared them to non-swingers living in the same California neighborhood. While the study (as well as most other studies on open marriages) was done in the 1970s before the spread of such sexually transmitted diseases as herpes and AIDS, a 1990 *New England Journal of Medicine* article suggests that sexual practices have not changed much since then: "There has been little change in sexual practices (including number of partners) in response to new and serious epidemics of sexually transmitted diseases, with the exception of an increase in the use of condoms."[16]

Gilmartin's comparison between swingers and nonswingers indi-cates that, like the Keristans, swingers seldom experience jealousy when their mates have sex with someone else. Swingers believe that it is possible to engage in frequent extramarital sex without being unfaithful or untrue to marriage partners. This is especially true, they say, when the sexual mate exchange happens "together," with both mates present at the particular social situation. Few non-swingers believe this is possible.

Swingers are not likely to respond with jealousy, even to this com-mon trigger of jealousy, because they don't perceive it as a threat. In their own system of beliefs, sex with another person doesn't mean being unfaithful or untrue; it simply means having harmless fun.

Three times as many nonswingers as swingers agree that when adultery occurs it is usually a sign that a marriage is not going well. Gilmartin argues that with this association in their minds, and with this interpretation of the meaning of adultery, it is not surprising that most middle-class suburbanites view the mere idea of their spouses engaging in any kind of extramarital sex as a strong threat to their egos as well as to their security, masculinity or femininity, and self-esteem.

Swingers manage to differentiate (both ideologically and emo-tionally) romantic sex from physical sex, or, in Gilmartin's termi-nology, "person-centered sex" from "body-centered sex." Sexual intercourse at a swingers' party is viewed as a valuable and reward-ing form of social recreation and convivial play. It has nothing to do with romantic or conjugal love and is very different from clandes-tine adultery. Therefore it doesn't pose a threat to the integrity and security of the marital bond.

For swingers, the analogy for a sexual mate exchange is a bridge party, in which it is quite common for participants to select some-one else's spouse for a partner. This is rarely perceived as a threat by the men and women involved.

To keep triggers for jealousy to a minimum, swingers (like the Keristans) structure the context of the extramarital sex. They have extramarital sex only as a shared leisure activity. They make sure that the couples they "swing" with are committed to preserving a rea-sonably happy marriage. Most swingers groups don't permit single men to participate, although many welcome single women. Even married men rarely are allowed to attend without their wives. The reason is that men are perceived as a greater threat.

Almost all swingers' groups have strong norms prohibiting mem-bers from expressing romantic feelings (such as saying "I love you") and falling in love with one another. Swingers can and do express warmth and friendship toward their sex partners, but they forbid any sign of desire for sexual or emotional exclusivity, which is part of the romantic experience of falling in love. These rules are aimed at pro-tecting the marital bond of all the couples involved.

Despite all these protections, swingers are not entirely free from jealousy. Most often, jealousy surfaces when one or more of the peo-ple participating in the sexual mate exchange has accepted the idea of swinging on an intellectual level, but not on the deeper and more significant emotional level.

At times, when people bored with marital sex hear about sexual mate exchange they get very excited and bring up the idea with their spouses. This, as noted earlier, tends to be the case for husbands more often than for wives. My research on marriage burnout also suggests that boredom in sex is a greater problem for men than it is for women.[17]

A man who is bored with sex at home feels the need for sexual variety. He has fantasies about the exciting sex he would enjoy as a swinger. In his zeal to persuade his wife, he often forgets to deal with the real implications of swinging—such as seeing his wife undress and have sexual intercourse with other men. If, as often happens, his wife at first objects vehemently to the idea but ends up enjoying the experience, such a man typically feels tremendous jealousy. One man who found himself in this situation describes it as the most intense experience of jealousy he has ever had. "I couldn't concentrate on the woman I was with. My ears were tuned to my wife, who seemed to be having a great time with the man she was with. It was horrible. I simply couldn't take it." This man decided that swinging was not for him, and instead found sexual variety in illicit affairs.

Experienced swingers also report occasional jealousy, but their experience tends to be milder than that of the novices and not necessarily negative. When jealousy happens, they typically don't mention it until they come home, and then share it as a tease and a sexual turn-on. Seeing or imagining their mates with another person reactivates swingers' sexual interest in their mates. Even when they are physically depleted after spending several hours having sex, the emotional charge produced by jealousy and by talking about it helps rejuvenate their desire.

This positive aspect of jealousy happens so often among swingers that it has become a part of the swinging ideology. When swingers hear their friends talk enthusiastically about how they come home from a party even more erotically charged toward their mates than when they left, they look for similar feelings in themselves. As is often the case, when people look for a particular emotional experience, they tend to find it.

Once again we can see that the experience of jealousy is moderated by the interpretation people give it. For swingers—members of a group whose ideology includes an interpretation of jealousy as a sexual turn-on—it is likely to become that, even if at some other period in their lives it was a response to a perceived threat.

The technique the swingers use is "reframing," and as noted before, people can learn to use it. Adopting new beliefs about the meaning of extramarital sex is only the first step in the complex process of overcoming jealousy. Even among people who manage to reduce their jealousy, chances are that not many will take the next step and agree to multiple extramarital relationships. In that respect, swingers are indeed unusual.

Certainly, one of the characteristics of swingers is that they are more interested in sex than are nonswingers. Swingers engage in extramarital sex more often than nonswingers, and they engage in more sex with their own spouses. Gilmartin asked husbands and wives separately about sex with each other. The discrepancies between their responses were small. The data showed that, among the swingers, 23% of the couples had sexual intercourse an average of six or more times per week, compared to only 2% of the non-swingers. Similarly, 32% of the swingers, as compared to 14% of the nonswingers, had intercourse four to five times per week. On the other hand, only 11% of the swingers, as compared 48% of the non-swingers, had intercourse an average of once (or even less than once) per week.[18]

While nonswingers didn't engage openly in extramarital sex, many did so secretly. In 34% of the couples, one of the partners had been involved in an extramarital affair, and in 5% of the couples, both husband and wife had affairs. Those people who had affairs had the lowest ratings of marital happiness. People who remained sexually faithful were far more likely to describe marriages that were happy and satisfying.[19] One can conclude either that poor marriages push people into extramarital affairs, or that having extramarital affairs destroys marital happiness.

Yet the swingers, who engaged in far more extramarital sex than the unfaithful nonswingers, were even more likely than the faithful nonswingers to describe their marriages as "very happy." Because the swingers do not associate extramarital sex with unfaithfulness or betrayal, it does not reflect problems in the marriage and does not generate jealousy.

In addition to having more sex with each other, swinging couples also tended to express more love and affection toward each other, spent more time in informal conversation, and showed greater interest in each other than did the nonswingers. This suggests that the swingers derived the love, security, and emotional nurturance they needed from their marital partners. This is why the "strictly physical" extramarital sex didn't trigger jealousy. On those rare occasions when the extramarital relationship became a threat to the marriage, it certainly evoked jealousy.

Lessons for Nonswingers

In this chapter, I have described three groups of people who have managed to reduce jealousy to a minimum: people in open marriages, the Keristans, and swingers. All three groups demonstrate that it is possible for people to be involved sexually with several people with little apparent jealousy.

Like the Keristans, swingers are quite conventional in some ways. The Keristans don't have sex unless there is a "current intention of a lifetime involvement," and afterward remain sexually faithful to each other. The swingers are likewise sexually faithful except for the mate exchange. Like people in open marriages, swingers believe in traditional marriage (and in what Gilmartin calls "residential and psychological monogamy"). They want to improve their marriages by opening the possibility of nonthreatening extramarital relationships.

All three groups believe in "togetherness"—the sharing of activities and interests between mates within the context of a committed relationship. All three groups value honesty in their relationships and derive a sense of security from them. At the same time, all three groups also believe in the value of sexual variety. The main difference among them, and between them and people in conventional marriages, is the social structure they created to achieve what they perceive as compatible goals: intimacy with their mates and sexual variety with others.

Even people who are satisfied in a monogamous marriage and would never be swingers, have an open marriage, or live in a commune such as Kerista can learn several lessons from these three unusual groups that can help reduce jealousy in their intimate relationships.

One lesson involves trying to eliminate jealousy triggers. Couples should discuss the things that are jealousy-provoking for them (in most cases each partner has different triggers) and explore together ways for each to do their "thing" without evoking jealousy in the other.

To be able to discuss such things, couples need to spend time together in informal conversation. This is one thing the Keristans, the swingers, and the open-marriage couples do very frequently. They also express love and affection toward each other and show a great deal of interest (sexual and nonsexual) in each other, which helps increase their sense of security in the relationship. While one may disagree with their method for keeping their interest in each other alive (that is, sexual involvement with other people), one can still apply their ideas of increasing security in a way that seems more appropriate. The three groups share the conviction that jealousy is a learned response. They know it can be unlearned because they have done it. The view of jealousy as learned is more conducive for coping than the sociobiological notion that jealousy is inborn and natural. Even people who are sure that they (or their partner) were born jealous can benefit from exploring the implications of the idea that jealousy may be learned. What will one need to unlearn and learn in order to reduce one's jealousy?

Consider the meaning of extramarital sex. For all three groups, it almost never means that "there's something wrong with the marriage." For most couples it means exactly that. Still, the affair and the jealousy it triggers don't have to be the end of a relationship. If couples learn to see the outside involvement as a message or a distress signal, the relationship can evolve into a deeper, more honest sphere.

The importance of feeling secure in intimate relationships as a way to prevent jealousy is one of the most important implications one can derive from the Keristans, the swingers, and the open–marriage couples. Without a sense of security, these three groups could not have maintained the quality of intimacy that they achieved in their different relationships.

Another valuable implication is the importance of social support and the power of social approval. In a couples' support group, a woman may describe the way her husband stares at every attractive woman he sees on the street as "outrageous" behavior that "makes her wild with jealousy." If the rest of the women in the group tell her that there is nothing wrong with this behavior, make a joke of it, and themselves start to express appreciation of attractive men they have noticed, chances are good that this woman will reevaluate the threat implied by her husband's behavior and respond with less jealousy in the future.

Finally, it is important to remember that even among these unusual groups, some jealousy occurs. It is hard to eliminate jealousy entirely in a culture that emphasizes possessiveness and exclusivity to the extent that our culture does. Yet the three groups show that it is possible to reduce jealousy and minimize the role it plays in peoples' lives.

While the three groups we have met in this chapter are unusual in their lack of jealousy, the group we will meet in the next chapter is unusual in its extreme response to jealousy. The groups in this chapter can teach what to do to overcome jealousy; the group in the next chapter can teach what not to do, so that jealousy doesn't lead to violence.

A Note to Therapists

"Reframing" is an important therapeutic tool and people can be taught to use it. In role playing, the couple can be instructed to use a situation likely to trigger jealousy. For example, the couple is at a party and the partner is flirting with someone else. The jealous person can be trained to reframe the jealousy (e.g., This pang of jealousy I'm feeling is actually a sexual turn-on"). The reward can be imagining all the things they can do together when they finally get home—instead of having a jealousy scene.

8
Crimes of Passion

For love is strong as death, jealousy cruel as hell. It blazes like blazing
fire, fiercer than any flame.
—*Song of Songs* 8:6

And I will judge thee, as women that break wedlock and shed blood are
judged, and I will give thee blood in fury and jealousy
—*Ezekiel* 16:38

[Jealousy] is the hydra of calamities, the sevenfold of death.
—Edward Young, *The Revenge*

Jealousy has produced violence and aggression throughout history.
"Crime of passion" has become so familiar a term that we rarely
consider how paradoxical it is—passion and crime, love and death. It
is the cruel paradox in which one murders the person one loves most.
"Love is strong as death," says King Solomon in the *Song of Songs*; and
Edward Young, the eighteenth–century English playwright, calls jealousy "the sevenfold of death." Shakespeare's Othello, the archetype of
the jealous husband, strangles his beloved wife, Desdemona, because
he suspects her of infidelity. Discovering that his suspicions were
groundless, he then kills himself. Shakespeare's tragic hero inspired
some psychologists to call delusional jealousy that leads to violence
the "Othello syndrome." (See, as an example, Leong et al. 1994.)

Studies of spousal murder followed by suicide list jealousy as one of the precipitating causes.[1] FBI statistics indicate that approximately one third of all solved murders involve spouses, lovers, or rivals of the murderer and either a real or a suspected infidelity as a major cause.[2] A wide range of hostile and bitter events has been attributed to jealousy, including murder, suicide, destruction of property, aggression, and spouse–battering.[3] Stories of murder and other violent acts triggered by jealousy often appear in newspapers and magazines. The popular interest in such stories suggests that although stories about passion and stories about violence each have a certain attraction, those about passion combined with violence are particularly fascinating.

Despite the great interest they generate, however, crimes of passion do not seem personally relevant to most people's jealousy problem. When I asked 607 people how they usually cope with their jealousy, only 1% said they respond with violence. When I asked another group of 103 people how they coped with their most extreme experience of jealousy, 7% mentioned an act of violence.[4] While many violent acts are attributed to jealousy, relatively few people resort to violence to solve their jealousy problems.[5]

Violent responses to jealousy deserve a serious discussion, however, because of the great harm they can cause. Even flying dishes (or, in the case of one couple I worked with, a flying watermelon) can cause great physical and emotional damage—much more so flying fists and bullets. It's important to know how to defuse the potential for violence in a jealousy situation. Indeed, Gregory Leong and his colleagues argue that the Othello syndrome often raises significant forensic issues, particularly dangerousness. Dangerous people suffering from the Othello syndrome may exhibit hostility that ranges from verbal threats to homicidal acts (Leong et al., 1994).

In this chapter I will describe the stories of men and women who are in prison for crimes related to jealousy. The men were part of a group of inmates I worked with as a therapist in one of California's state prisons (Pines, 1983). The women are in prison in Israel and I interviewed them individually (Pines, 1992b). In addition, a group of my University of California, Berkeley students interviewed twelve American women inmates in one of California's women's jails.

As is the case for other violent crimes, crimes of passion are most likely to be committed by young males from low socioeconomic classes and minority ethnic and racial groups, who are subject to economic and social deprivations.[6] Most of the men I worked with in prison were no exception; each had a high predisposition for jealousy and for violence. More significant for the prevention of jealousy-related violence, however, is the dynamic of situations that provoked their violence. As we will see, the dynamic of these situations is very similar for men and for women, for blacks and whites, for poor and well-to-do.

Stan

On September 3, 1979, Stan, 18 years old, shot and killed his girlfriend Kathy. Stan's background is different from that of most of the other men in the group I worked with. He is white and comes from a middle-class family. In high school he was the running back for the football team and a member of the Block Club, the Service Club, the Spirit Club, the school newspaper, and the yearbook. Stan was also active in the school government and was the class president during his sophomore and junior years. He maintained a 3.8 grade point average and became a lifetime member of the state's scholarship federation. One year he received the Scholar/Athlete Award, presented to him by the High School Hall of Fame, based on his excellence in studies and sports. He was also chosen as a Junior Republican delegate by one of the state's senators. He could not exercise his duties, however, because of his arrest.

At 8:00 P.M. on September 3, Stan and Kathy had a date to meet on the university football practice field. They had a heated argument—one of many. The reason was always the same: Stan wanted a more serious and committed relationship than Kathy was ready for. Kathy told Stan she wanted to devote herself to her studies and be able to see other men. Stan was so emotionally dependent on Kathy that the thought of losing her was horrifying:

> I could never talk to my family. Kathy was the one person I was able to open up to. I felt I was losing her. . . . I was more involved with her than she was with me. It was very scary. I was trying to hold on.

Stan was caught cheating on his college application for an Ivy League school and got into serious trouble. This, combined with

Kathy's withdrawal, made him panic. He needed her desperately. The more he fought to hold on, the more Kathy struggled to get away. Their argument on the night of the murder became increasingly heated:

> She told me to stay away from her and her family. I felt rage ... violence ... I felt I was losing her. She hit me twice with her fist on my cheek.... She tried to pull the gun out of my hand. We struggled.... I heard a gunshot and saw Kathy fall to the ground. I panicked and started running. I threw the gun into a body of water nearby.

The "body of water" was never identified and the gun never found. The .38 caliber handgun that killed Kathy was taken from her father's store. Stan had stolen it while working for Kathy's father the summer before. His reason for stealing the gun and having it with him on the night of the murder, he said, was to be able to protect Kathy.

When Kathy fell to the ground she was severely injured, but still alive. She was discovered some time later and was taken to a nearby hospital, where she was pronounced dead the following day. Hospital records indicate that she died of a single gunshot wound.

I met Stan in prison, where he was serving a life sentence. He looked like an all-American college kid with blond hair, blue eyes, and an athletic build. He has been working as an EKG technician, receiving straight As in all his premed classes, exercising, and attending Catholic services regularly.

I worked with Stan in group therapy and interviewed him individually about his jealousy as a precipitator of the murder. I discovered that Stan had little emotional connection with his parents. His father was a football coach and a "very dominant figure." Stan admired his father, but perceived him as critical and demanding. Stan had worked hard all his life to gain his father's approval, but nothing he did, nothing he achieved had seemed enough. Although he had a somewhat closer relationship with his mother, he had a great deal of difficulty communicating with either of his parents. During the three years that Stan had dated Kathy, he had spent so much time at her parents' house that they started to treat him as a member of the family. He had felt closer to them than to his own family.

Stan was in love with Kathy and could not imagine life without her. "She was like a dream come true." Loving Kathy more than she loved him made Stan feel weak and dependent. When I asked him who had the control in their relationship, Stan said "Kathy!" and explained, "She was like a crutch."

For all his athletic and academic successes, Stan felt "very dissatisfied" with himself. The standards he set for himself (the internalization of his father's severe standards) were so high that he couldn't help but fail: "I always wanted to improve myself. I wanted to be perfect." Unlike Stan, Kathy was sure of herself. "She wasn't afraid to voice her opinions. I was insecure because of my shyness." Kathy was Stan's crutch and connection to people.

Both Stan and Kathy were 15 years old when they first met. From the start, Kathy felt secure enough in the relationship to encourage Stan to go out with other people. At first he did it a few times. Sexual liaisons with other women were easy for Stan because of his involvement with football. But they paled in comparison with the love he felt for Kathy. He was attracted to her physically and emotionally. Unfortunately, Kathy was much less attracted to him. Stan described himself as "extremely jealous," and explained, "It was a result of my loneliness, dependency on Kathy, and insecurity about her." Over time, Stan's jealousy became a growing problem in the relationship. He became possessive of Kathy and was envious of anyone she spent time with:

> She would go away for the weekend with her family, and it really bothered me. I felt lonely. I felt emptiness in my heart. She was the only person I could express feelings to. I always had a need to have control, and I didn't have control over any decision she was making, whether to go away for a weekend with her family or which school to go to.

Stan's reaction to the jealousy he experienced was extreme, and at times it took a violent form:

> I was more emotional than Kathy. I just kept the pain in. When I got really frustrated, I'd get it out, the rage, physically, by hitting the wall or something. . . .

On the night of the murder, Stan was nervous and shaky, and felt close to a nervous breakdown. His heart was beating fast, blood was rushing to his head, and his hands were sweaty and trembling. He felt anxious, terrified at the thought of losing Kathy, possessive, enraged, confused, and frustrated. His self-esteem was low and his self-pity high. With Kathy he felt such extreme jealousy often, and when he did, it lasted for days. She gave his whole life a sense of meaning. If he lost her, he felt his life would be empty and meaningless. He could not accept it. He could not let her go. The total rejection and disdain Kathy expressed during their fight caused Stan's frustration, pain, and rage to explode in violence.

My clinical experience suggests that overt disdain or rejection expressed toward the jealous partner is an important precipitant of the violent outburst. The critical role played by a humiliating rejection is evident in the case of Goldie, a woman who is in prison for the attempted murder of her ex-lover.

Goldie

Goldie's story appeared in the papers in the summer of 1992. I visited her in prison and interviewed her at length. Goldie, 51 years old, was awaiting trial for the attempted murder of her ex-lover Nathan. Nathan, 43, told the police that Goldie confronted him in the street holding a gun in both her hands. Shaking all over, she screamed: "This is your end," then she started shooting. Nathan's life was spared miraculously, despite the six bullets that Goldie shot at him from the small gun she had stolen several hours before from her ex-husband. Nathan suffered a minor wound in his hand from one of the bullets and was taken to a hospital. Goldie, who is divorced and the mother of two adult children, was taken by the police for questioning.

The love story between Nathan and Goldie, which could have ended in murder, started some years before when Nathan separated from his wife. During the height of their romance, Nathan moved in with Goldie. Then, some months before the violent attack, there was a warming in his previously tense relationship with his estranged wife. As a result, Nathan left Goldie's house and moved with his children to his parents' house. He started working on his relationship with his wife with the intent to move back into his house and resume the marriage.

"Goldie did not like this," said Nathan. "She would call me hundreds of times, and refused to hear about the possibility of us breaking up. She even came to my parents' house, screaming and embarrassing me. One day when I met her she said she had in her purse a loaded gun and that she will kill my wife. Instead, she almost killed me."

On the day of the attack, at about 6:00 A.M. Nathan left his parents' house on his way to work, when Goldie appeared in front of him, dressed in dark clothes. "Suddenly she pulled out a gun, screamed at me, and started shooting. I did not believe what was happening. I saw death in front of me. I heard the thunder of a gunshot, and felt my right arm go numb. Somehow I managed to get back to my senses. I threw on her the bag I was holding, then I flung myself on her and dropped her on the floor." In the struggle that followed, Nathan pushed Goldie's head to the concrete with his knee, but she continued to shoot five more shots that whizzed by his stomach. "She fought like a wild animal, breathing heavily and screaming at me, "That's the end of you!" recounted Nathan.

Hearing Nathan's shouts and the gunshots, his mother came running out of her house. She threw herself on top of Goldie, and using all her strength managed to pull the gun out of her hands. Neighbors that arrived at the scene beat Goldie up and called the police.

During the police questioning it was revealed that on the previous night Goldie had visited her ex-husband's house, and used the opportunity to steal his 7.65 millimeter gun. She left his house early in the morning and went to Nathan's parents' house, where she waited for him.

Goldie told the police the Nathan met her that morning with curses and insults and even started hitting her. "He attacked me, hitting my head against the wall while using foul language. I was scared, that's why I pulled out the gun and shot him." When I met her in prison, she told me another story. As in Stan's case, Goldie's story is one of a great obsessive love.

> I loved him so much that I could not imagine life without him. I knew that he suffered terribly in his marriage, and was really happy when he lived with me. When I came to meet him that morning I wanted to tell him that I love him and cannot live without him and if he refused to come back to me, I was going to shoot myself, so my soul will stay with him forever. But when he saw me he started cursing me and insulting me. I just went mad

and shot him. But I never meant to hurt him. I could have killed
him if I wanted to. I was close enough. I still love him and I know
he still loves me. He is the one who is paying for my lawyer....

Although Goldie was a woman of 51 at the time of the crime, and
Stan a young man of 18, there were important similarities in the circumstances leading to their crime. Both were deeply in love with
their partner in a relationship that gave meaning to their lives and
made them feel complete. Both became very dependent on their
lovers. Both wanted a formal commitment and were refused. Both
felt needy and powerless in their relationship. They were willing to
accept the asymmetry only because of their great dependency on
their lovers. When they discovered—in a cruel and insensitive
way—that they were going to be jilted, their despair, rage, and pain
made them attack the person they loved more than themselves. In
both cases there was a component of envy in the jealousy. It was
expressed in the impulse to destroy the beloved—who had the ability to make them happy, yet refused to.

Once again we see how the fatal combination of the loss of an
asymmetrical "total" love, combined with an insulting and humiliating rejection, triggers violence. A similar dynamic can be found in
most jealousy-related violence.

Of course, this does not mean that Goldie and Stan's crimes are justified. It means that the way in which a jealousy crisis is handled plays
a critical role in determining whether or not the crisis will escalate to
violence. Goldie and Stan are not very different from other people
who are completely dependent on a romantic relationship. Their
crimes were the result of an escalation that could have been avoided.

Not every jealousy-related violent outburst is directed at the
rejecting partner. And at times there is a way back even after an out-
break of violence. Neil is an example.

Neil

Unlike Stan and Goldie, who are serving life sentences for killing or
attempting to kill their lovers, Neil was serving time for killing his
ex-girlfriend's lover.

Like Stan, Neil was a shy and insecure young man. The only time
he got into trouble was during adolescence, when together with a

group of boys he was caught shooting a BB gun at street-lamps. After finishing high school, Neil enlisted in the army and was sent to Vietnam.

When he was released from the service, for the first time in his life Neil was able to afford an apartment of his own. It was also the first time in his life he had a girlfriend. Since he was very much in love with his girlfriend, and dependent on her emotionally, he invited her to move in with him. She agreed, and for a while it seemed as if his dreams were coming true. But only for a while.

After several months his girlfriend started an affair with a security officer and eventually broke up with Neil. Then she kicked Neil out of his own apartment. When Neil returned from a trip out of town, he discovered that his ex-girlfriend and her new lover had moved his belongings back to his parents' house. Neil went there and spent several hours turning the events over in his head. Then he took his father's old gun, went back to the apartment, and burst into the bedroom, where he found the girlfriend and her new lover in bed.

During the trial, Neil claimed that he didn't mean to kill either his girlfriend or her lover; all he wanted was to scare them with his gun so they would get out of his place. But the security officer, seeing the pointed gun, came at him naked. During the struggle that followed, in which the officer tried to get the gun out of Neil's hand, a shot was fired by mistake and the officer was killed. Neil's first instinct was to flee. His girlfriend came with him and they drove for hours, both of them crying. Eventually she persuaded him to turn himself in to the police. At the trial, the girlfriend supported Neil's story. As a result of her testimony, the verdict he received was second-degree murder rather than first-degree.

Today, Neil is a free man. He is working as an engineer, is married, and has two children. Jealousy is not a problem in his marriage, and he is convinced that he will never again respond with violence to jealousy or to any other problem.

While Stan, Goldie, and Neil did something that most people never do—respond to a jealousy crisis with violence—they are "normal" enough for their crimes not to be blamed on such things as mental illness, drugs, alcohol, an abusive childhood, or poverty. One of the most noteworthy things they all had in common, besides a predisposition toward jealousy and a jealousy-related crisis, was a gun. They are people who, if it weren't for the crimes they committed, could have been seen as successful members of society. For the people I will present next, violence was not a one-time event, but a way of life.

Mike

Mike, a 30-year-old man, is serving a life sentence for rape and murder. He describes the events that led to his crime:

> I met Rosemary after getting out of a very painful relationship with Pat. I was extremely jealous of Pat. I could get killing mad about her. I didn't want people to even look at her.
>
> The worst jealousy I ever felt was when I came back after ten days, and I found out she got married. I knew the guy. She told me he was just a friend.... I know her, she was up to no good. I was never comfortable with her seeing other men. There was lots of insecurity on my part. If I had married Pat, I would have ended in prison much sooner.

While Mike wasn't in love with Rosemary the way he had been with Pat, he still became very emotionally dependent on her:

> Rosemary was there, and it helped in terms of Pat. I got married at 17. She was 21. I thought I couldn't live without her. I was dependent on her emotionally. I felt she really cared about me.

Mike was totally unprepared for what he found out:

> Rosemary and I were living with Ann who was a friend of Rosemary before our marriage and after that too. It was comfortable for all of us. We were happy together. When I found out that Rosemary and Ann were lovers, I was really shocked. I just got into the car and split. I felt that she'd rejected me. I felt abandoned. I couldn't handle it.

Abandonment is a core issue for Mike:

> I felt abandoned by my mother. I don't remember my father. He committed suicide when I was 3 years old. He shot himself

because of another woman. No one ever talked about him. I was the only child for a long time. But it was difficult for my mother—being single and a black woman—to make a living. When I was 6 she started dating. Until then we were together. I got very jealous. I attacked the men she was dating. I would steal from them. I would curse them. I tried to beat one of them up, but he moved out of the way, and I fell down the stairs. I still have a scar.... When I was 8 she took me to my grandmother who used to beat me up regularly.

At the time of his father's death, Mike was in his Oedipal stage, experiencing the first stirrings of sexual feelings and in love with his mother. Most boys have to compete with their father for their mother's love. Mike didn't need to do that. Mother was his. They were together, and close. He was her only one—a young boy's heaven. Things changed when his mother started dating. Suddenly he had competition for her love. Mike responded with tremendous jealousy.

He expressed his jealousy in violence—not toward himself, the way his father did, but toward his competitors for Mother's love. His violence caused the ultimate rejection: Mike was sent away to live with his abusive grandmother. These childhood experiences had a profound impact on his predisposition toward jealousy. As an adult, Mike attempted to excuse his mother's betrayal, but the little hurt boy in him still felt terribly abandoned. Mike sees the feelings of abandonment as the root cause of his jealousy:

I have the gravest fear of abandonment. This is probably why I am so jealous. Mom, Pop, Coot [a friend]—in one way or another I lost all of them. Even the pets. Somebody poisoned my ducks, my dog was given away, another was taken. They gave my dolls to a cousin [a girl]. Everything I ever cared about, I ended up losing. When I love, I expect total fidelity. I know I don't handle infidelity very well, and I say it up front. A close, intimate relationship has to be monogamous. If not, it's like a betrayal to me. I could never be with someone who is open to have casual sex with others. That would hurt me too much. I couldn't live with that. To me sex isn't casual. If there's no emotional involvement, to me it's nothing.

Sounds reasonable, doesn't it? A man who has a fear of abandonment and a problem with jealousy makes sure the women he gets involved with don't make him feel abandoned and don't trigger his jealousy. Why is it, though, that Mike chose to fall in love with Pat, a woman he knew was "up to no good," a woman who caused him to feel insecure, and eventually abandoned him in a most cruel and inconsiderate way? Why is it that Pat triggered more jealousy in Mike than did Rosemary, his wife? ("I wasn't threatened by Rosemary's relationship with Ann, but could get killing mad about Pat.") The reason is that Pat fit Mike's negative romantic image better.

As noted earlier, romantic images develop early in life and are particularly powerful because of it. They are based on the significant features—positive and, even more so, negative—of the people who were most influential in our early childhood. For most people, these are the parents. We internalize the image of the people who taught us the meaning of love by the way they gave us love, or withheld it from us. As adults, we look for a person who fits that internalized image. When we meet such a person, we project our internalized romantic image onto him or her and experience it as falling in love.

Why do men like Mike, Stan, and Neil, who fear rejection and abandonment, choose to fall in love with women who reject and abandon them? The reason is that the women they choose represent a painful part of their romantic image, and thus provide them with an opportunity to heal a childhood injury. The relationship may seem like a living hell—and in extreme cases may trigger violence—but it actually represents a hope to master a childhood trauma.[7]

Mike fell in love with Pat because he knew she wouldn't make him number one just as he wasn't number one for his mother. If Pat had returned his love, it would have helped heal his childhood wound. Unfortunately for Mike, she did not.

Mike cared less about Rosemary, yet got a sense of security from her love. When she too betrayed him, he was devastated. Just then he thought he was failing in his work too. He knew he was going to destroy everything, the way he had as a child.

> My supervisor at work came and mentioned something about me being moved. I felt like a failure. I was very angry. That morning I put my gun in my lunch-box. [Mike is an electronics

technician and was sent out to customers' homes to make repairs.] I knew I was going to kill someone. When I got into the house and saw it was a woman, I decided to rape her too.

She was very brave. I admired her. At a certain point I had second thoughts about killing her. But I knew I had to kill some-one. I wanted to get it over with.

It was a cold–blooded murder. In a world where he felt he had lost everything, the only power Mike had left was the power to destroy.

Jealousy as a Trigger of Murder

Mike is black, Stan is white. Mike belonged to a lower socioeconomic class than Stan. Yet there were several important similarities that brought them both to prison with a life sentence.

For both, control was extremely important. The reason, as their childhood histories suggest, is that as children they felt powerless to get the love and recognition they so desperately wanted. Despite their need for control, both actually felt insecure and inferior (none of Stan's successes helped change that). They frequently felt isolated and lonely. This made them emotionally dependent on the women they finally allowed themselves to fall in love with, and thus very susceptible to jealousy.

When the women they depended on to give their life a sense of meaning were leaving them for someone else, the feelings of pain and despair were overwhelming. Violence was their way to gain back some sense of control. When nothing was left to lose, the only thing left to do was to destroy everything. In Stan's case, that meant killing Kathy, in Mike's case—killing anyone. In both cases, the impulse to destroy represented the component of envy in the jealousy situation.

Chuck's crimes were rape and robbery. Yet the events that led to his crimes resemble those in Mike's story in many ways.

Chuck

Chuck, a short, husky man, grew up in the South. He was the oldest of six children born to a religious Baptist family. When he married, Chuck expected his wife to be faithful. The reason, as he readily admits, is that he is "a very jealous man" and has been jealous throughout his life. When his wife had an illicit affair with another man, Chuck became "violently jealous":

> I tried to push the picture of the two of them together from my head, I wanted to erase the picture from my mind, but I couldn't do it. I was very upset. I would ask her questions.... I wanted to know all the details. I started making threats of what I would do to her. Once I punched her.

His violent outbursts of jealousy were the cause of their subsequent separation:

> After that, everything went downhill. I made up my mind that the marriage wouldn't work. I got very depressed. I let the house and everything else go. I went back to the military. But I still loved her.

After the separation, things started falling apart in other areas of Chuck's life:

> After my wife and I split, I got into trouble for using dope and going AWOL, and had to leave the army. I had given up on the hope of getting back with my wife. I was living with my grandfather. It was a low period in my life. Nothing was going right. I tried to commit suicide, but the gun wouldn't fire. I didn't want to do anything with anybody. I just gave up on life.

It was at this time that Chuck started breaking into houses:

> I started burglarizing. When I went in I didn't know someone was there. I came in through the window at 1:00 A.M. A woman was asleep in the bedroom. I got scared and tried to escape quietly. All of a sudden she woke up. When she saw me she had such a terrified look that I changed my mind. I raped her. I felt in control. I knew I could do to her anything I wanted. I stayed there the whole night raping her again and again and again. With her pants on, and with her pants off, in the bedroom and in the bathroom, in every position I could think of. I'm not trying to justify

my crime, but it wasn't like I tried to hurt her. I told her I didn't want to hurt her. I was there for eight hours. We talked a lot. In the next burglaries I was already hoping someone would be there. It went on for three or four months. I was convicted of two rapes, but there were actually five. I contacted the first rape victim, and the phone was tapped. I called her to tell her that I was sorry. I felt I loved her. I felt she understood me.

It may be worth noting that during the time of those rapes, Chuck (like many of the other rapists I talked to) actually had a girlfriend. Clearly, it wasn't sex alone he was after, but something else, something he had lost when he discovered his wife's affair—a sense of control, especially over a woman:

I didn't have much control over the relationship with my wife. The lack of control was particularly painful in terms of jealousy. During the rape I had complete control. Having total control was one of the most important things in the rape. I definitely don't want to go back to it, but if those feelings are still there when I get out, I'm afraid of my jealousy and my need for control.

Like Mike, Chuck is black and comes from a low-income background. Like Mike, he was emotionally dependent on his wife, and extremely susceptible to jealousy.

For Chuck, as for the others, the pain over losing a love relationship was exacerbated by problems in other spheres of life: Chuck got into trouble in the army, Stan got into trouble in school, and Mike was convinced he was about to lose his job.

For each of them, the relationship that was lost promised to heal some painful childhood wounds that in all three cases were related to problematic relationships with their fathers. Chuck had never lived with his father; Stan had a distant, critical, demanding father; Mike's father committed suicide when he was 3. At the beginning, the relationship seemed to heal these childhood wounds. Consequently, when the relationship ended, the loss was devastating.

Why is it that Chuck robbed and raped a series of random victims in response to his jealousy, Mike murdered and raped another chance victim, and Neil killed the interloper, while Goldie and Stan killed or attempted to kill their lovers? Despite differences in their personalities and backgrounds, the most significant reason seems to be the cruel and humiliating way Goldie and Stan were told the relationship was over. In Stan's case, Kathy hit him in the face and told him to get away from her and her family. In Goldie's case, Nathan responded to her despair with irritation, ridicule, and total insensitivity. Once again we see that the way a jealousy crisis is handled determines whether it will escalate to violence.[8]

Three Rapists

Besides Chuck, several other rapists I spoke with committed their crimes as a result of jealousy. I will describe three of them. All three men were white, blue-collar workers in their twenties. Ed had alcoholic parents, started college, but left after one year, and until his arrest worked as a carpenter. Ken grew up Baptist and worked in construction until his arrest. Al, a Mormon, had a father who married six times, had nineteen brothers and sisters, and worked as a driver until his arrest. All three men described themselves as "very jealous," and the events preceding the rape started with a betrayal by a woman they loved.

Ed lived with his girlfriend for over a year before the rape and his arrest. He describes the relationship:

> It was intense, both good and bad. Sometimes I had the control, and sometimes she. We both were very needy. I really loved her. I was always afraid it wouldn't last, based on relationships I'd had in the past. For the whole year and a half I was afraid the relationship would crumble. I was insecure about myself and my identity. Several times I wanted to get married and was rejected.

The discovery of her betrayal was devastating:

> When she thought the time was right she told me about being involved with my best friend. That really hurt me. As if I wasn't enough. There was an emptiness in my chest, a heavy lump. I couldn't handle hearing the details. I had nightmares about her leaving me—driving her car and going away. I felt a tremendous love for her. I was scared. Someone I cared about was slipping away. When you love someone and the love that they felt for you

is gone, that's the greatest pain in the world. I saw no way of con-
trolling the situation.

The discovery started a process of deterioration that eventually led
to a rape of a woman on the beach:

> The reality was hard, and I started being more involved in
> fantasy than in the real world. I was involved with drugs and
> alcohol. Once I tried to commit suicide. I had a deep sense of
> helplessness. I was passionate and needy, but I didn't feel she
> really loved me. The crime was intended to destroy the
> relationship. I felt inadequate as a man. I had a lot of anger
> toward women going back to my past. I was very scared during
> the rape, more than she was. It was scary to be out of control
> that way.

Ed is aware of his jealousy and his tendency to respond to it with
violence. Even after his trial and incarceration, jealousy continued to
be a difficult issue in his relationship:

> I'm a jealous person. I feel it very intensely. I was always an emo-
> tional person. I punched a guy once, right in the throat (in a jeal-
> ous rage). I have a lot of emotional involvement in the
> relationship. I can feel when she's with someone, and couldn't
> continue subjecting myself to this kind of pain. It's a cruel pun-
> ishment. When I went to prison she started seeing other people,
> and I always knew. Last week she told me she met someone else
> she wants to date. I gave her back all her pictures and letters. I
> couldn't handle my jealousy.

Ken was also living with a woman he loved, and experienced
tremendous jealousy when she showed interest in other men:

> We were living together three and a half years and were going
> to get married. I was very attracted to her physically and emo-
> tionally. I loved her. I wanted to spend all my time with her.
> Everything was great until about a month before my arrest.
> In the last month, my brother told me he saw her with two
> guys. It kind of hurt me. I didn't understand it. She told me she

was pregnant, but she didn't want me next to her. She pulled away. I felt terrible pain. I couldn't fall asleep. I thought I was losing her.

Like Ed and all the other inmates described earlier, Ken felt he was losing control over the relationship at a time when other aspects of his life were falling apart too. It was a difficult and scary feeling:

> I was 18 at the time. I lost my job. I lost my car, my dad went to jail, my mother was kicked out to the street, and my girlfriend was withdrawing from me. I was on "crystal" about five or six days, driving my friend's car. I was mad at myself for letting all these things happen. I lost control with my girlfriend. I was afraid I was losing her. She never believed my crime. She cried and cried and cried. I told her I didn't understand it myself. She told me she still loved me.

The events leading to Al's crime were similar to those that led Ken and Ed to violence. Al loved his girlfriend ("I always felt that she was a very attractive woman and a great person"). They lived together four years. Al hoped their relationship would last forever, yet felt extremely insecure about it:

> Things went from terrible to excellent and back again. I never trusted her. She always flirted, flaunting herself. She's an exhibitionist.

The jealousy crisis that eventually led to rape started when Al discovered he had been cuckolded:

> I found out at the hospital about her going to bed with this guy. That meant that the baby she had is probably not mine, because my sperm count is very low. After we talked, I went and got loaded on grass. I felt empty. I was afraid I was losing her. I started going out with different women and taking them to bed. The woman that called the police on me was one of these women. My crime was a revenge toward my old lady. I was telling her, "You can do it, I can do it." I didn't care during the trial. I thought about suicide. I still loved her.

Al had responded to jealousy with violence in the past:

> I know that jealousy is a problem for me. I am very jealous. Too jealous. Almost all my relationships ended because of it. I was always jealous of this one dude. I kept my old lady away from him. I told him if he does something to my lady, I'll fuck his. One time at a party she disappeared for a long time. At first I was worried, then I found out she was talking to this dude. I kicked his ass and I got really mad at her. I was very jealous, very angry. If I thought she was having an affair, I'd try to catch them and hit her or split. After I found out, it would come to a stop. Either I would leave or she would.

All four rapists described themselves as "extremely jealous." All four needed desperately to feel in control, yet were extremely dependent on their partners. Each felt devastated by the discovery that "his" woman was involved with another man. Other crises made them feel that they were losing control over their lives. The use of drugs exacerbated the problem. Rape gave them a sense of control over a woman, control they felt they had lost in their own life and relationship.

This explanation is not an excuse for the crimes these men committed. It also does not mean that the women in their lives deserve blame for their crimes. Instead, it means that men who have an unusually high predisposition to jealousy and violence and are otherwise unstable emotionally, who are dependent on their intimate relationship and feel betrayed—especially when they are in a crisis and using drugs—are likely to respond to their jealousy with violence.

What Causes Crimes of Passion?

Mike, Chuck, Ken, Ed, and Al are typical of criminals who serve time in prison for violence related to jealousy. As noted earlier, such criminals tend to be male, young, and from a low socioeconomic class.[9] In virtually every case the crime was a result of an extreme predisposition to jealousy combined with an extreme jealousy trigger: withdrawal or actual betrayal by a woman they loved and depended on emotionally.

During group therapy and individual interviews with these men, we explored the roots of their jealous predisposition (Pines, 1983).

The exploration revealed two shared experiences in virtually all of their backgrounds. The first was a traumatic experience of aban- donment in early childhood. At times the abandonment was by the mother, at times by the father, at times by both parents (in one case the young boy arrived home from kindergarten to discover the house locked and both parents gone). In some cases the parent left the family; in others he or she died of illness, committed suicide, or withdrew emotionally. In all cases the boy experienced panic, rejec- tion, abandonment, loss, and total helplessness. As adults these men tended to be especially dependent on their intimate relationships. When they felt that their lover was withdrawing—because of inter- est in another man, or because of problems in the relationship—the withdrawal triggered tremendous jealousy marked by emotions closely related to the traumatic childhood experience.

The second experience shared by most of these men had to do with the lack of a positive masculine role model during childhood. At times it was caused by the absence of a father altogether, other times by the presence of an abusive father or one who was distant, cold, and critical.

The lack of a loving, "normal" father—strong sometimes, weak other times, supportive sometimes, angry other times—caused the men to internalize instead a sex-role stereotype of a man who was a macho caricature. Consequently, when his lover began to with- draw, the withdrawal was perceived as a serious threat to his mas- culinity. In his extreme jealousy, the man felt the need to do something that would prove to his lover, and even more so to him- self, that he was a "real man." His feelings of powerlessness in his relationship and life in general made him desperate to feel power- ful, and he regained his feeling by attacking his victim.

The crimes that the jealousy triggered had two primary charac- teristics: They gave the men a sense of control, and they "proved" their masculinity. Most of the men admitted that having control over their victim was the most exciting part of the crime. The crime itself—whether a murder, a robbery, or most particularly a rape—enabled the men to prove their masculinity to the women who made them doubt it. The crime often involved a high level of daring and risk (e.g. robbing a house while the owners were eating dinner in the dining room); the "masculine" risk-taking was a great source of pride for these men.

Women and Crimes of Passion

While women are less likely to commit violent crimes than men, on rare occasions women also respond to jealousy with violence. In another study of jealousy and violence, I compared the responses to *The Romantic Jealousy Questionnaire* (see Appendix B) of twelve women inmates who described themselves as having a jealousy problem to those of twelve women who were similar to the inmates in age and socioeconomic status.[10]

The results of the comparison indicated that the women in prison described themselves as jealous, and believed their intimate partners perceived them as jealous, to a much greater degree than the control group. When describing their most intense experiences of jealousy, the women inmates reported feeling more rage, aggression, anxiety, humiliation, grief, frustration, depression, and pain. They also reported feeling possessive, self–righteous, and close to a nervous breakdown. When asked how they coped with their jealousy, the women in prison were far more likely to say that they used violence. They also reported being more likely to suffer silently but visibly or to leave their mates.

When asked about their childhoods, the women in prison described a more troubled home life; a relationship between the parents marked by violence; having a jealous mother; and being beaten while growing up. They were also likely to feel less secure in their current intimate relationships.[11]

Like the men who committed crimes of passion, these women had traumatic childhoods that contributed to their extreme predisposition to both jealousy and violence. An extreme case of such a childhood marked by abandonment and loneliness, was described by a gay woman I interviewed in prison who killed another woman by hitting her head with a rock. The reason for the attack was a pass that this woman made toward her lover.

Hidden Crimes of Passion

So far, the discussion of the relationship between jealousy and violence has focused on people who were incarcerated for committing crimes of passion. However, not all people who act violently as a result of jealousy end up in prison. How likely are people with a serious jealousy problem to act violently?

A study conducted by Paul Mullan of 138 people referred for psychiatric assessment for a serious jealousy problem (none of the referrals came from the courts) revealed that while only 1% had ever been charged with a violent crime, a mere 19% had *not* acted aggressively toward their partners. Close to 57% had a history of committing acts of violence, including threats to kill or maim (24%), accompanying threats by brandishing knives (nine men and two women, together 6%), underlining threats by waving blunt instruments such as pokers (nine men, or 7%), and holding a gun to the partner's head while issuing threats (one man) (Mullen & Maack, 1985).

Fifty-six percent of the men and 53% of the women inflicted assaults on their partners. The seriousness of the attacks varied. Ten of the men throttled their wives with homicidal intent. Twelve people stabbed or slashed their mates with knives. Nine men and two women struck their partners with clubs or other blunt instruments on one or more occasions, causing multiple fractures in four instances. The most common pattern of violence was repeated attacks involving hitting, punching, and kicking the partner. This catalog of violence had never come to the notice of the police, despite the hospital treatment a number of the partners received for their injuries.

In a later article on crimes of passion, Paul Mullen argues that in recent years jealousy has been transformed from a sanctioned response to infidelity into personal pathology. In making jealousy a symptom of psychopathology, it ceases to be the responsibility of the individual and allows claims of diminished capacity with respect to crimes of passion (Mullen, 1993).

Implications

Most readers can probably understand to a certain extent why the people described in this chapter did what they did, but would never do such things themselves. They would never kill, rob, or rape because of jealousy, and would not hit, punch, or kick their partner. Nevertheless, as noted at the beginning of the chapter, it is important to know how to defuse the potential for violence in an extreme jealousy situation whether one is being jilted, doing the jilting, or is a concerned observer.

It is extremely important to be aware of emotionally charged situations that could lead to violence. People who find themselves involved with an emotionally dependent partner and have fallen out of love should be very careful not to just come home one day and say, "I've found someone else I love, and I'm leaving." Jilting a desperately loving and dependent partner without an opportunity to discuss the matter is an invitation to violence. Such a situation can unleash jealous rage with an enormous destructive potential. This can be avoided by treating ex-lovers with sensitivity and respect.

People who are jilted and who feel that without their mate their life will have no meaning need to know that the greatest danger facing them is their own jealousy. The best way to deal with it is by getting away. Clinical experience suggests that a prolonged separation usually results in the amelioration or even the disappearance of jealousy, particularly if the jealous person can come to accept the separation as permanent and begin to disengage. Separation is especially advisable for people with a history of extreme jealousy or violence.[12]

It is also crucial for people in a jealousy crisis to be able to discuss their jealousy openly and gain control over themselves and their life. There are workshops and books aimed at helping people deal with their jealousy, heal their broken hearts, and let go of destructive relationships.[13] Three of the most important things such workshops can do are to make jealous people realize that (1) they are not alone in this predicament, (2) there's life even after a lover leaves, and (3) it is possible to turn even a jealousy trauma into a growth experience. All three may seem impossible in the midst of a jealousy crisis, but should be kept in mind even if only as theoretical options.

People who find themselves unable to deal with their own or their partners' jealousy, and are concerned that either they or their partners may resort to violence, should not hesitate to ask for professional help. Otherwise they may find themselves in the kind of situations that the men and women described in this chapter found themselves.

Most important: If there are firearms in the house, they should be gotten rid of right away. Police records show that when there's a gun in the house, the people living in the house are the ones most likely to be hurt by it.

These recommendations apply to coping with situations in which the jealousy has a high violence potential. The next chapter addresses techniques for coping with jealousy in general.

A Note to Therapists

Therapists should be sensitive to emotionally charged situations that could lead to violence. These situations almost always involve couples in which one mate is extremely dependent on the relationship while the other one is trying to withdraw or get out. In work with such couples it is important to help both partners take responsibility for their part in this unhealthy dynamic.

The withdrawing partner should see the role he or she may have played in creating their partner's dependency on them. This can be addressed by such questions as: "What was it that attracted you to your partner when you first met?" "Could it have been the intensity of his or her feelings for you which made you feel secure, loved, and adored—the center of his or her world?"

It is equally important to help the jealous partner figure out what role he or she may have played in creating the jealousy crisis. This can be addressed by questions such as: "Is your jealousy related in some way to some aspect of your mate's personality that attracted you when you first met?" "Could it have been the fact that all women seemed drawn to him?" "That she is a sexy and flirtatious woman? That you felt excited?"

It is also important to help such jealous people focus on the things in their life that are in their control (such as the decision to take a few days off and get away), on things that they enjoy, and on people they love aside from their partner (making a list of people they love and who love them can be very helpful).

9
Coping with Romantic Jealousy

৯৯ ৯৯ ৯৯

There are palliatives [for romantic jealousy]: the first is the recognition of
the problem (disease) and the second is the wish to cure oneself.

—A. R. Orage, *On Love*

৯৯ ৯৯ ৯৯

One of the most common questions asked by people with a jealousy
problem is: Can jealousy be overcome? The answer, as evidenced
throughout this book, is yes, but with great effort. Like most other
difficult emotional experiences, jealousy, if treated correctly, can be a
trigger for growth. It can be the first step in increased self-awareness
and greater understanding of both the partner and the relationship.

People tormented by jealousy can find comfort even in the mere
knowledge that their response is normal, universal, and motivated
by a need to protect a valued relationship. Awareness alone, however, is not enough.

Since this chapter is devoted to coping, it is appropriate to start
with a clarification of what coping is and what it is not. Coping is not
the same as treatment. There are many different methods for treating
jealousy cited in the scientific literature, including hypnosis, the use
of drugs, behavior therapy, cognitive therapy, rational–emotive therapy, systems therapy, couples therapy, psychoanalysis, a combination
of couples therapy with individual therapy, and a combination of
psychodynamic, systems, behavioral, social–psychological, and evolutionary approaches.[1]

In all these treatment approaches, the individual or couple suffering from jealousy goes to an expert and is treated for the problem. Going to an expert is just one form of coping.

What Is Coping?

Richard Lazarus, a leading expert in the field of stress and coping, defines coping as "efforts to master conditions of harm, threat or challenge when an automatic response is not readily available."[2] Coping does not necessarily imply success in overcoming the harm, threat, or challenge, but is only an effort to master it. A person who takes a sleeping pill for a temporary escape from the unbearable pain caused by a partner's unfaithfulness is making an effort (even if an unsuccessful one) to cope.

Different coping strategies vary in their effectiveness. Some are almost always useful—such as talking about the problem with one's partner in an open and honest way, or learning about oneself to understand one's jealous response. Others, such as acts of violence, are almost always disastrous. Still others fall somewhere in between, only serving to delay the inevitable. Taking sleeping pills, drinking alcohol, and using illegal drugs are some of the more negative examples of this last category.

Whether a certain coping strategy is useful or disastrous can be determined by its consequences. As a result of the actions taken in response to jealousy, does the individual have increased self-awareness or a greater understanding of the partner's perspective? Does the relationship as a whole seem more loving, harmonious, and satisfying for both partners? If the answer is no, the coping strategy has not been useful.

In the remainder of this chapter I will present different strategies for coping with jealousy. Some of them may already be familiar, others probably will be new. Some of those will seem more appropriate than others. Even if a certain technique or exercise does not seem right, it is important not to reject it right away. The more coping strategies one has in one's arsenal, the better able to cope one will be.

Effective coping always involves four parts or stages:

1. being aware of the problem
2. taking responsibility for doing something about it

3. achieving clarity about what needs to and can be done
4. developing new tools for coping, and improving the range and quality of old tools[3]

Adequate coping is impossible without *awareness* that there is a problem. Some people hide from the problem and try to avoid thinking about it. When there is an illicit affair, the betrayed partner almost always knows about it at some level, but at times chooses "not to know."

Other people who are aware of their "jealousy problem" tend to think that the jealousy is all their own fault ("I'm simply a jealous person"). This reaction does not show true awareness of the problem, because it fails to put the jealousy in the context of the relationship and the particular situation that triggered it.

Awareness has two parts: One is the simple realization that a problem exists; the other is the ability to recognize that the problem is a function of certain dynamics in the relationship or the particular situation, rather than the fault of the "jealous person." Once people recognize this, the focus of their coping efforts shifts from "What's wrong with me as a person that makes me so jealous?" to "What can I do to change the situation so that my jealousy is not triggered so easily?"

To effect a change, an individual must be willing to *take responsibility* for changing the relationship or the situation. This is usually quite difficult. Yet taking responsibility for effecting a change in a difficult situation is therapeutic in and of itself, because it reduces the debilitating effects of feeling helpless.

When people are aware of the existence of a problem in their relationship, and are willing to take responsibility for trying to change it (instead of waiting for their partner to change), the third necessary step is to achieve *clarity about what needs to be done and what can be done.*

Most people in the midst of a jealousy crisis cannot easily discriminate between what they can change in the relationship or situation and what they cannot. Some assume that everything in themselves, their mates, and their relationships can be changed. When they discover, the hard way, that this is not always so, they feel hopeless and helpless and come to believe that nothing can be changed. There are also people who believe from the outset that nothing can be changed. These individuals never attempt to change anything. "That's life," they say. The slogan may reduce their stress to some extent, but it also prevents them from actively seeking positive change.

The truth is that some things in a relationship cannot be changed or would be extremely difficult to change—for example, the basic personalities of both mates. But many triggers in a jealousy-provoking relationship or situation—certain behaviors, for example—can be changed with varying degrees of effort. The most important advantage of achieving clarity is the ability to distinguish between those aspects of the relationship and the situation that can't be changed, and those that can. This allows people to channel their efforts where there will be the greatest likelihood of important progress.

Jealousy has been described as "the eruption of attachment that can be transcended only through awareness."[4] As people move (with awareness) into the core of their jealousy, they may discover such unpleasant things as ungrounded expectations, projections, fears, and insecurities. The awareness of their existence is the first step in overcoming them.

In a jealousy crisis, people first need to determine what is at the heart of their jealousy. Is it fear of loss? Is it a humiliation? Is it feeling excluded? Is it something else? (What is the most painful thought associated with the jealousy? Does it hurt to know that your wife had a wonderful time with someone else, and you were excluded? Do you feel humiliated because your husband has flirted all night with a stunning woman, and everyone at the party saw it? Or do you feel a terrible pain of loss because you know you have lost your mate's love and the relationship?) While feeling excluded is no doubt painful, it is not as painful as losing a love relationship. People who don't bother to clarify what hurts them most can respond to a trivial incident as if they had lost the relationship.

Once people have identified the focus of their jealousy, they need to figure out why they are responding the way they are. Is it a result of their sensitivity, or of a real threat to the relationship? Even people who are especially prone to jealousy should make an effort to avoid labeling themselves "a jealous person" instead of a person with a predisposition to jealousy. The predisposition can be a result of a particular family background, a cultural background, or a past history of intimate relationships. After clarifying what exactly they are feeling and why, they can proceed to examine their various options for coping.

Coping with Jealousy?

Recall your most extreme experience or experiences of jealousy. To what extent did you use each one of the following coping strategies: never, once or twice, rarely, occasionally, often, usually, always?

- Talk to your partner about the situation and your response to it in a rational manner?
- Use sarcasm?
- Accept the situation because you felt there was nothing you could do about it?
- Avoid the issue and try not to think about it?
- Use "stony silence," clearly indicating that you were aware of the problem but refused to talk about it?
- Use denial (e.g. you knew that your partner was involved with someone, but you chose not to know)?
- Cry, either in front of your partner to make your suffering obvious, or when you were all alone?
- Use verbal assault, screaming at your partner, cursing, swearing?
- Retaliate, making your partner jealous either by flirting, having an affair, or by telling your partner about other lovers?
- Attack your partner physically, with fists, nails, dishes?
- Leave your partner, either temporarily or forever?
- Suffer silently and covertly, so neither your partner nor anyone else knew about your pain?
- Suffer silently but visibly (making sure your partner knew you were in pain)?
- Try to find the funny side when thinking about the situation?
- Make a joke of it to your partner or to others?
- Think through your own role in the situation and assess rationally what you stood or feared to lose?

I presented the question "How do you cope with jealousy?" in two different studies.[5] In one of these studies, 285 men and 283 women were shown a list of seven coping strategies and asked which one of these strategies they were most likely to use when jealous. The response chosen most frequently was, "I talk about it with my partner." The least frequently chosen response was, "I respond with violence." Here are the percentages of the responses, in rank order:

- I talk about it with my partner—34%
- I let my partner know I'm hurt—25%
- I try to ignore it—22%
- I scream—7%
- I get away—5%
- I respond in some other way—5%
- I respond with violence—1%

The problem with these percentages is that they tell us only the primary strategy the person uses, when in many cases people use different strategies at different times, and even simultaneously. In the second study, 103 men and women were asked whether or not they use each of sixteen different coping strategies presented earlier. Once again, "rational discussion" was one of the two most frequently reported strategies, the second being "I think through my role in the situation and assess rationally what I stand or fear to lose." And again, "physical violence" was the least frequently mentioned strategy. Here are the percentages of people who answered "yes" when asked whether they use a particular strategy for coping with extreme jealousy:

- I think through my role in the situation and assess what I stand or fear to lose—80%
- I use rational discussion—79%
- I use verbal assault—60%
- I use sarcasm—56%
- I accept the situation—55%
- I cry—44%
- I use stony silence—42%
- I suffer silently but visibly—36%
- I try to find the funny side of the situation—36%
- I avoid the issue—33%
- I retaliate, making my partner jealous—33%
- I leave my partner—29%
- I suffer silently and covertly—27%
- I make a joke of it—26%
- I use denial—18%
- I resort to physical violence—7%

In two different studies, using two different groups of people and two different questions, the most frequent strategy reported for coping with jealousy was rational discussion; the least frequent strategy was violence.

Does this mean that people really are most likely to talk about their jealousy in a rational manner or think through their role in the situation? Not necessarily. More likely, they answer according to what they know is the most acceptable way to deal with their jealousy whether or not they actually do it.

When asked to recall the most intense jealousy they have ever experienced, and then how they would have liked to respond to the situation that triggered that jealousy, chances are that most people would have said that they wished they had a cool, rational discussion with their partner or thought through the situation and their role in it. Chances are also good that in fact they did something different, which is part of the reason they recall it as their most extreme jealousy.

The fact of the matter is that talking with one's partner and thinking through one's role in the jealousy crisis are indeed the best coping strategies, because they are the most likely to produce positive results. The practical question is: How to do it?

Since it is difficult to think clearly and compare options when in the midst of an emotional turmoil, it is best to get away temporarily from both the person and the situation that triggered the jealousy (if at all possible, to get out of town).

The person in the midst of a jealousy crisis needs to consider several questions. These questions were mentioned earlier in this chapter and throughout the book, but they bear repeating:

- First, what is it exactly that's making you jealous? The fact that he's going out without you? That he seems to have more fun with her than with you? That he had an affair?
- Second, what is at the heart of your jealousy? Envy of your rival? Fear of loss? Fear of abandonment? Humiliation? A threat to the relationship? A threat to your ego?
- Third, why are you experiencing that particular component of jealousy so intensely? Is it related to an old experience you might have had in your childhood? How is the old experience related to what

you are experiencing now? Could the current threat be related to what you found most rewarding about your mate's love at the beginning of your relationship?

Once people have identified their own role in the jealousy problem, they can consider their options for responding. They should consider, too, how their partner is likely to respond to each of those options, and what they themselves want to happen. A man who wants more than anything else for him and his wife to be close again should realize that attacking his wife is not the best strategy. Expressing his love and pain is likely to have a much more positive outcome. The best setting for that is an open and considerate discussion that gives both partners the opportunity to describe their feelings and explain whatever needs to be explained without being attacked.

One way to do it (which works best with couples who like structure) is for each partner to take exactly five minutes to make one point (only!) as the other partner listens and tries to understand. The speaker is not allowed to attack the listener. The listener can only ask for clarification and, at the end of the allotted five minutes, must repeat back the main point to the speaker's satisfaction.[6]

Hurt feelings and counter-attacks can be avoided if both partners are careful to follow these three steps:

1. Describe what the partner is probably feeling. ("You must feel constrained when I'm with you at a party.")
2. Describe what you are feeling. ("I feel left out when you have long conversations with other people, and threatened when you seem attracted to them.")
3. Express clearly what it is that you want. ("I would really appreciate it if you would include me in some conversations when we are at a party.")

When the situation is too explosive for talking of any kind, couples may want to consider writing what they want to say to each other—in the form of a love letter. People who feel overcome by jealousy and think they are likely to do "something crazy" should remember the important distinction between what they feel and what they do. Even when they feel crazy, they don't have to act crazy;

even if they feel out of control, they don't have to act that way. In fact, behavioral therapists believe that it is possible to change feelings by changing the thoughts or actions associated with them.

People don't always realize, or want to admit, that they have a wide range of response options in a jealousy situation. As evidenced earlier, they can show their partners how important the relationship is to them; they can get out of the situation or the relationship; they can ignore what is going on; they can show their partners how much they are suffering; they can laugh it off; they can make a scandal; or they can talk to their partner about their feelings and wishes.

The Behavioral Approach to Jealousy

The focus of the behavioral approach, as its name implies, is on observable behavior.[7] Unlike the psychodynamic approach and like the systems approach, the behavioral approach has no interest in the unconscious. Behaviorists assume that the causes for, and solutions to, a jealousy problem exist in the current environment, even if the jealousy–triggering event happened at another time and place. Behavior is the result of learning and psychological problems are always the result of inappropriate learning.

Like writers who advocate open marriages, behaviorists disagree with sociobiologists' view that jealousy is natural, instinctive, and inevitable. They believe, instead, that it is learned. And since jealousy is learned, behaviorists maintain, it can also be unlearned and a new (and better) response can replace it.[8]

Behavioral therapists define a problem exactly the way the person who comes for treatment defines it. They do not assume that the therapist knows the "real" problem better than the person experiencing it. The treatment goal is to help the person change inappropriate responses and dysfunctional habits by unlearning them and replacing them with more appropriate responses. Treatment can accommodate either an individual or a couple.

According to behaviorists, in every interaction people try to get as many rewards as they can for the lowest possible cost. In couple therapy, couples are taught to negotiate contracts that enable each partner to get more rewards from the other. The only cost is doing something the other wants.

Desensitization is one of the behavioral techniques that can be used to treat jealousy.[9] The process comprises several steps. First, the person is asked to make a list of the things that trigger jealousy and rank them according to the degree of jealousy they create. Second, the person is taught progressive relaxation by learning to relax different parts of the body. Third, the person is trained to remain relaxed while imagining different items on the list, starting with the item at the bottom of the list, the one that triggers the least jealousy. Once the person is able to think about this item and remain relaxed, the next item on the list is introduced. If the person cannot remain relaxed while imagining it, the instruction is to return to the relaxation exercises and then try again. This way, the person can gradually learn to confront the triggers that produce the most extreme jealousy, and remain calm.

In jealousy workshops I use a variation of this exercise, which involves people revisiting their most intense experience of jealousy. I ask participants to lie down on the floor (if that is possible) and make themselves as comfortable as possible. Next I ask them to imagine themselves in their favorite place (it can be inside or outdoors); the day is sunny and they are relaxed and happy. A deep breath is bringing calm and comfort to every cell in their body. As they exhale, they imagine all feelings of discomfort, tension, and pain leaving their body. They concentrate on relaxing each part of their body separately, starting with the toes and moving up slowly to the face and head, until they feel completely relaxed.

When total relaxation is achieved, I ask them to flip through the pages of their personal history book until they reach the incident that triggered their most extreme jealousy and try and remember as many details as they can about this incident. (Who were the people involved? How did they look? What exactly happened? When? Where? What did they do in response?) When they have an urge to escape the pain, the rage, the panic, I ask them instead to let these difficult feelings flood them, stay with the pain for a minute, then take a deep breath, slowly bring their mind back to the present, and sit up. After sitting up they write down as many details of their experience as they can remember and tell three other workshop participants about it. For a behavioral therapist, accumulating such details is an essential step of treatment.

The second part of this exercise starts the same way as the first, with participants lying on the floor and imagining they are in their favorite place (a beautiful sandy beach or next to a cool stream in the forest). As they imagine lying there, the sun warming them gently, the wonderful feeling of relaxation is back. But, this time, they are asked to imagine that the sun is not only warming them, but also energizing and empowering them with its rays. They are strong and in control. Time has passed since they experienced their most intense jealousy, and during that time they have learned more about themselves and about their relationships. They are wiser, more experienced, and more powerful now. When they feel their inner power and wisdom, they are instructed to hold on to them as they would to a shield, a magic weapon.

Now they are ready to go back in time and revisit their most intense experience of jealousy. I ask them to imagine that they have been given a chance to go back to that incident and relive it any way they want—remembering that now they are armed with wisdom, experience, and power. What do they choose to do? How do they respond this time? Is it the same way they responded originally, because the experience taught them so much, despite the pain? Or differently, the way they have wished so many times they had responded—cool, gracious, in complete control of themselves and of the situation?

After workshop participants have completed the guided imagery, they are given a chance to discuss their experiences and share insights they have gained. People who do the exercise on their own can write down both their experiences and their insights.

People who respond differently when revisiting the site of their most extreme jealousy need to understand that the ability to respond in this new way is within them. The feelings of empowerment, of experience, wisdom, control, are a part of them that they can call up at any time, even if it requires greater effort in times of stress. The next exercise can prove this.

In this exercise people are asked to take a sheet of paper and fold it lengthwise, then write the letter *A* on top of one side, and *B* on top of the other side. Recalling the thoughts that ran through their head during the first (traumatic) part of the exercise, they are asked to list as many of these thoughts as they remember on the side of the paper labeled *A*. Next, they are asked to recall their thoughts during the second part of the exercise, and write as many of them as they can remember on the side of paper labeled *B*. When they can unfold the paper, they compare the two columns. For example:

A	B
He doesn't love me, that's why he did it. I'm unlovable.	I know he loves me, and he probably has his reason for doing what he did.
I'm all alone. Nobody loves me.	I'm not alone. There are people I love who love me.
This is so painful, life is not worth living.	This is painful, so I'll do something nice for myself.
I'm in so much pain that I can't control what I do.	I'm in pain, but I'm strong and in control. I want to learn something from all this.

The person who suffers from a jealousy problem can repeat the *B* sentences over and over again for several days, so that the next time jealousy strikes they are familiar and easily accessible.

Albert Ellis uses a similar approach in the application of his Rational Emotive Therapy to the treatment of jealousy.[10] Ellis differentiates between rational and irrational jealousy. Rational jealousy is reality based, while irrational jealousy is the result of irrational thoughts such as "It's awful that my beloved is interested in someone else! I can't stand it!" Like all other emotional upsets, Ellis argues, jealousy follows an ABC scheme. At point *A* there is an *Activating* event (e.g. your beloved shows interest in or attention to someone else.) At point *C* the person feels an emotional *Consequence*—intense jealousy. Quite commonly the person falsely attributes *C* to *A* (e.g. erroneously concludes that "Because my mate is carrying on a hot affair with so–and–so, that makes me jealous"). Actually, contends Ellis, there is no magic by which any outside event, even a traumatic event such as your spouse's affair, can cause you to experience jealousy. Only your *Beliefs* (the *B* in the ABC scheme) can do that. *Disputing* the irrational beliefs is the *D* in rational emotive therapy. Instead of the irrational and easily disputed beliefs such as "It's awful" and "I can't stand it!" the person is taught to say "I don't like this situation very much. I wish my beloved would be devoted only to me. What a pain in the ass this is!" If people choose to believe this, and nothing but this, promises Ellis, the emotional *Consequence* at point *C* may be disappointment, regret, or irritation, but not insane jealousy.

People tormented by jealousy almost always have a specific "traumatic scene" that causes them the sharpest pain each time they think of it. For men, it tends to be a sexual scene: "She is having sex with her new lover, and both of them are making fun of me." For women, it tends to be a scene of great intimacy: "They are walking together in the park with a baby carriage." "They are looking at each other lovingly after making love, smiling and touching tenderly." "He is offering her marriage. " The behaviorist Zeev Wanderer believes that by eliminating the emotions associated with this traumatic scene, one can eliminate the jealousy problem.

Wanderer developed a technique he calls Physiologically Monitored Implosion Therapy (PMIT).[11] PMIT is an improvement on a well-known behavioral technique called "Implosion therapy" (or "flooding"), which has been used successfully in treating phobias and PTSD. In implosion therapy, patients are asked to imagine their worst fear or most traumatic experience again and again until the fear is reduced. In PMIT, the therapist monitors the patient's blood pressure with an electronic instrument that records subtle changes. The patient talks about difficult situations, and the therapist keeps a tape recording of the scene the patient described just preceding a peak in blood pressure. This scene is considered the source of the problem. Repeated exposure to the recording reduces the scene's power over the patient, and blood pressure gradually returns to normal. Here is an example of how this process works: A man in his mid-thirties with a job in radio broadcasting had a girlfriend who worked in the same office. One day she terminated their relationship to start a romantic involvement with one of their coworkers. The man's job required that he interact frequently with both of them. His intense jealousy caused him to avoid this contact, to the detriment of his work.

During PMIT, the man was asked what he found most difficult about seeing his girlfriend with her new lover. "The fact that they are making love," he responded. What was it about their sex life that disturbed him most? Wanderer measured the man's blood pressure as he recounted his fantasies of the couple's sex life.

Analysis of the blood-pressure data indicated that the largest rise in blood pressure occurred when the man described the special sounds his ex-lover used to make when she reached orgasm. At the time of their own sexual involvement, he thought he was the only man who could make her produce these sounds. Now he was most tormented by the thought that she was making those sounds with her new lover.

The therapist recorded a session on tape in which the man was asked to imagine in great detail his ex-lover's new sexual liaison, dramatizing her orgasms, how "she's making those sounds with him.... He's touching her body in all the places that arouse her, they are laughing." The man was instructed to listen to the tape for an hour a day. After less than a week of listening to the tape, the scene no longer pained but bored him. He was able to have work-related contact with both his ex-lover and her new man without discomfort.

Another case that Wanderer treated involved a stockbroker who came to therapy because he felt he needed to stop being jealous. He said his jealousy had caused him to lose several girlfriends. The last girlfriend, whom he liked a great deal, was especially nice and understanding, and he was pained by her loss, which he considered his own fault: "One day I saw her coming out of a movie house with a lawyer friend of hers, and I made a terrible scene. She became very angry, and told me she can't have a relationship with someone who behaves that way."

His PMIT revealed that his worst scene was imagining the girlfriend leaving him for that lawyer friend. The man was taught how to relax while imagining this terrible scenario over and over and over again. After several therapy sessions he saw his girlfriend again with the same lawyer. This time he felt calm. He approached them and said a polite, "Hello, how are you?" to both of them. His girlfriend was so impressed by the change in his behavior that she called him up and they started dating again.

In both examples Wanderer describes, repeated exposure to the painful scene severed its connection to the jealous response and replaced it with a new connection between the scene and boredom.

I must add a word of caution to this very glowing account of the use of implosion therapy. I have seen a number of people who ran away from a therapist who tried to use this approach without adequate preparation. The traumatic scene is extremely painful, and people cannot be flooded with it without proper preparation and support.

"Scrupulous Honesty" (which was described in chapter four) is another, less traumatic version of implosion therapy.[12] In this technique, the nonjealous partner is instructed to "flood" the jealous partner with every detail of the day's experiences. The flooding inundates the jealous mate with information that helps dispel anxiety and insecurity.

Another version of implosion therapy used specifically for the treatment of jealousy is the "Dutch cow" technique described to me by the Israeli therapist Tsafy Gilad.[13] Gilad used the technique in treating the jealousy problem of a middle-aged couple.

Jealousy became a problem after the wife discovered that her husband had had a year-long affair. Although the affair was long over, the wife couldn't stop thinking about it. During the process of therapy the couple learned that the wife's discovery of the affair devastated her sense of security in the marriage. Security was what she looked for when she married her husband and was the most important thing the marriage gave her. To restore her sense of security, she wanted to know her husband's whereabouts every moment he was away from her, so she wouldn't worry that he might be spending time with the other woman.

The husband, who was ready to do anything to restore the marriage, was instructed to call his wife every hour whether she was at home, at work, with friends, or shopping. The instruction also meant, however, that the wife had to tell her husband where she would be every hour so he would know where to call her. The technique is nicknamed "Dutch cow" because the telephone calls serve the same function as the bells Dutch cows carry around their necks: They let their owner know where they are at every moment, so that no fences are needed.

After several weeks of this ordeal, the wife had had enough. She started dreading the phone calls, which intruded on her life. But her husband didn't mind them at all. He was ready to go on long after she said she couldn't take it anymore. While it is not clear whether the technique helped the wife genuinely trust her husband again, it clearly helped sever the connection between the husband's temporary absence and the wife's jealousy, and replaced it with a connection between his phone calls and annoyance.

Another behavioral technique for helping a couple cope with the aftermath of an affair was developed by behavior therapist Bernie Zilbergeld.[14] It involves asking the betrayed spouse to write a convincing defense of the spouse who had the affair. When I use this technique, I also ask the spouse who had the affair to write a defense of the betrayed spouse's jealousy. These defenses are extremely difficult to write, but are very effective in helping couples make the empathic leap that is required in order to understand each other's perspective. Here, for example, is part of a defense written by a female attorney of her boyfriend's involvement with other women:

> A contract is not binding when one party has been coerced or fears negative repercussions for failure to enter the contract. Such is the case here. When Jack agreed to maintain an exclusive relationship with me, he believed that he must acquiesce to my terms or lose me.
>
> When the first breach occurred, I sent an ambiguous message: I hate your behavior, but I will never hate you, and so I will forgive you and put this behind us and resume our relationship. Again, I exacted the term of an agreement to remain exclusively committed to each other and added that truth was essential to the maintenance of the relationship.
>
> Repeatedly the pattern has been that promises are made, broken, forgiven, cajoled, questioned—unpleasant and painful for both, but put aside. Jack could easily have concluded that I was making empty threats to leave or to require him to leave. He saw how distressed I was, but saw, too, that I could bounce back and behave as if business as usual was the rule. When he was honest and revealed that he had been with a woman all night, coming home at five in the morning, my behavior didn't change. The pattern was so set that even then I did not act on my threats to end the relationship. These were storms we weathered.
>
> Since he prizes his autonomy and freedom above all else, he was willing to endure these painful confrontations because he knew that they would pass and he would be able to maintain his life according to his preferred pattern. The lies necessary to maintain that lifestyle were lies he told to protect me from hurt

> rather than to protect himself, he thought, and since his affairs
> had nothing to do with his love for me, he told me about them
> to stabilize our life together.

After both partners read each other's defenses, they are more able and willing to see the other's point of view in the jealousy situation. This is a version of the role-reversal technique (also described in chapter four) in which partners take turns describing each other's point of view. At the basis of both the written defenses and the role-reversal techniques is the power of behaving "as if," which is also evident in a third technique, called "Pretend" (Im et al., 1983).

In this technique, the jealous person is instructed to act as if he or she were not jealous. The underlying assumption—one of the basic assumptions of the behavioral approach—is that if a jealous person can control his jealous behavior and act in a nonjealous manner, he can learn to perceive himself as a nonjealous person. In addition, behaving in a nonjealous manner is likely to evoke a more favorable response from the nonjealous partner. As systems therapists argue, jealous behavior, with its attendant demands, interrogation, whining, and fault-finding, usually evokes a negative reaction from the partner. By behaving more reasonably and positively toward the partner, despite feelings to the contrary, couples can reverse their downward spiral of interaction.

The counterpart of the "Pretend" technique is another technique (mentioned briefly in chapter four), called "Turning the Tables," in which the nonjealous partner is instructed to act the part of the jealous partner. Couples therapists Won Gi Im, Stefanie Wilner, and Miranda Breit (1983), who developed this technique, describe an example of its successful use.

The husband, a physician in his mid-forties, sought help because his marriage of twenty-one years was in trouble as a result of his wife's jealousy. His wife expressed her unfounded jealousy by raging at him and harassing him on the telephone at the hospital where he worked, which caused him a great deal of embarrassment.

The husband was instructed to act the part of a jealous spouse and to keep this strategy secret from his wife. Having learned over many years how a jealous person behaves, he was able to perform the role of the jealous husband so skillfully and subtly that his wife didn't realize he was role-playing. While he had seldom called home in the past, he now called his wife frequently to check on her, to see whether she was home and to ask exactly what she was doing. He made suspicious and critical remarks about any new clothes she wore, and expressed displeasure when she showed the slightest interest in another man.

The result was dramatic. The wife, now feeling flattered by her husband's attentiveness and newfound interest, stopped her jealous behavior completely. She became pleasant and loving toward her husband and expressed remorse over her earlier behavior. At an eight–month follow–up, the husband reported that his wife continued to behave more lovingly toward him, but as a precaution he still played the role of the jealous husband from time to time.

In both the "Pretend" and "Turning the Tables" techniques, one partner is instructed to behave differently (more like the other partner) as a way of changing the dynamics surrounding a jealousy problem. The following exercise is aimed at getting both partners to work on a jealousy problem together:[15]

Each partner needs three sheets of paper for this exercise. On top of the first page, the jealous partner is instructed to write the heading "Behaviors That Trigger My Jealousy" and the nonjealous partner is instructed to write "Jealous Behaviors That Get on My Nerves." Under this heading, the jealous partner lists all the things the nonjealous partner does that trigger jealousy; the nonjealous partner lists all the things the jealous partner does that trigger anger, frustration, hurt, or feeling caged. For example, an item on a jealous partner's list may be, "When you are honey–dripping sweet to every woman you meet on the street after being nasty to me." An item on the nonjealous partner's list may be, "Your suspicion about every woman I happen to bump into on the street."

On top of the second page the jealous partner writes: "The Needs at the Base of My Jealousy" while the nonjealous partner writes: "The Needs at the Base of My Annoyance." Under this second heading the partners name the different needs at the heart of their jealousy or annoyance. For example, at the heart of the jealousy triggered by seeing him act sweet to other women may be her need to feel special, to feel that she is his "one and only." At the heart of the anger at her suspicion may be a need to feel trusted.

At the top of the third page, both partners write: "Wishes." Under this heading, they write what the other partner can do to fulfill their need. They are encouraged not to ask for things that are too general, such as "Make me feel special" or "Show that you trust me," but rather, to ask for specific and concrete things that their partner is capable of giving, things that have special significance for them. For example, "Take me out for a romantic dinner"; "Tell me that you trust me." Note that both examples are positive statements—things to do, not things to avoid. Note, too, that both examples involve observable behavior—this behavior is the focus of the behavioral approach.

After writing their lists of wishes, both partners go over those lists and rank their requests from 1 to 10 in terms of their importance. A score of 10 means very important, a score of 1 means minor importance. (For example, how important is going out for a romantic dinner? 8? 6? 9? 3? What about an intimate dance at a party? Is it more or less important? How important is it to hear that your partner trusts you?)

Once both partners have ranked their requests, they are instructed to exchange their lists, examine each other's wishes, and then rank them in terms of the difficulty in fulfilling them. Again, the most difficult request gets the score of 10, the least difficult gets the score of 1. (How difficult is it for you to tell your partner that you trust him? 8? 6? 3? How difficult is it to take your partner out for a romantic dinner?)

It is important to emphasize that requests are not demands, and should never be expressed or understood as such. They are wishes. When a partner fulfills a wish, it's a gift and should be perceived and received that way.

A couple who struggles with a jealousy problem should try to give each other at least three gifts a week. This probably will not be easy. If it were easy, the couple would have done it before. The things the partner asks for may be difficult. (It may be hard to look straight into his eyes and tell him that you trust him, when deep in your heart you don't—which is why you respond with jealousy when he is too friendly toward other women.) Couples don't have to give gifts they have rated high in difficulty. It is better to start with those they have rated least difficult. As the relationship becomes more loving and trusting, couples usually find it easier to give each other the more difficult gifts.

Finally, a note about assumptions. One of the most damaging assumptions in couple relationships is that something asked for is worthless. ("If I have to ask for it, what kind of a gift is it?") Another dangerous assumption is that the gifts the partner wants are the same things you want. The exercise described here can help couples break free of these assumptions and give each other what they both really want. This way, both partners will get more rewards from the relationship. And, as noted earlier, getting as many rewards as possible for the lowest possible cost is one of the goals of behavioral couple therapy.

An Evaluation of the Behavioral Approach to Jealousy

One of the major contributions of the behavioral approach is its emphasis on observable behavior and its view of jealousy as a learned response that can be unlearned. The behavioral techniques and exercises described in this chapter have in common the assumption that if people change their behavior (even when they are only role-playing at first) they can change their feelings and attitudes. Such behavioral techniques can be very effective and far less time-consuming than psychodynamically oriented psychotherapy.

One of the major criticisms of the behavioral approach (similar to a criticism of the systems approach) is directed at its disregard for the role of traumatic childhood experiences and unconscious processes in the development of psychological problems such as jealousy. According to the psychodynamic approach, unless these childhood experiences are addressed and the unconscious processes brought to consciousness, the jealousy problem will not be cured. These critics see the changes brought about by behavioral techniques as superficial and temporary. Behaviorists, on the other hand, believe that insight is not necessary for a lasting change in behavior to take place. Because they focus on observable behaviors, their interventions can be studied and, indeed, have been proven effective.[16]

Coping Strategies and Theoretical Approaches

The coping strategies presented in this chapter were inspired primarily by the behavioral approach. Throughout the book, however, numerous exercises and coping strategies were presented that were inspired by other theoretical approaches.

The psychodynamic approach, which views romantic jealousy as occurring in the mind of the jealous individual, inspired the exercise called "Jealousy as the Shadow of Love." This exercise requires introspection aimed at making a connection between the adult jealousy and childhood experiences. The systems approach, which views jealousy as occurring in the dynamic of a particular relationship, inspired the role-reversal exercise, which requires both partners to work jointly on their jealousy problem. The social–psychological approach, which views jealousy as influenced mainly by cultural forces, inspired the shift from dispositional to situational attribution. The sociobiological approach, which views jealousy as innate and shaped by evolutionary forces, and different for men and for women inspired the "relationship sociodrama," a technique designed to break people's fallacy of uniqueness and discover the universal nature of jealousy. The cognitive–behavioral approach inspired a variety of techniques and exercises aimed at helping individuals and couples learn new responses to jealousy triggers. Each approach and strategy can help people understand and cope with a jealousy problem more effectively.

A Final Word about Coping

The exercises in this chapter assume that people truly want to be rid of their jealousy problem. This assumption may or may not be true. It is possible that, despite all appearances to the contrary, the jealousy problem serves an important function in the relationship, a function the couple would rather not acknowledge. If this is the case, chances are that the coping strategies recommended here will not work.

Nevertheless, exercises that give couples an opportunity to learn about themselves and about each other, and that increase the number of rewards couples give each other, can only benefit the relationship, and therefore deserve a good try.

Even if the techniques and exercises recommended in this chapter don't solve a particular jealousy problem altogether, they are guaranteed to increase self-knowledge and enhance growth of both the individual and the couple.

A Note to Therapists

All the coping strategies presented in this chapter can be used (and will no doubt be most effective when they are used this way) by professional therapists. Some exercises can be used in the context of individual therapy (e.g. "flooding"), some can by used in the context of couple therapy (e.g. writing the defense for the affair/jealousy), and some can be used in the context of a couple workshop (e.g. the "relationship sociodrama"). Once again I would like to caution therapists about the use of implosion therapy.

Can Any Good Come Out of Romantic Jealousy?

გა   გა   გა

Jealousy is always born together with love, but it does not always die
with love.... We are happier in the passion we feel than in that we
arouse.

—La Rochefoucauld, "Reflections"

გა   გა   გა

Can any good come out of jealousy? My own answer—as evidenced
in the preceding chapters—is a definite yes. To find out what other
people think about this question, I asked 103 men and women to
rate their agreement with the following statements (on a 1 to 7 scale
ranging from 1 = Disagree strongly to 7= Agree strongly):[1]

Jealousy is a sign of love.
Jealousy is an instrument for inducing commitment.
Jealousy brings excitement to listless relationships.
Jealousy teaches people not to take each other for granted.
Jealousy makes life more interesting.
Jealousy makes relationships last longer.
Jealousy makes one's partner look more desirable.
Jealousy makes people feel alive.
Jealousy makes people examine their relationship.

Here are the mean ratings for each statement, in descending order
of agreement with the different statements:

Jealousy makes people examine their relationship: 4.7
Jealousy teaches people not to take each other for granted: 3.1
Jealousy is a sign of love: 3.0
Jealousy is an instrument for inducing commitment: 2.8
Jealousy makes one's partner look more desirable: 2.6
Jealousy brings excitement to listless relationships: 2.4
Jealousy makes life more interesting: 2.3
Jealousy makes people feel alive: 2.3
Jealousy makes relationships last longer: 1.5

The respondents agreed most strongly with the statement that jealousy is positive in that it forces people to examine their relationship. Yet, as can be seen by their mean rating (4.7), they agreed with it only to a certain extent. The same rating (4.7) was given to a statement describing a negative effect of jealousy with which the same respondents agreed least: that jealousy makes people feel guilty. They agreed much more strongly with statements about the other negative effects of jealousy:

Jealousy causes emotional distress: 5.9
Jealousy puts a strain on relationships: 5.9
Jealousy can block thought and distort emotions: 5.9
Jealousy wastes valuable time: 5.8
Jealousy causes physical distress: 5.5
Jealousy restricts the partner's freedom: 5.2
Jealousy may result in violence: 5.0
Jealousy can cause social embarrassment: 5.0
Jealousy drives the partner away: 4.8

Agreement about the negative effects of jealousy did not necessarily correlate with a respondent's own level of jealousy. In other words, whether or not people perceived themselves as jealous had little effect on their rating of these negative effects of jealousy. On the other hand, agreement about the positive effects of jealousy was significantly correlated with self-perception—the more jealous one perceived oneself to be, the more likely one was to agree with the positive effects of jealousy. This means that while everyone agrees on the negative effects of jealousy, only people who perceive themselves as jealous agree that it has positive effects. There are several possible explanations for this.

People who perceive themselves as jealous may want to describe jealousy in a positive light. By the same token, people who perceive jealousy as a more positive experience may admit more readily to feeling jealous. It is also possible that when people have a traumatic experience with jealousy they need to convince themselves that something positive came out of it. The final possibility is that because people who view themselves as jealous tend to experience jealousy more often, they have more occasions to discover its positive effects.

While all four of these explanations probably have a grain of truth in them, for the remainder of this chapter I will take the approach suggested by the last explanation—namely, that some good can come out of jealousy. Let us examine this "good" more closely.

Jealousy Makes People Examine Their Relationships

Most people don't examine their relationships very often, if at all, after they pass the stage of courtship and romance. Similarly, most people don't examine their work situation or their relationship with other family members often. All this self-examination takes time and energy most people don't have to spare. As noted before, the common response of people who tried an open relationship and decided against it was that it was too time-consuming: "You have to talk about the relationship all the time. You have to examine and reexamine rules you made that for some reason are not working. It's exhausting. It leaves no time or energy for anything else."

Romantic jealousy, with all the emotional and physical turmoil it generates, provides people with an opportunity to examine their relationship without extra effort. To put it another way: People who have already suffered the pains of jealousy should not waste the opportunity to learn something valuable about themselves and about the relationship. The jealousy can serve as a guide in examining such questions as: "What does this experience tell me about myself? What does it tell me about my partner and our relationship?" Examination of this sort is most productive if followed by more action-oriented questions such as: "Is this the kind of relationship I want for myself?" And if the answer is no, "What can I do to change things?"

Jealousy Teaches People
Not to Take Each Other for Granted

Romantic love is not an eternal flame. If fuel is not added to it, sooner or later the flame will burn out.[2] When people first fall in love and their love is reciprocated, they feel fortunate to have such a wonderful person return their love. When they are not sure whether or not their love is reciprocated, insecurity and doubt intensify their emotions. They are ready to do anything to have this wonderful person love them back. Yet all too often, when they feel assured of their partner's love and commitment, they start to take this love for granted. They make demands they would not have made during the courtship stage, and would never make of other people. Their partner becomes the person in their life who is "supposed" to understand their work pressures, their all-absorbing involvement with their children, with their friends, with community work. "Who else can I expect to understand and be supportive if not my partner?" they ask self-righteously. Dealing with continuous stress at work, with children, with a parent, or with voluntary activities in effect gives these concerns a higher priority than the relationship. No romantic relationship can withstand this kind of assault for long. Taking each other for granted erodes love.

Paradoxically, the threat of involvement with a third person stops this overinvolvement with people outside the relationship and brings the focus back to the couple. Suddenly people's security in their partner's love and commitment is shaken, as they wonder once again: "Does he [she] love me? Does he [she] not?"

Jealousy Is a Sign of Love

Whether or not romantic jealousy is seen as a sign of love varies in different cultures and different periods of history. Therefore, whether or not people agree with the statement at the head of this section tends to be influenced by the norms of their culture. Yet even people who don't see jealousy as a sign of love may still respond with jealousy when they perceive a threat to a valued romantic relationship. In this way (as noted in chapter one), jealousy is the shadow of love.

Contrary to the people who believe that "There's more self-love than love in jealousy," or "Jealousy is caused by possessiveness and by a sense of inferiority, not by love," I would argue that even if self-love, possessiveness, and inferiority are a part of jealousy, couples can deal with these feelings more effectively if they focus on love. A person who is on the receiving end of a partner's jealousy and is convinced that the jealousy results from the partner's possessiveness or inferiority complex can do little to change things. But if, instead, the person sees the jealousy as a sign of love, related to the things both partners found most attractive about each other initially, that person is more likely to realize that jealousy is part of a dynamic in the relationship to which both partners contribute, and that both partners can work to change. As noted earlier, viewing jealousy as a response to a perceived threat to a valued love relationship, or to its quality, eliminates guilt and blame and frees energy for more constructive coping.

Jealousy Is an Instrument for Inducing Commitment

When Gary reached 40, he felt that he had only a limited number of erections left. With this in mind, he wanted to enjoy as many of those erections as possible. Although he was happy in his marriage of fifteen years to Sara, he wanted the freedom to experience other women sexually. Since he saw himself as an enlightened and liberated man, he was happy to allow Sara to have sex with other men, too. Sara was not at all interested in an open marriage and was jealous of every woman she thought Gary might be interested in. "When I walk down the street and I see these young, beautiful women, I panic," she said. But since she felt she had to be as enlightened and liberated as Gary was, she accepted his extramarital sexual liaisons.

Many months later, after much hesitation on her part and encouragement on Gary's part, she agreed to spend a weekend with an attractive male friend whom she had dated in her college years. The weekend turned out to be a very positive experience for Sara. But to her (and his) great surprise, hearing that, Gary "freaked out." Sara described the strange experience: "He started following me around the house like a puppy, begging me to assure him that I love him and would not leave him for that man." To her great relief he no longer wanted an open marriage.

A similar process often happens to people, most often men, who fear commitments.[3] A jealousy crisis, which makes the person aware of a competitor for his partner and the chance of losing the relationship, can become the trigger that induces commitment. This might also explain why women try to induce jealousy more often than men do.

Jealousy Intensifies Emotions

As Gary discovered, jealousy makes one's partner look more desirable. At times this happens because, like the children we all were once, we find the toy we ourselves have neglected to be more interesting when someone else shows an interest in it. At other times people's fear of losing what they have come to take for granted makes them realize just how desirable it is. All of a sudden they notice the wonderful qualities that made them fall in love with their partner.

Jealousy can bring excitement to listless relationships. In the midst of a major jealousy crisis, one thing people never complain about is boredom. They may talk about the pain of the experience, they may say it is infuriating, they may say it's humiliating—but they never say it's boring. And where there is emotional energy, there is an exciting occasion for growth. The intense emotions serve as fuel for the exploration. Most people would probably never do so much self-examination if they were not in the midst of an emotional turmoil.

People who are willing to explore their intense emotions, positive as well as negative, may even discover that jealousy can make life more passionate and interesting. As swingers know from their experience with sexual mate exchange, a sting of jealousy, if interpreted positively as a tease, can make couples sexually excited about each other. The sphere in which all these positive effects can be seen most clearly is sex.

Jealousy Adds Passion to Sex

Despite the great pain most people associate with jealousy, it sometimes has a positive effect on the quality of their sex lives. Ben and Stacy's story is a good example.

I met Ben and Stacy at an intensive five-day jealousy workshops I lead.[4] Ben was fifteen years older than Stacy. They had met as boss and employee, and Stacy continued to adore Ben and treat him as a mentor. Ben had been divorced for over five years when they became romantically involved. Before that, he had been married for many years, and was monogamous the entire time. When he became single again, Ben wanted to make up for things he had missed in his youth (he married young), so he had many affairs.

Stacy had had several boyfriends prior to her romantic involvement with Ben, but she was still a virgin when they met. The difference between them in age and sexual experience created problems in the relationship. The main problem, from Ben's point of view, was that sex had become boring. While he still loved Stacy, was flattered that such a young and beautiful woman was in love with him, and was committed to the relationship, her "lack of experience" made their sex life "unexciting." Ben wanted to be able to see some of his former girlfriends and have sex with them. He encouraged Stacy to get sexually involved with other men, which he said would be good for her and for their relationship. "It would help her become more experienced and sexually sophisticated," he argued.

Stacy, for her part, was very jealous of Ben's former girlfriends and felt inferior to them. Although she was extremely attractive and had ample opportunities to date other men, she would have been happiest in a monogamous relationship with Ben. It was painful for her to realize that sex with her was not enough for him.

During the first days of the workshop, Ben brought Stacy's jealousy and insecurity to the group's attention on several occasions. On all these occasions he presented himself as understanding of "Stacy's problem," while he flirted openly with other women in the group. Then something happened that changed things dramatically.

Following a particularly intense session, in which one of the men in the group accused Stacy of being cold and emotionally unresponsive, Stacy broke down in tears. The group responded to her tears with understanding and support and gave her very warm feedback. The man who initially attacked her—one of the more attractive men in the group—sat next to her, hugged her, and stroked her back.

The man had indicated his attraction to Stacy several times before, without a response from her. This was the real reason for his earlier attack and accusation of her "coldness." Now he was extremely sorry for the pain he had caused her, and was doing his best to comfort her. He was still hugging her and stroking her back when the session was over and the rest of the group, including Ben, left the room.

His comforting gradually became more sexual. They both were emotionally aroused by the events that had taken place in the session, and physically aroused by their close contact. Their stroking and kissing became more passionate. Eventually they made love, right there on the carpet. Since they hadn't planned it, neither of them used contraceptives.

Ben was furious. He had seen Stacy and the man becoming physical with each other, and became extremely jealous. "How could you do this to me?" he demanded. The focus of his anger (so he claimed) was not that Stacy had sex with another man, which was what he had said all along that he wanted her to do. Rather, he objected to her carelessness about contraception. "You hurt me more than any other woman has ever done," he said accusingly, "and I trusted you to protect my feelings."

Stacy, tears rolling down her cheeks, said that she'd never intended to hurt Ben's feelings. Nevertheless, she was stubborn in her insistence that she was not sorry for what she had done, and that it had been a wonderful experience.

While processing the experience with Ben and Stacy, helping him examine his jealousy and her conflicting feelings, I asked them whether anything positive had come out of the incident. I was not surprised to hear Ben say, with great amazement, "When we made love afterward, it was the most passionate sex we ever had. It was unbelievably intense and exciting. I can't figure why." Stacy, still crying, nodded in agreement.

The reason their sex was so exciting was that it happened in the intensely emotional context of a jealousy crisis. For both Ben and Stacy, the security of a committed relationship had been shaken. Their perception of themselves and of each other suddenly changed. Ben, who until that time considered himself a "nonjealous" person, experienced intense jealousy marked by anger, envy, rivalry, betrayal, fear of loss, and feelings of exclusion. Stacy, who until that time perceived herself as the one with the "jealousy problem," felt not only empathy for Ben's pain but also a new, powerful, and exciting experience of being desired by two attractive men.

Ben and Stacy's story is not unusual. I have seen many similar cases in which one partner (usually the man) pushed to open the relationship because sex had become boring, but who responded with great shock and jealousy when the other partner actually became involved with someone else. To the surprise of both partners, the painful shock and the intense jealousy it generated helped revive the sexual passion in the relationship. Passionate sex depends on emotional arousal, and jealousy, as we well know, can be extremely arousing emotionally.

Jealousy doesn't always result in passionate sex, however. The jealous person may be terrified at the prospect of losing the relationship, and anxiety is the antithesis of passion. This tends to happen when jealousy is a chronic problem in the relationship.

When a relationship has strong roots of trust and security, a temporary jealousy crisis can serve as a reminder to both partners of how important they are to each other. For couples who take each other for granted, or whose relationship has become boring and listless, jealousy can restore the relationship as the number-one priority. Even if these changes are associated with the negative side of jealousy, they can intensify feelings between partners, and thus enhance the experience of sex.

On the other hand, when jealousy is a lasting problem, it threatens the fabric of security and trust at the foundation of a relationship. An example is a marriage in which the husband says he loves his wife, yet continues to have extramarital affairs. The wife responds to the affairs with jealous tantrums, yet remains in the marriage. The best thing that can result from this type of a jealousy problem is an occasion to examine the relationship and the role each partner plays in it: Why did she choose to marry someone who is interested in other people? Why is he staying in a relationship that doesn't satisfy his needs? Does the marriage satisfy other needs (for example, a need for continuous drama)? This kind of self-examination is most beneficial if it leads to constructive action. The important question to address is: What can be done to change things?

Jealousy Protects Love

At the beginning of the book I suggested that jealousy is a response to a perceived threat to a valued relationship or to its quality. In other words, jealousy aims to protect romantic relationships. It is not a useless flight of irrationality, but a useful signal people can learn to interpret correctly. It is also a shock absorber that can facilitate both personal growth and relationship enrichment.[5] Every one of the positive effects associated with jealousy discussed in this chapter can be seen as a love–protective function of jealousy.

Jealousy makes people examine their relationships, with the implicit hope that the relationship and its quality will remain intact. It teaches couples not to take each other for granted; in this way it ensures that they continue to value each other and to express it in their daily interactions. It is a sign of love; it indicates that people value the love relationship it protects. This is true even in those extreme situations in which jealousy leads to violence. It is an instrument for inducing commitment; it protects the boundaries of intimate relationships. It intensifies emotions—and thus keeps the spark alive in intimate relationships. It adds passion to sex; in this way it helps maintain the quality of sex in romantic relationships.

The next story demonstrates many of the positive effects of jealousy. It also demonstrates several of the issues discussed throughout the book.

A Story of Love and Jealousy: Alan and Linda and Gail

When Alan met Linda, she was in her first year of law school and he had a small house–painting business. Linda was a brilliant student and is an exceptionally attractive woman. Despite all her acknowledged success, however, she was very insecure. Alan, a virile, earthy, and affectionate man, calmed her. His love made her feel safe. No other man had ever made her feel that secure. Alan was the man who could take care of her and give her the loving attention her successful father never had time to give.

Alan, for his part, couldn't believe a woman like Linda would even look in the direction of a simple man like him, yet she was actually reciprocating his love. He was thrilled. He admired Linda's intelligence and identified with her academic success. She gave him an entrance into a world he had always considered beyond his reach. Their love for each other was passionate. Linda was the "wings" (intellectual, flighty, temperamental) and Alan the "roots" (simple, down to earth, stable). Together they felt complete. Things were going so well that they soon decided to get married.

Their marriage was passionate and turbulent. The areas in which they complemented each other intensified their mutual attraction, but the difference in their social status created a growing number of problems and conflicts. Linda complained that she couldn't talk to Alan the way she did to men in school. Alan complained that she was too involved with her studies. With a moment's reflection it becomes clear that Alan's and Linda's complaints about each other were related to the things they found most attractive when they first met. Linda was attracted to Alan's earthiness and simplicity; now he was too earthy and simple. Alan was attracted to Linda's intelligence and academic involvement; now he thought she was too involved academically.

Alan's complaints made Linda feel that he was criticizing her career goals. His lack of support made her withdraw even further into her academic world. Linda's complaints hurt Alan's pride. He became increasingly more uncomfortable in social situations involving Linda's fellow students and law professors and tried to avoid these situations as much as he could.

Given the growing distance between Alan and Linda, and the intensity built into the relationships among law students, who spend long hours studying together, what happened was almost inevitable: Linda had an affair with another student in her program. She felt that this man, unlike Alan, was her equal. They shared similar goals and she could talk with him about things she could never talk about with Alan.

Alan was terribly hurt by Linda's affair and responded with tremendous jealousy. The affair was particularly painful for him, because it took away what he found most rewarding about Linda's love—her acceptance of him as an equal.

Linda's lover was someone with whom Alan felt unable to compete; he wasn't enough as a man or as a mate. The "wings" Linda's love gave him had been clipped. Now she shared with someone else what he considered an even greater intimacy than the intimacy she had with him—the intimacy of minds. Alan's pain was unbearable.

To help himself overcome the pain, Alan started playing tennis several times a week. His good looks and excellent skills made him a desirable tennis partner. After tennis, the players often would go to a nearby coffee shop. Alan found himself talking with the attractive women he had played tennis with. Unlike Linda, these women seemed to appreciate him, to share his values, and to delight in his company. It didn't take him long to get sexually involved with one of them, and later on with two more. The sexual liaisons restored his self-confidence.

Now it was Linda's turn to experience the pain of jealousy. By this time her own affair was over. The law student had returned to a committed relationship he had with someone else; his affair with Linda turned out to be only a diversion. Linda was crushed. She had failed with a man who was her equal. This reinforced her belief that anyone she found desirable would never want her in the long run. She longed for the security of Alan's love, but now Alan was giving his love to other women. Linda couldn't bear it, even though she considered the other women "stupid fools."

Linda's jealousy focused on the most important thing Alan's love gave her, the thing she was now most afraid to lose: the feeling of secure ground under her feet. If she lost Alan's love, her life would not be worth living.

Linda started to woo Alan back, using every charm she knew would attract him. Alan was delighted, and happy to return to her. His encounters with women who were "less liberated" than Linda, however, made him aware of his need for a home—not the kind of home that Linda provided, but a "real home" complete with a hot meal waiting when he came home from work. They decided to hire a live-in housekeeper who would stay in a spare room in exchange for cleaning and cooking. That housekeeper was Gail.

Gail was new in town and almost penniless. For her, the arrangement with Alan and Linda, which gave her a roof over her head in addition to a job, was ideal. As a hardworking woman, she had no problem with the house cleaning and cooking her job required.

The new arrangement worked wonderfully for everyone. Alan felt that now the house became a real home. He loved Gail's home cooking and tidiness. On nights when Linda studied in the library, he and Gail sat at the kitchen table and talked. Gail, who had a history of troubled relationships with men, found Alan to be similar to herself. They became good friends. Like Alan, Linda appreciated having a neat house and great meals to come home to. She and Gail were also becoming good friends.

All three seemed happy with the arrangement. It ended only because Gail decided it was time for her to go back to her hometown.

After Gail left, Alan and Linda discovered that her presence had been hiding a growing estrangement between them. Linda complained again about Alan's intellectual inadequacies and Alan felt again that this was not the "home" he wanted. They decided on a trial separation, and Linda moved to another apartment in their building. Despite their separation, Alan and Linda continued to see each other regularly.

When Linda left for a professional convention one week, Alan decided to go out of town too. It just so happened that the relatives he wanted to visit lived close to Gail's hometown, so he called her up and suggested that they meet. The meeting was more moving and emotional than either of them expected. Both of them discovered how much they really meant to each other and how much fun it was to spend time together. Alan told Gail that he and Linda were separated and seriously contemplating divorce.

Gail, who had previously held back her feelings for Alan out of loyalty to Linda, gave in after hearing about the planned divorce. What hadn't happened during all the time they had shared a household happened now; they became lovers. Alan felt that this time he had found a woman who was truly perfect for him. They were so much alike. It felt so comfortable, so easy, so different from the eternal struggles in his marriage.

Gail, too, felt that she had found her "match made in heaven." Unlike the men she had known in the past, Alan was a friend and kindred spirit. She could talk to him. She could trust him. And now that he and Linda were separated, she could let herself feel passion for him, something she had never let herself experience before.

When Alan returned from the trip, he told Linda he wanted a divorce and that Gail was coming back to live with him. Linda, who until then had been searching for a more appropriate mate, was overcome with jealousy. It was "the most awful, consuming, heart-wrenching pain" she had ever felt. She felt betrayed by Alan and by Gail. She telephoned Gail, weeping and screaming, "How can you do this to me? And I thought you were my friend!" "This is not something I did," Gail responded. "You were going to divorce Alan anyway. I had nothing to do with the problems between you two." The verbal brutality of Linda's attack made Gail even more determined to give her relationship with Alan a chance.

Linda was inconsolable. She couldn't accept that she had lost Alan to a woman she cared for and trusted. She cried incessantly and was ready to promise Alan anything he wanted. She threatened: "I'll never let the two of you be alone in peace. I'll never let you make love. I'm going to stand at the window, scream, and throw stones. When I see Gail, I'm going to bash her face." Alan was patient and understanding. He held Linda in his arms when she cried. Yet he remained determined to give his relationship with Gail a chance.

On their way home from the airport, Alan started talking to Gail about getting married and having children. Gail had to slow him down and remind him that they needed to find out if they could live together as a couple before deciding to have a family. But his enthusiasm was contagious.

The idyll between Alan and Gail was shorter than anyone had anticipated. Almost immediately after she moved in with Alan, Gail sensed his change of attitude. At first she tried to ignore it, but soon things became intolerable and the confrontation unavoidable. "What's going on with you?" she asked, afraid to hear his answer. "This is not working out for me. It's not the way I imagined it would be," said Alan. "How can you say that, when I've been here only two days?" Gail asked in tears. "You need to give us a chance to make it work." "I'm sorry. I think this is all one big mistake," Alan said quietly, and left.

Gail sank to the floor. This was a nightmare come true. This was exactly what had kept her from getting involved in relationships with men before. How had she let Alan get through her defenses? Why did she think that being kindred spirits was an assurance for anything? What was she going to do now? She couldn't go back home—the humiliation would be too great. She couldn't stay. Maybe it would be better to end it all right now. Life wasn't worth living with so much pain. When the phone rang, Gail hesitated, but thinking Alan might have changed his mind again, she picked up the receiver. It was Linda.

Since her arrival, Gail had called Linda several times. She had left messages for her at home and at school, but Linda hadn't returned her calls. Now, in her hour of despair, she was on the line.

Linda knew what was going on because Alan had told her about his change of heart the minute it happened. Now that she had Alan back, she could allow herself to feel empathy with Gail's pain. She knew that pain intimately.

The two women started talking. After starting, it was difficult to stop. Both of them had so much to talk about, so much that needed to be said, to be clarified. Suddenly Linda said, "I have this weekend off. How about us going skiing? That will give us a chance to talk as much as we want." Gail couldn't imagine anything she would rather do. At the ski resort, Linda and Gail had a chance to compare notes. What had Alan told Gail to convince her that his relationship with Linda was over? What had he told Linda at the same time to keep her tied to him? Two women had been betrayed by the same dishonest and undeserving man ... "and to think that he almost managed to turn us against each other." Carried away by their excitement over renewing their friendship and sharing the pain they both experienced, they hugged each other affectionately.

In the romantic atmosphere of the ski resort (they were in a hot tub at the time) hugs and kisses of excitement gradually turned more passionate. Finally they made love. For both, it was their first sexual encounter with a woman.

Gail fell in love with Linda in a way she had never loved before. She had never opened up to a man the way she did to Linda. She had never felt so understood. She adored Linda. She wanted to take care of her. She moved in with Linda and started once again cleaning the apartment and cooking Linda's favorite meals. When Linda was exhausted after a long day at court or in the library, Gail would drive her home.

While this was going on, Alan was wild with jealousy and was doing what Linda and Gail described with great delight as "crazy things." He came to Linda's apartment raving and raging, threw her clothes out the window, screamed at the top of his lungs that they were "filthy, disgusting sluts." Now it was Alan's turn to feel betrayed, rejected, and left out by two women he loved and considered his best friends. But he also felt he was competing against something beyond him, beyond his comprehension. Only perverts were doing the kind of things Linda and Gail were doing. How could they do it? How could they do it to him?

Linda and Gail felt sorry for Alan, yet felt united as women against this man whom both of them had loved, trusted, and felt betrayed by.

The joy of sharing their love, their pain, and their power as women fueled Linda and Gail's relationship for a while. But it was not enough of a foundation for a long-term relationship—not for Linda, that is. Soon she started longing for the safety of Alan's arms. Gail's arms weren't strong enough to make her feel safe, to calm her fears and insecurities. Eventually, Linda went back to Alan.

Once again Gail had a chance to experience jealousy. This time she was not jealous of Linda for having Alan, but of Alan for having

Linda. The loss of Linda's love was far more painful than the loss of Alan's love. Gail had never allowed herself to be as vulnerable with a man as she had been with Linda. The loss was devastating.

Linda was supportive and understanding of Gail, yet clear about wanting to make her marriage work. After a while she found Gail's pain and emotional dependency increasingly more difficult to handle. She suggested that Gail go to therapy, and told her she was willing to help her cover the cost.

Through therapy, Gail was able to understand her obsession with Linda and the reasons for her problematic relationships with men. A year and a half later she moved in with another woman, with whom she developed a very satisfying relationship. Yet she still cared deeply about Linda and wanted to be a part of her life. When Linda had a baby, Alan, Linda's doctor, and Gail were with her in the delivery room.

Alan, for his part, came to realize the impact his lack of formal education had on his self-image and on his relationship with Linda, and decided to go to college—something he had dreamed about all his life.

A Case Analysis

For the purpose of this chapter, the most important point this complicated case demonstrates is that something good can indeed come out of jealousy. In the study mentioned earlier, the effect of jealousy that respondents found most positive was that jealousy can make people examine their relationships. Did the jealousy each of them experienced cause Alan, Linda, and Gail to examine their relationship? Most definitely yes! As a result of their different jealousy crises, all three spent long hours talking about themselves and about their relationship.

Although the results of such exploration can be rewarding, the process it involves can be both difficult and emotionally demanding. It points to the personal vulnerabilities that make people susceptible to jealousy, and to the repeated patterns that keep jealousy alive in their relationships. Some couples can explore their jealousy problem on their own; others need the professional help and support of a therapist.

By examining the love they felt for each other (those qualities that had initially attracted them to each other and the most important thing they gained from the relationship) and by examining the shadow this love had cast when threatened (the threat or the loss that triggered their jealousy) Alan, Linda, and Gail were able to identify the function that the love and the jealousy served in their inner lives, and in the dynamics of their relationship.

Regardless of the approach, or combination of approaches, used to analyze this complex relationship, the story portrays jealousy as the shadow of love. We can start with Linda's love and jealousy of Alan. Both of Linda's parents were intellectuals and successful professionals. They were also very close to each other, and their closeness didn't leave much space for Linda. In addition, Linda's emotional life was marked by competition with a brilliant and cold older brother and by identification with her mother's unhappiness. As a result of these childhood experiences, Linda was sophisticated intellectually, but full of emotional insecurities. Alan, a simple earthy man, gave her the adoration and intimacy she was longing for because of her childhood deprivation. Only after Alan met her deeper emotional needs was Linda able to look for someone more like herself (and like her father and brother). When Linda had the affair, Alan's jealousy focused on his intellectual inferiority to her lover.

Alan's parents were farmers and uncomplicated, practical people. Alan felt loved, yet was desperate to get away from the world they represented. When Linda had her affair, he felt not only devastated by the betrayal of the woman he adored, but also rejected by the world she represented. Alan had to be comforted by women who were more like himself. He needed someone who would appreciate him, and his female tennis partners met that need. During the second crisis in his marriage he was looking for the same thing, and found it in his relationship with Gail.

Linda's jealousy was dominated by the feeling of exclusion she had experienced often in her childhood: "The two of them" (her parents) shared a wonderful intimacy that did not include her. The security of being loved and adored by a stable man like Alan was gone. She no longer felt safe and special. He was giving other women (especially Gail) what she considered as hers alone: the affirmation she was not able to get as a child, the assurance that she was "number one."

A different kind of love bound Alan and Gail. They were two of a kind; their family backgrounds were similar, and an easy friendship developed between them long before they felt any passion. When Alan went back to Linda, Gail's jealousy focused on the loss of this friendship. Alan's romantic betrayal was especially painful for Gail because he was someone she had considered a trusted friend and a kindred spirit.

The love between Gail and Linda was fueled by sharing powerful emotions: love, jealousy, rage at Alan, and camaraderie as women. It also had another powerful element: Gail and Linda complemented each other in much the same way Linda and Alan did. Gail was the "roots" and Linda the "wings." This proved, once again, a powerful combination. The combination, however, was much more powerful for Gail than for Linda, because Alan, with whom Linda had a similar relationship, was physically stronger and more able to make her feel secure.

When Linda returned to Alan, Gail's jealousy focused on the loss of the intimate bond the two women had shared. She was certain she would never have this kind of a bond again. She later discovered that while she couldn't have such a bond with a man, she could have it with another woman.

A psychodynamic analysis of the relationship between Alan, Linda, and Gail focuses on the unconscious needs brought out by their jealousy and on the childhood experiences at the root of both their jealousy and their love.

Looking at romantic jealousy as a couple issue (in all three permutations) is an example of the systems approach. In Linda and Alan's case, for example, they fell in love because each represented a lost part in the other (Linda was Alan's "wings" and Alan was Linda's "roots"). With time, however, the missing part in the other became a source of repeated conflicts. Each wanted the thing the other was least able to provide: Linda wanted Alan to become more intellectual, and Alan wanted Linda to become less involved with her career. When Alan and Linda recognized this destructive pattern, they were able to work on developing the lost parts in themselves. For Linda, motherhood provided an especially rewarding opportunity to develop her "roots"; for Alan, the possibility of going to college provided an opportunity to develop his "wings." Once they took steps to develop these "missing parts" in themselves, they were less dependent on each other to provide them.

From the sociobiological point of view, the differences between Linda's relationships with Gail and Alan demonstrate the inherent difference between the male and the female response to jealousy. When Gail and Linda were jealous, they felt devastated and responded with desperate attempts to save the relationship. When it was Alan's turn to experience jealousy, however, he responded in the typical masculine way: with rage and lashing out, protecting his ego more than the relationship.

According to the social–psychological perspective, the threesome's need for exclusive monogamous relationships reflects the North American value of monogamy. In another culture the threesome could have found a solution in the form of a triangle family. In a polygamous society, Alan could have taken both Linda and Gail as wives. Jealousy is a culturally accepted reaction to many of the situations described in the story. None of the same jealous reactions would have happened in a culture such as the Toda.

Returning to the definition of jealousy, I think it is rather clear that every time Alan, Linda, or Gail experienced jealousy, each was responding to what he or she perceived to be a threat to a valued relationship. Jealousy, as the story demonstrates, is indeed a complex response with many influences: childhood experiences, relationship dynamics, learned responses, cultural norms, and inherent differences between the sexes.

Postscript

The jealousy crisis taught Linda not to take Alan for granted and also gave her the incentive to commit herself to the relationship—both very positive effects. While their marriage had never been listless, jealousy brought so much excitement into it that once the crisis passed, both Linda and Alan were ready for some peace and quiet.

Since they no longer needed jealousy to make life more interesting, Linda and Alan arrived at a relatively calm stage of their relationship. Instead of using jealousy to fuel their passion and intensify the emotions in their relationship, they could focus their energy on their young child and therefore delight in something positive and hopeful.

Alan is a doting father who built the baby's crib and first toys with his own hands. Linda appreciates Alan's help and devotion. She too adores her beautiful child and discovered that she can be a good mother. Linda finds motherhood a rich and rewarding experience.

Working on their jealousy problem made Alan and Linda aware of each other's needs and vulnerabilities. Both are trying hard to be sensitive to these needs. Although they are not always successful, the overall atmosphere in their little family is one of warmth and caring. Linda concludes, "All this taught Alan and me how much we really care about each other. We decided to stop hurting each other and just enjoy the good thing that we have. And we do."

Gail, who started therapy as a result of the jealousy crisis, has made important discoveries about herself that have enabled her to live a more honest and satisfying life. As an introverted woman who grew up in a blue–collar family, self-examination was something she had never before considered. The therapy offered her the chance to work through her relationship with Linda and discover the conscious and unconscious roots of her problem in relationships with men. If it were not for the crisis prompted by her jealousy of Linda and Alan, she probably would have continued to avoid this very painful but ultimately healing process.

Since Alan no longer perceived Gail as a threat to his relationship with Linda, he didn't object to her presence in their life. With time, some of his warm feelings toward Gail returned. Linda continues to maintain a close friendship with Gail.

Jealousy itself did not cause these positive changes in Alan, Linda, and Gail. The changes came from the way they coped with their jealousy. Instead of treating it as a traumatic experience they had to get over as quickly as possible, they used it as an opportunity for growth.

My goal in writing this book has been to give individuals, couples, and professionals working with individuals and couples the information, tools, and examples they need to turn jealousy into such a positive experience. The case of Alan, Linda, and Gail is just one example.

A Note to Therapists

Alan, Linda, and Gail's case demonstrates an obvious point that can't be overemphasized. Professionals who work with individuals and couples with a jealousy problem have to shed their own assumptions about relationships and be nonjudgmental in their dealings with their clients. People who are troubled by jealousy think that there is something terribly wrong with them. The therapist has to provide a supportive and nonjudgmental milieu in order to help them turn the problem into an experience of personal growth. Because breaking the fallacy of uniqueness and the blame frame are much easier when people can see that they are not the only ones struggling with this problem, a jealousy workshop may be very helpful. Suggestions for leading such a workshop can be found in Appendix A.

A Final Word about the Five Approaches to Jealousy

In describing the five primary approaches to jealousy, I have underplayed the aspects in which they contradict each other. I value and use each one of the five approaches, but part company with them when they dismiss each other—which they routinely do. Many of the theoreticians and practitioners of each approach would be extremely uncomfortable at the prospect of being lumped together with approaches they oppose.

For a psychodynamically oriented therapist, behavioral techniques can't possibly cure the "real issue" underlying a jealousy problem. To a behavioral therapist, the psychodynamic preoccupation with the unconscious and with traumatic childhood experiences is unnecessary and cannot possibly help cure a jealousy problem. To a systems therapist, the focus of both behavioral and psychodynamically oriented therapists on the individual makes no sense in the treatment of such obviously "couple" issues as jealousy. To a social psychologist, the notion that jealousy is a product of a particular individual mind or a particular relationship is absurd when it so clearly is determined by cultural norms and mores. In addition, the sociobiologist's notion that jealousy is innate and that sex differences in jealousy have evolved in an evolutionary process is not only ridiculous, but dangerous as well. Sociobiologists don't understand how anyone can deny the existence of an innate element in jealousy when the evidence for it is so overwhelming.

The picture of jealousy that I have presented incorporates the perspectives of all five approaches in expanding concentric circles.

In the center is an individual who experiences jealousy. The individual's jealousy is related to childhood experiences and his or her personal history of intimate relationships. It is expressed in learned responses. The next circle is the couple, of which the jealous individual is a part. The couple's dynamic determines whether and how a jealousy problem will be expressed. The third circle is the situation. It includes the culture in which the couple lives, which in turn determines how jealousy is experienced and expressed. The fourth circle is the genetic programming that is different for men and women.

My discussion of the five approaches has focused on those aspects that are most relevant for coping with jealousy. Each approach has something valuable to offer. It is illuminating for people to discover how jealousy is related to unresolved childhood experiences. It is helpful to discover how their jealousy is maintained by the dynamics of their relationship. Sometimes they need to unlearn some inappropriate responses to jealousy triggers and learn more appropriate responses. They can take comfort in knowing that no matter how crazy they think they are when jealous, they are not unique; other people respond the way they do, and there may be a culture that considers their response the most appropriate. It is also comforting to realize that some of the troublesome differences between one's own sex and the opposite sex in response to jealousy may be related to different genetic programming.

People who assume that there is only one way to cope with romantic jealousy deprive themselves of the benefits that other approaches can offer. Even if a particular coping strategy is successful in a certain situation, one does not have to use this strategy exclusively. The person best able to cope has many arrows in the quiver, is able to deal with jealousy in a variety of ways, and uses the most effective strategy or combination of strategies for each given situation.

Appendix A
Jealousy Workshops

Since some people may be embarrassed to admit they have a jealousy problem, it may at times and with certain groups be better to advertise the workshop as addressing other emotions as well. Here, for example, is an ad for a jealousy workshop I conducted some years ago with my friend and colleague, the sociologist Gordon Clanton.

Emotions of Desire
Protecting the Limits of Love and Commitment

Love, jealousy, envy, anger, hurt, and other powerful emotions are generated in intimate relationships. These emotions are not useless flights of irrationality. Emotions are useful. They are signals we can learn to interpret. They are also shock-absorbers that can facilitate personal growth and relationship enrichment.

Jealousy is a protective reaction to a perceived threat to a love relationship. Jealousy is love's shadow but it is also love's bodyguard. Envy (which is often confused with jealousy) is hostility toward someone who has something or some personal quality we don't have and probably cannot get. Anger is often a legitimate protest against unfair treatment, against accumulating injustice that hurts and crushes the spirit, and makes the rebellion of divorce more likely later. Through group discussions, gestalt work, role-playing, and guided imagery, in the supportive, nonjudgmental workshop context, participants will learn and practice constructive ways of protecting love relationships and positive ways of expressing legitimate hurt and anger, thus minimizing the pain of jealousy and envy.

The workshop is for everyone who seeks to gain better understanding of the variety of emotions of desire. It is especially helpful for couples who are seeking to define and protect the limits of their relationship and for therapists and marriage counselors who work with people for whom these issues are important.

And here is another ad, addressing jealousy directly. This was the ad that the Kerista Villagers (members of the commune described in chapter seven) read, which prompted them to call me and suggest they come to the workshop and share with the group their insights about overcoming jealousy.

Sexual Jealousy and Personal Growth

What is sexual jealousy? Is it a sign of love or an indication of insecurity? What are the reasons for it? How prevalent is it? What are some of the emotional, physiological, and attitudinal reactions to it? What people and situations are likely to elicit jealousy? What are its negative and positive effects, and most important, how can it be coped with more effectively? These are some of the questions addressed in this workshop.

Through lectures, group discussions, personal exploration, and role playing, participants will explore critical issues related to jealousy and gain better understanding of what it is and how to better cope with it.

The workshop is intended for couples who wish to deal with the issue of jealousy in their relationship, for individuals who experience jealousy as a personal problem, and for therapists and marriage counselors.

Here is the description of a jealousy workshop for mental health professionals:

Romantic Jealousy
Theoretical Perspectives and Clinical Applications

There are five major theoretical approaches to jealousy: psychodynamic, systemic, behavioral, sociopsychological, and sociobiological. An integrated approach that combines all five of these very different theoretical perspectives with their different clinical applications is proposed as the most effective way to treat romantic jealousy. Through lectures, discussions, structured exercises, and guided imagery, workshop participants will explore each of these approaches, their clinical applications, and how to apply an integrated approach to the treatment of romantic jealousy.

The workshop is primarily recommended for mental health professionals who work with individuals and couples with a jealousy problem and for anyone else who seeks a better understanding of love and its shadow: romantic jealousy.

Workshop Participants

While the specific content of a jealousy workshop differs according to the composition and needs of the participants, the basic workshop I will be describing here can and has been used successfully with individuals and couples in both homogeneous and heterogeneous groups.

In homogeneous groups participants are either individuals or couples, of a similar age, similar life circumstance, and similar background. In heterogeneous groups some people are single and some are coupled. Some participants are young and some are old, some are at the beginning stages of their relationship, and some have been married many years. In addition, in most workshops some of the participants are mental health professionals who come to learn more about jealousy. At the end of the workshop, participants in such heterogeneous groups invariably express great surprise at the benefit that they feel they have gained from people who are so different from them.

The workshop is best suited for a weekend format (two hours on Friday evening, two three-hour sessions on Saturday, and a two hour session on Sunday morning for a total of ten hours), but it can be shortened to half a day or be expanded to five days. In the longer workshops participants have more time to get to know each other and to explore in depth their own individual or couple issues.

The workshop can be used with groups as small as eight people and as large as forty, but the ideal number is between twelve and twenty.

A Workshop Format

The workshop progresses through three stages. The initial stage involves a formal presentation, including a definition of jealousy and an explanantion of the difference between jealousy and envy, between normal and delusional jealousy, and between chronic and acute jealousy. The second stage involves a series of structured exercises that help group members understand their jealousy problem better in a supportive small group atmosphere. The third stage involves an open discussion of participants' individual issues. The progression from the formal, structured (and safe) to the more open-ended exercises and in-depth examination helps preempt resistance.

Introductions

If the group includes less than twenty-five people, it is important that participants begin by introducing themselves, and stating the reason for their interest in jealousy and their expectations from the workshop. This process gives group members an idea of the human resources available to them in the workshop and the range of issues different people bring. As participants listen to each other, they should note who seems to be struggling with issues similar to their own, with whom they may want to work later in a small group. In addition to serving an important function for the participants, the introductions can give the group leader invaluable information about participants' expectations.

The only problem with this process is that it can be rather time consuming. This time should definitely be taken for a weekend or a week-long workshop. There is definitely not enough time for it in a half-day workshop. In a one-day workshop participants can be limited to one-minute presentations.

For a workshop that includes over twenty-five participants, another mode of introduction is called for. An example is a drawing of love and jealousy. After a brief introduction that explains the format of the workshop and introduces jealousy as the shadow of love, participants are provided with large sheets of drawing paper and crayons, and asked to draw their love on one page and their jealousy on another. Afterwards (at times after several attempts) both drawings are hung on the wall and group members move around the room and receive explanations of the work from the "artists." The advantage of this approach, as with other nonverbal approaches, is that people's drawings are less controlled by their conscious mind. As group members examine each other's drawings they can see the connection between love and jealousy, and between both these emotions and deeper issues.

After the introductions (which in a weekend or a week-long workshop means the next morning) comes the formal presentation. A short lecture can incorporate much of the material presented in chapter one, including the definition of jealousy and envy, and the differentiation between normal and delusional jealousy, and between chronic and acute jealousy. At some point during this session, participants can be given a copy of *The Romantic Jealousy Questionnaire* (see Appendix B) to sensitize them to the various issues related to jealousy. Another session can then be devoted to a discussion of their responses to the questionnaire (which they may fill out during the break between the morning and evening sessions) and to the material presented in chapter two.

Structured Exercises

The second stage of the workshop involves a series of structured exercises, many of which can be found througout this book. The first exercise, "Romantic Jealousy as the Shadow of Love" (presented in chapter one), is done in groups of four. Group members are asked to choose (based on what they heard each other say in the introduction session) one person whose problem seems related to their own. Couples are then instructed to choose another couple and make a foursome. (Husbands and wives should not be in the same foursome.) Once the foursomes have been formed, they are asked to tell, in turn, how they met their partner, what was it that most attracted them to their partner, and what was the most important thing the relationship with their partner gave them. Foursomes are given about half an hour (about seven minutes per person) for this part of the exercise. In the second part of the exercise, foursomes are asked to describe, in turn, their jealousy problem. They are given forty minutes (ten minutes a person) for this part of the exercise. In the third and most important part of this exercise, participants are instructed to try and discover, with the help of the other members of their foursome, a connection between their original attraction to their partner, and what turned out later to be the core of their jealousy problem. They are given about half an hour for this part. When all foursomes are done, the participants are invited to an all–group discussion and sharing. The workshop leader can sit with one of the foursomes during this exercize, but be available to all foursomes for questions.

In a short (half-day) workshop this may be all there is time for. In a longer (weekend) workshop, the next stage can be an exploration of, "The Romantic Image and Its Relationship to Jealousy" (also described in chapter one). If at all possible, this part of the exercise should be done following a relaxation exercise (in which group members lie down on the floor if at all possible, focus on their breathing, and then, starting with the head and ending with the toes, focus on every part of their body and relax it). Participants are asked to recall their room (or favorite place in the house) as children, and then recall their parents (or parental figures). What were they like? What did they give and not give as parents? How did they express love? What was their relationship with each other like? Was there a traumatic experience of some sort? Foursomes are given about forty minutes to tell each other about these childhood experiences.

In the next, and last, part of this exercise they are asked to help each other find a connection between the jealousy problem and these childhood experiences. Finding such connections helps workshop participants "self-focus"—which is to say, shift from pointing a blaming finger at their partner for the jealousy problem to taking responsibility for their own part in it.

After either "Romantic Jealousy as the Shadow of Love" or "The Romantic Image and Its Relationship to Jealousy" couples can spend time discussing (with partners taking turns talking and reflecting what they hear the other say) things they can do to help each other better cope with their jealousy problem.

Another exercise, described in chapter nine, is "Revisiting Your Most Intense Jealousy." This exercise also starts with relaxation. Participants are invited to imagine themselves relaxing in their favorite place as they imagine the sun's rays warming different parts of their body. Next they are asked to flip through the pages of their personal history book until they reach the incident that triggered their most intense feelings of jealousy. What exactly happened? How did they respond? What did they feel and think? (This can be very difficult for some people in the group and may cause an outburst of tears.) After they open their eyes and sit up, participants tell their story to their foursome (or to the group, if it is a group numbering less than ten people). Since some of the stories can be rather complicated and painful, a whole hour should be allotted to this part of the exercise.

The second part of the exercise starts the same way as the first, with participants lying on the floor and imagining they are in their favorite place. They imagine themselves lying there, the sun warming them gently and relaxing every part of their body. But this time the sun is not only warming them, but also energizing and empowering them with its rays. They feel strong and in charge. Time has passed since they experienced their most intense jealousy, and during that time they have learned more about themselves and about relationships. They are wiser and more experienced. When they can feel their power and wisdom, they are instructed to hold on to them as they go back in time and revisit their most intense experience of jealousy. They have miraculously been given a chance to go back to that incident and relive it any way they want—remembering that now they are armed with wisdom, experience, and power. What do they choose to do? How do they respond this time? Is it the same way they responded originally, or differently, the way they have wished so many times they had responded? Participants describe what happened when they revisited their jealousy to their four-some, and later, if they so choose, to the entire group in an open summary and sharing segment.

"From Twosome to Threesome" is an exercise not previously described in this book. Its goal is to demonstrate what happens when a third person enters a diadic relationship. Group members are assigned the letters *A*, *B*, or *C*. (The group leader goes around the room pointing to people and saying: "You are *A*, you are *B*, you are *C*." It is important that there will be equal numbers in each of the letters.) *B*s are asked to leave the room and wait outside, while the *A* and *C* dyads are instructed to talk openly about a current problem they are strug-gling with. As the discussion progresses and deepens, the *B*s are instructed to return to the room and join in the conversation. What happens typically is that the *B*s find it difficult to barge in, and when they succeed, the "intimacy" of the *AC* couple is broken.

"Sociodrama" is an exercise mentioned in chapter five and is aimed at exploring conflicts related to jealousy, especially those that tend to be divided by gender (e.g. is it better for couples to be monogamous or to have open relationships). An imaginary line is drawn across the room. On each end of the line is one extreme posi-tion ("only a monogamous relationship can offer true intimacy" vs. "true love is only possible if both partners give each other complete freedom"). Two volunteers are asked to present these two positions convincingly, even if they are more extreme than their own posi-tions. Once the two extreme positions have been elaborated, group members are asked to place themselves on that part of the imagi-nary line that best reflects their position on the issue, and move along the line if they change their position during the discussion.

"Role Reversal" (described in chapter four) is the basis of yet another fun exercise. Participants are asked to go on a date (with their partner if possible, and with someone who can easily role play their partner if they are alone). On that date (they decide jointly where to meet, and arrive at the meeting place dressed in any way they see fit) they are instructed to behave the way their partner typically behaves. This makes it possible to feel how their partner usually feels (either jealous or harassed by jealousy), develop greater empathy for their partner and explore the possibility of change in that direction for themselves.

Individual Issues

The third stage of the workshop, which is only possible in weekend or week–long workshops, involves an open discussion of participants' individual issues. Couples who volunteer to present their issue to the group are asked to describe the issue from their different perspectives. Once they have done so to their own satisfaction, group members who feel that they have a personal understanding or involvement with their issue are asked to elaborate on each partner's perspective. (This process was described in chapter five in Ron and Carol's case.) Once the perspectives have been clarified, the question of coping is raised, with both group members and the couple trying out various modes of coping with the problem.

The Final Session

The final session of the group (for which at least an hour should be allotted) is devoted to personal summaries and feedback. As in the introduction session, participants are invited to share with the group anything of significance that has happened to them, and commit themselves to changes they plan to make. This is also the occasion for workshop participants to tell the group leader what they think and feel about the workshop.

The Romantic Jealousy Questionnaire

A. Background Information

Sex: _____   Age: _____

Last grade/degree completed in school: _____

Occupation: _____

Race: Asian _____   Black _____   Hispanic _____   White _____

   Other (please specify) _____

Religion: None/atheist _____   Catholic _____   Jewish _____

   Protestant _____   Other (please specify) _____

Number of older brothers: _____   Older sisters: _____

   Younger brothers: _____   Younger sisters: _____

B. Home/Childhood

1. Who was primarily responsible for rearing you?
   a. mother and father
   b. mother only (state reason)
   c. father only (state reason)
   d. other relative (explain who and why)
   e. other person (explain who and why)

2. Are your parents currently together?
   a. yes
   b. no

3. If your parents are not together, what is the reason?
   a. death
   b. divorce
   c. other (please explain)

4. If your parents are separated, how old were you when the separation occurred? _____

5. Were either of your natural parents absent from the home while you were growing up? (If so, please state the reason.)

    a. no

    b. father absent part of the time

    c. mother absent part of the time

    d. both father and mother absent part of the time

    e. father absent all the time

    f. mother absent all the time

    g. both father and mother absent all the time

6. How would you describe your family's financial situation while you were growing up?

1	2	3	4	5	6	7
poor			managed to get by			rich

7. How would you describe your relationship with your mother while you were growing up?

1	2	3	4	5	6	7
terrible			mixed			excellent

8. How would you describe your relationship with your father while you were growing up?

1	2	3	4	5	6	7
terrible			mixed			excellent

9. How would you describe your home life when growing up?

1	2	3	4	5	6	7
terrible			mixed			excellent
abusive			O.K.			loving

10. How would you describe the relationship between your father (or father figure) and your mother (or mother figure) while you were growing up?

1	2	3	4	5	6	7
terrible			mixed			excellent

11. Was your father ever physically violent with your mother?

1	2	3	4	5	6	7
never			once a month			every day

12. Was your mother ever physically violent with your father?

1	2	3	4	5	6	7
never			once a month			every day

13. Were you ever beaten while growing up?

1	2	3	4	5	6	7
never			once a month			every day

14. If you were beaten, what was the usual excuse?
    a. something you did (if so, what?)
    b. something the beater did (if so, what?)
    c. no apparent reason

15. Was/is your father (or father figure) a jealous man?

1	2	3	4	5	6	7
not at all			average			extremely

16. Was/is your mother (or mother figure) a jealous woman?

1	2	3	4	5	6	7
not at all			average			extremely

17. Were there jealousy scenes between your parents?

1	2	3	4	5	6	7
never			several times			regularly

18. While growing up, did you have a very close (best) friend?

1	2	3	4	5	6	7
never			part of the time			always

19. While growing up, were you ever rejected by a group of kids you wanted to belong to?

1	2	3	4	5	6	7
always			several times			never

(Please describe any such incidents.)

20. While growing up, were you ever rejected by a boy/girl you loved?

1	2	3	4	5	6	7
always			several times			never

(Please describe any such incidents.)

21. How did you feel about yourself, most of the time, while growing up?

1	2	3	4	5	6	7
terrible			average			great

C. Current Situation

1. How would you describe your financial situation?

1	2	3	4	5	6	7
insecure			manage to get by			secure

2. How would you describe your physical condition?

1	2	3	4	5	6	7
terrible			average			excellent

3. How would you describe your emotional condition?

1	2	3	4	5	6	7
terrible			average			excellent

4. How do you feel about your life in general?

1	2	3	4	5	6	7
dissatisfied			average/ambivalent			very satisfied

5. How do you feel about yourself in general?

1	2	3	4	5	6	7
terrible			average			excellent

6. How do you feel about your looks in general?

1	2	3	4	5	6	7
dissatisfied			average/ambivalent			very satisfied

7. How do you feel about your general desirability as a sexual partner?

1	2	3	4	5	6	7
very dissatisfied			average/ambivalent			very satisfied

The next series of questions will address your most significant intimate relationship. If you are currently not involved in such a relationship, please answer all the following questions as they relate to your most important past relationship.

D. Intimate Relationship

1. Are you currently in an intimate relationship?
   a. yes
   b. no

2. How long, in years and months, have you been with your partner? _____ years _____ months

3. How long do/did you expect the relationship to last?

1	2	3	4	5	6	7
short time			several years			forever

4. How would you describe the relationship?

1	2	3	4	5	6	7
bad			mixed or average			excellent

5. Who has/had the control in the relationship?

1	2	3	4	5	6	7
your partner			equal control			you

6. How secure do you feel in the relationship?

1	2	3	4	5	6	7
very insecure			moderately secure			very secure

7. How do/did you feel about your partner in general?

1	2	3	4	5	6	7
very dissatisfied			average/ambivalent			very satisfied

8. How physically attracted are/were you to your partner?

1	2	3	4	5	6	7
not at all			moderately			very

9. How emotionally attracted are/were you to your partner?

1	2	3	4	5	6	7
not at all			moderately			very

10. How sexually desirable do you feel your partner is/was?

1	2	3	4	5	6	7
not at all			moderately			very

11. If you found someone else, would you leave your partner?

1	2	3	4	5	6	7
definitely not			possibly			definitely

E. Attitudes and Feelings Related to Jealousy

1. Do you believe in monogamous (one–on–one) relationships for yourself

1	2	3	4	5	6	7
definitely not		to a certain degree				definitely

2. Have you ever been sexual with someone else while in the relationship?

1	2	3	4	5	6	7
never			a few times			all the time

3. If so, did your partner know about it?
    a. yes
    b. no

4. If yes, how did your partner respond?

1	2	3	4	5	6	7
badly			mixed			very well

5. Have you been unfaithful to your partner any other way?

1	2	3	4	5	6	7
never			a few times			all the time

(If so, please explain in what way.)

6. Has your partner ever been sexual with someone else while in the relationship with you?

1	2	3	4	5	6	7
never			a few times			all the time

7. If so, how did you feel about it?

1	2	3	4	5	6	7
very bad			mixed			good

8. Has your partner been unfaithful to you any other way?

1	2	3	4	5	6	7
never			a few times			all the time

(If so, please explain in what way.)

9. Would you be (were you) open with your partner about other sexual experiences?

1	2	3	4	5	6	7
definitely not		to a certain degree				definitely

10. Would your partner be (was your partner) open with you about other sexual experiences?

1	2	3	4	5	6	7
definitely not		to a certain degree				definitely

11. How jealous is your partner?

1	2	3	4	5	6	7
not at all			moderately			extremely

12. Is jealousy a problem in your relationship?

1	2	3	4	5	6	7
not at all			moderately			extremely

13. How often has jealousy been a problem in previous relationships you had?

1	2	3	4	5	6	7
never			a few times			always

F. Jealousy Prevalence

1. How jealous are you?

1	2	3	4	5	6	7
not at all			moderately			extremely

2. Do you consider yourself a jealous person?
   a. yes
   b. no

3. How jealous were you during childhood?

1	2	3	4	5	6	7
not at all			moderately			extremely

4. How jealous were you during adolescence?

1	2	3	4	5	6	7
not at all			moderately			extremely

5. Do people with whom you were intimate consider you jealous?

1	2	3	4	5	6	7
not at all			moderately			extremely

G. Jealousy Triggers

Please use the following jealousy scale for all the questions in this section:

1	2	3	4	5	6	7
no jealousy			moderate jealousy			extreme jealousy

1. How much jealousy would you experience if you found out that your partner had been having a sexual relationship with:

   a. someone you don't know personally, and of whom you have a low opinion?

   b. someone you don't know personally and know nothing about?

   c. a family member?

   d. someone you don't know personally and of whom you think highly?

   e. someone you know personally and distrust?

   f. someone you know and find to be similar to you?

   g. someone you know, trust, and consider a friend?

   h. your best friend and confidant?

   i. someone you know and envy?

2. How much jealousy would you (did you) experience in each of the following situations?

   a. Your partner is being flirtatious and spends a great deal of time during a party dancing intimately and behaving provocatively with someone else.

   b. Your partner spends a great deal of time during a party dancing with someone else.

   c. Your partner spends a great deal of time during a party talking to someone else.

    d. Your partner disappears for a long time during a party.

    e. Your partner disappears briefly during a party.

    f. You answer your phone, and the caller hangs up after hearing your voice.

3. How much jealousy would/did you experience if/when your partner:

    a. had another lover?

    b. had a close friend of your sex who was single and eligible?

    c. had a close friend of your sex?

    d. was friendly with single and eligible people?

    e. expressed appreciation of, and interest in, someone s/he knows casualty?

    f. expressed appreciation of an attractive stranger passing by?

    g. expressed appreciation of a movie or television star?

4. How much jealousy would you experience if your partner:

    a. announced s/he had fallen in love with someone else and was thinking about leaving you?

    b. had a serious long–term affair?

    c. had an affair, but was open about it and assured you it was caused by a need for variety that in no way would affect your relationship?

    d. was open to, and frequently had, casual sexual experiences?

    e. recently had a casual one–night affair?

    f. had a love affair a long time ago, when already partnered with you?

    g. had a love affair many years ago, before being partnered with you?

    h. had an affair many years ago, when already partnered with you, with someone who is now deceased?

    i. had an affair many years ago, before being partnered with you, with someone who is now deceased?

5. How much jealousy would you experience if you discovered that your partner was having a love affair and:

    a. was extremely indiscreet about it; a scandal erupts in the middle of a big party, you are cast in the role of the betrayed lover and are expected to respond?

b. was extremely indiscreet about it; a scandal erupts, you are cast in the role of the betrayed lover, but you hear about it when you are alone?

c. everyone but you has known about it for a long time, but no one has said anything?

d. everyone knows about it?

e. only you and a few close and trusted friends know about it?

f. your partner is discreet, the three of you are the only ones who know about it, and they know that you know?

g. your partner is discreet, no one knows about it, and your partner doesn't know that you know?

Try to recall, in as much detail as possible, your most extreme experience of jealousy. Who were the people involved? How did they look and act? What was the situation? How did you feel? What did you do? Please describe the experience.

H. Reactions to Jealousy

1. Recalling your most extreme experience of jealousy, to what extent did you experience each one of the following physical and emotional reactions? Please use the following scale to respond to all items.

1	2	3	4	5	6	7
not at all			moderately			extremely

Physical Reactions

a. heat
b. headaches
c. shakiness
d. empty stomach
e. shortness of breath
f. blood rushing
g. high energy
h. coldness
i. fainting
j. nausea
k. cramps

l. nightmares
m. feeling of impending nervous breakdown
n. exhaustion
o. dizziness
p. no appetite
q. hands/legs trembling
r. fast heartbeat
s. insomnia
t. sexual arousal

Emotional Reactions

a. rage
b. humiliation
c. self–pity
d. confusion
e. pain
f. possessiveness
g. blame
h. feeling excluded

i. inferiority
j. frustration
k. fear of loss
l. envy
m. anger
n. aggression
o. passion
p. understanding

q. anxiety
r. depression
s. guilt
t. grief
u. helplessness
v. vulnerability
w. excitement
x. emotional exhaustion

Cognitive Reactions:

a. "How could you do this to me?"
b. "Everybody must be laughing at me."
c. "You couldn't possibly love me and still do this."
d. "You lied to me!"
e. "Where have I gone wrong?"
f. "I knew something was going on."
g. "How could I not notice that something was going on?"
h. "I would never have done such a terrible thing to you."
i. "This is the end of the relationship."
j. "What is missing in me that you're looking for in him/her?"
k. "I wish I were as attractive, smart, sexy."
l. "If you leave me I'm going to die."
m. "How dare you treat me this way."
n. "I wish you [or the other person] were dead."
o. "I can't take this much pain."
p. "I wish I were dead."

(Please give any other thoughts you may have had.)

2. How long did your most extreme jealousy last?

1	2	3	4	5	6	7
seconds	minutes	hours	days	weeks	months	years

3. How long does your most common jealousy last?

1	2	3	4	5	6	7
seconds	minutes	hours	days	weeks	months	years

4. How often do you experience extreme jealousy?

1	2	3	4	5	6	7
never	once	rarely	occasionally	often	usually	always

I. Coping with Jealousy

1. Recalling your most extreme experience of jealousy, how well do you think you coped with it?

1	2	3	4	5	6	7
poorly			average			very well

2. If you could rewrite history, would you have responded differently?

1	2	3	4	5	6	7
definitely			not sure			definitely not

3. How have you coped with jealousy? Please use the following scale to respond to all items:

1	2	3	4	5	6	7
never	once	rarely	occasionally	often	usually	always

a. rational discussion
b. screaming
c. crying
d. physical violence
e. suffering silently and covertly
f. finding the funny side
g. acceptance
h. sarcasm
i. using the occasion for thinking through my role in the situation and what it is I stand or fear to lose
j. avoiding the issue
k. "stony silence"
l. throwing things
m. denial
n. retaliating by making partner jealous
o. leaving partner
p. suffering silently and visibly
q. making a joke of it

J. Effects of Jealousy

1. Do you consider your jealousy a problem?

1	2	3	4	5	6	7
not at all			moderately			extremely

2. Do you like being jealous?

1	2	3	4	5	6	7
not at all			moderately			extremely

3. If you could get rid of your jealousy completely, would you like to?

1	2	3	4	5	6	7
definitely not			not sure			definitely yes

4. Do you like your partner to be jealous?

1	2	3	4	5	6	7
definitely not			not sure			definitely yes

5. Do you think jealousy is a normal response in certain situations?

1	2	3	4	5	6	7
definitely not			somewhat			definitely yes

6. Do you consider your own jealousy in extreme situations an appropriate response?

1	2	3	4	5	6	7
definitely not			somewhat			definitely yes

7. Would you believe someone who told you s/he is not jealous in such an extreme situation?

1	2	3	4	5	6	7
definitely not			somewhat			definitely yes

8. How desirable do you think jealousy is as a personal trait?

1	2	3	4	5	6	7
undesirable			mixed			desirable

9. Can you make yourself stop being jealous?

1	2	3	4	5	6	7
definitely not			to a certain degree			definitely yes

10. What are some of the positive and negative effects of jealousy?
    Please use the following scale to rate all items:

1	2	3	4	5	6	7
definitely not			to a certain degree			definitely yes

    Positive Effects of Jealousy:
    a. Jealousy is a sign of love.
    b. Jealousy is an instrument for inducing commitment.
    c. Jealousy brings excitement to listless relationships.
    d. Jealousy teaches people not to take each other for granted.
    e. Jealousy makes one's partner look more desirable.
    f. Jealousy makes life more interesting.
    g. Jealousy makes relationships last longer.
    h. Jealousy makes one examine one's relationship.

    Negative Effects of Jealousy:
    a. Jealousy drives one's partner away.
    b. Jealousy causes physical and emotional distress.
    c. Jealousy may result in violence.
    d. Jealousy puts a strain on relationships.
    e. Jealousy wastes time that could be spent more enjoyably.
    f. Jealousy restricts partners' freedom.
    g. Jealousy can block thoughts and distort emotions.

11. Have you ever been the object of someone's jealousy?

1	2	3	4	5	6	7
never			a few times			all the time

12. Did you like the experience?

1	2	3	4	5	6	7
not at all			somewhat			very much

K. Reasons for Jealousy

1. What do you think causes people in general to experience
   jealousy? Please use the following scale to rate all items:

1	2	3	4	5	6	7
definitely not			to a certain degree			definitely yes

Jealousy is:

a. a normal reaction accompanying love

b. the result of personal insecurity

c. the result of feeling excluded and left out

d. the result of weakness in the relationship

e. the result of fear and loss

f. the result of being afraid to lose face

g. the result of being afraid to lose control

h. reaction to grief and pain over losing partner's love

i. an instinctive reaction to threat to a love relationship

j. a result of one's own impulses toward infidelity

k. a result of feeling inadequate as a woman or man

l. a result of childhood deprivation and abandonment

m. a fear of being considered inadequate by others

n. the result of self-blame, feeling that if your partner is attracted to someone else or having an affair, you probably deserve it because you brought it on yourself

o. the result of feeling envious resentment of another's success or advantage

p. the result of a threat to the privacy of your intimate relationship (intimate acts, secrets, and so on)

2. After answering the questionnaire, what is your definition of jealousy?

3. Using your own definition, how jealous are you?

1	2	3	4	5	6	7
not jealous at all		moderately jealous			extremely jealous	

Romantic Jealousy Research

Research

The criterion question "Are you a jealous person?" in *The Romantic Jealousy Questionnaire* (Pines & Aronson, 1980) was shown to be significantly correlated with self-reported jealousy, relationship jealousy, chronic jealousy, projective jealousy, interpersonal jealousy, dependency, and romantic love (Mathes et al., 1982).

Tables 1–8 present the different antecedents, correlates, and consequences of romantic jealousy. These tables were first published in Pines, A. M. & Aronson, E. (1983). Antecedents, correlates and consequences of sexual jealousy. *Journal of Personality*, 1, 108–136, and are reprinted by permission of the *Journal of Personality*.

Table 9 shows the difference between people who answered "yes" and those who answered "no" to the question: "Are you a jealous person?"

Table 10 presents correlates of projected jealousy.

Table 11–19 present various aspects of gender differences in jealousy.

Table 1. Subject and Relationship Variables

	Mean	Standard deviation
Subject Variables		
Financial situation (1 = highly insecure; 7 = highly secure)	4.9	1.4
Physical condition (1 = very poor; 7 = excellent)	5.7	1.0
Mental condition (1 = very poor; 7 = excellent)	5.8	1.0
How do you feel about yourself in general? (1 = very dissatisfied; 7 = very satisfied)	5.5	1.0
How do you feel about your looks in general? (1 = very dissatisfied; 7 = very satisfied)	5.3	1.0
How do you feel about your desirability as a sexual partner? (7 = very desirable)	5.7	1.0
How do you feel about life in general? (7 = very satisfied)?	5.8	0.8
How do you feel about your partner's desirability as a sexual partner? (7 = very desirable)	6.1	1.0
How do you feel about your sexual partner in general? (7 = very satisfied)	5.9	1.0
How physically attracted are you to your partner? (7 = very attracted)	5.7	1.2
How emotionally attracted are you to your partner? (7 = very attracted)	6.2	1.0
Relationship Variables		
How long do you expect the relationship to last? (1 = very short time; 7 = forever)	5.3	1.7
How would you describe your relationship? (1 = very bad; 7 = excellent)	5.8	1.2
Who has the control in the relationship? (1 = your partner; 7 = you)	4.1	1.0
How secure do you feel about the relationship? (1 = extremely insecure; 7 = extremely secure)	5.4	1.4
If you found another person, would you leave? (1 = definitely yes; 7 = definitely not)	5.2	1.8
Would you be open to your partner about other sexual experiences? (7 = definitely yes)	4.6	2.1
Would you expect your partner to be open with you? (7 = definitely yes)	4.8	1.9
Has your partner ever been unfaithful to you sexually? (1 = definitely not; 7 = definitely yes)	2.8	2.1
Has your partner ever been unfaithful in any other way? (7 = definitely yes)	2.2	1.7
Have you ever been unfaithful sexually? (1 = definitely not; 7 = definitely yes)	2.3	1.8
Have you been unfaithful in any other way? (1 = definitely not; 7 = definitely yes)	2.0	1.6
Have you fantasized sexual involvement with others? (1 = never; 7 = all the time)	4.4	1.5

Table 2. Jealousy Variables

	Mean	Standard deviation
How jealous is your partner? (1 = not at all jealous; 7 = extremely jealous)	3.8	1.8
How jealous are you now? (1 = not at all jealous; 7 = extremely jealous)	3.3	1.7
How jealous were you during childhood?	3.6	2.0
During adolescence?	4.3	1.8
During young adulthood?	4.1	1.9
During advanced adulthood?	3.5	1.8
Average physical reaction (3-point scales: 1 = none at all; 3 = very intense)	1.6	0.4
Average emotional reaction (3-point scales: 1 = none at all; 3 = very intense)	2.0	0.4
How often do you experience extreme jealousy? (1 = never; 2 = once; 3 = rarely; 4 = occasionally; 5 = often; 6 = usually)	3.3	1.0
How long did your most extreme jealousy last? (1 = seconds; 2 = minutes; 3 = hours; 4 = days; 6 = months; 7 = years)	3.7	1.5
How long does mild jealousy last? (1 = seconds; 2 = minutes; 3 = hours; 4 = days; 5 = weeks; 6 = months; 7 = years)	2.6	1.1
Do you consider your jealousy a problem? (1 = not at all; 7 = yes, a very serious problem)	2.7	1.7
Do you like being jealous? (7 = dislike it very much)	6.0	1.3
Would you like to get rid of your jealousy? (7 = definitely yes)	5.8	1.6
Do you like your partner to be jealous? (7 = definitely yes)	2.9	1.9
Have any intimate relationships ended because of jealousy? (1 = none; 7 = all)	1.4	0.8
Do most people who know you well consider you a jealous person? (7 = definitely yes)	2.5	1.6
Do people you have been intimate with consider you jealous? (7 = definitely yes)	3.3	1.8
What percent of people answering the questionnaire will admit to being "a jealous person"?	57	25
What percent are actually jealous?	75	24
Who are more jealous—men or women? (4 = equal jealousy)	4.1	1.0
Is jealousy a normal response in certain situations? (1 = definitely not; 7 = definitely yes)	4.8	1.8
Do you consider your jealousy in extreme situations an appropriate reaction? (7 = definitely yes)	5.1	1.8
Do you believe someone who will tell you s/he is not jealous in such extreme situations? (7 = definitely yes)	3.8	2.0
How desirable is jealousy as a personal characteristic? (7 = very desirable)	3.0	1.6
Can you make yourself stop being jealous? (7 = definitely yes)	3.9	1.6

Table 3. Jealousy Elicitors

	Mean	Standard deviation
People eliciting jealousy (1 = no jealousy; 7 = extreme jealousy)		
Someone you don't know and have a low opinion of.	3.2	2.0
Someone you don't know and know nothing about.	3.5	2.0
A family member.	4.3	2.0
Someone you don't know and think very highly about.	4.3	2.0
Someone you know and find similar to you.	4.5	2.0
Someone you know and distrust.	4.6	2.0
Someone you know, trust, and consider a friend.	4.7	2.0
Your best friend and confidant.	4.9	2.0
Someone you know and are envious of.	5.4	2.0
Love affair of partner as a jealousy elicitor (1 = no jealousy; 7 = extreme jealousy)		
Your mate is extremely indiscreet, a scandal erupts, and you hear about it when you are alone; everybody else *but* you has known about it for a long time.	5.7	1.8
Your mate is extremely indiscreet and a scandal erupts in the middle of a big party and you are there.	5.4	2.0
Your mate is very discreet, no one else knows about it, and s/he doesn't know that you know	5.4	1.8
... and everybody knows about it.	5.3	2.1
... and only you and a few close friends know.	5.1	2.0
Your mate is very discreet, but knows you know.	5.0	2.1

Table 4. Coping with Jealousy (in Order of "Yes" Responses)

	Percentage yes
How do your cope with jealousy?	
Use the occasion for thinking and processing	80
Rational discussion	79
Verbal assault	60
Sarcasm	56
Acceptance	55
Crying	44
Stony silence	42
Suffer silently but visibly	36
Avoidance of issue	33
Retaliation	33
Leave mate	29
Suffer silently and covertly	27
Make a joke of it	26
Denial	8
Physical violence	7

Table 5. An Object of Jealousy

			Percentages		
	Mean	*Standard Deviation*	Definitely not	To a certain degree	Definitely yes
How did you feel being the object of someone's jealousy?					
Feeling good	2.1	0.6	63	29	8
Feeling pity	2.0	0.7	17	57	26
Feeling guilty	1.9	0.7	51	38	12
Feeling weak	1.8	0.7	46	42	12
Feeling happy	1.8	0.5	75	21	4
Feeling sad	1.8	0.5	79	20	2
Feeling helpless	1.8	0.7	35	45	20
Feeling anxious	1.8	0.6	55	37	8
Higher self-concept	1.8	0.6	67	26	7
Feeling angry	1.8	0.7	65	26	9
Feeling empathetic	1.8	0.7	50	38	12
Feeling strong	1.7	1.4	54	35	11
Feeling depressed	1.7	1.1	79	16	4
Feeling bad	1.6	0 7	41	42	16
Feeling excited	1.6	0.7	33	45	22
Feeling vulnerable	1.6	0.7	40	43	18
Feeling pained	1.5	0.7	58	32	10
Feeling confused	1.5	0.8	39	38	23
Feeling superior	1.5	0.8	44	34	22
Feeling uncomfortable	1.4	0.6	63	32	4
Feeling victimized	1.4	0.7	35	50	15
Feeling passionate	1.4	0.7	24	55	21
Feeling frustrated	1.4	0.6	63	32	4
Feeling irritated	1.4	0.6	60	33	7
Feeling self-confident	1.3	0.7	42	42	17
Feeling self-assured	1.3	0.8	39	39	23
Feeling lucky	1.2	0.8	40	40	20
Overall	2.5	.6	8	37	56

Table 6. Jealousy Correlates

Variables	Kendall/ two-tailed r	p
Background		
Age	−.19	.007
Number of older brothers	.25	.001
Number of younger brothers	−.15	.028
Physical condition	−.23	.001
Mental condition	−.31	.001
How long do you expect the relationship to last?	−.24	.002
How secure do you feel about the relationship?	−.29	.001
If you found someone else, would you leave?	−.23	.002
Do you believe in monogamy?	−.16	.022
Has your partner ever been unfaithful sexually?	.17	.020
Has your partner ever been unfaithful in any other way?	.32	.001
Have you ever been unfaithful?	.22	.003
Have you fantasized sexual involvement?	.22	.002
Your general desirability as a sexual partner	.17	.011
General feeling about sexual partner	−.22	.002
Prevalence		
How jealous were you during childhood?	.18	.013
adolescence?	.23	.001
young adulthood?	.50	.001
advanced adulthood?	.72	.001
Have any intimate relationships ended because of jealousy?	.15	.023
Do most people consider you jealous?	.50	.001
Do people in intimate relationships consider you jealous?	.59	.001
Percentage of people answering the questionnaire who will admit to being jealous	.14	.043
Who are more jealous, men or women?	.18	.008
How often do you experience jealousy?	.54	.001
When you experience jealousy, how long does it last?	.19	.009
Jealousy elicitors		
Average response to people eliciting jealousy	.33	.001
Average response to incidents eliciting jealousy	.43	.001
Average response to partner's behaviors eliciting jealousy	.51	.001

Table 6. Jealousy Correlates (*continued*)

Variables	Kendall/ two– tailed r	p
Average response to partner's affairs as a jealousy trigger	.31	.001
Average response to discovering partner's affair	.36	.001
Reactions to jealousy		
Average physical reactions to jealousy	.24	.002
Average emotional reactions to jealousy	.37	.001
Do you consider your jealousy a problem?	.48	.001
Do you like your partner to be jealous?	.35	.001
How desirable do you think jealousy is?	.23	.002
Can you make yourself stop being jealous?	−.35	.001
Positive effects of jealousy		
Teaches people not to take each other for granted	.37	.001
Makes relationships last longer	.36	.001
Indicates you love your partner	.35	.001
Brings excitement to listless relationships	.33	.001
Makes partners look more desirable	.31	.001
Jealousy is a sign of love	.29	.001
Makes one examine one's relationship	.24	.001
Makes one feel alive	.23	.001
Reasons for jealousy		
Instinctive reaction to threat	.25	.001
Normal reaction accompanying love	.20	.005
Wards off infidelity impulses	.18	.009
Self-blame	.18	.010
Immaturity and a defective self	−.17	.017

Note: Correlations with responses to the question: How jealous are you at this stage of your life? (1 = not jealous at all; 7 = extremely jealous) The different *p* values to identical *r* values are the result of different *ns*.

Table 7. Reasons for Jealousy (in Order of Magnitude)

	Mean	Standard deviation
Reasons for jealousy (7 = definitely yes)		
The result of personal insecurity	6.0	1.2
The result of fear of losing face	6.0	1.1
The result of weakness in the relationship	5.3	1.6
The result of feeling excluded	5.2	1.6
A simple grief and pain reaction	5.0	1.9
A threat to privacy of one's intimate relationship	4.7	1.9
A result of competitiveness	4.4	1.7
The result of feeling inadequate as a man/woman	4.4	1.8
An instinctive reaction to threat	4.4	1.9
The result of fear of losing control	4.4	1.8
The result of fear of loss	4.2	1.7
The result of fear of being considered inadequate	4.2	2.0
Used to ward off impulses toward infidelity	4.2	2.0
A normal reaction accompanying love	4.0	2.0
The result of feeling envious resentment	3.9	1.7
A sign of immaturity and a defective self	3.9	1.7
The result of childhood deprivation	3.6	1.8
The result of self-blame	3.1	1.7
Used to ward off impulses toward homosexuality	3.1	1.8

Table 8. Negative and Positive Effects of Jealousy
(in Order of Magnitude)

	Mean	Standard deviation
Negative effects of jealousy (7 = definitely yes)		
Causes emotional distress	5.9	1.3
Puts a strain on relationship	5.9	1.2
Can block thoughts and distort emotions	5.9	1.3
Wastes time	5.8	1.4
Causes physical distress	5.5	1.5
Restricts partner's freedom	5.2	1.7
Can cause social embarrassment	5.0	1.5
May result in violence	5.0	1.7
Drives one's partner away	4.8	1.4
Makes one feel guilty	4.7	1.8
Positive effects of jealousy (7 = definitely yes)		
Makes one examine one's relationship	4.7	2.0
Teaches people not to take each other for granted	3.1	1.8
A sign of love	3.0	1.8
An instrument for inducing commitment	2.8	1.7
Makes one's partner look more desirable	2.6	1.6
Brings excitement to listless relationships	2.4	1.6
Makes love more interesting	2.3	1.5
Makes one alive	2.3	1.5
Makes relationship last longer	1.5	0.9

Table 9. Are You a Jealous Person?

Variable	Yes Mean	No Mean	F	p
Partner was unfaithful	3.0	2.1	6.1	.01
Unfaithful in other ways	2.5	1.7	6.0	.02
Secure in relationship	5.2	6.0	10.3	.002
Expected length	5.1	6.1	9.5	.003

Note: F is the result of an analysis of variance comparing the means. Small p is the probability of the result being an error.

Table 10. Correlates of Projected Jealousy

	r	p
Partner was unfaithful	−.24	.002
Would leave if found someone else	.23	.002
Has been unfaithful	.22	.002
Fantasized sexual involvements	.22	.002

Table 11. Mean Gender Differences in Reported Jealousy

Variables	Men Mean	Women Mean	F	p
Jealousy level	2.9	3.0		
Frequency	2.9	3.0		
Duration (extreme)	3.5	3.8		
Duration (mild)	2.6	2.3		

Table 12. Mean Gender Differences in Physical Reactions to Jealousy

Variables	Men Mean	Women Mean	F	p
Hot	1.5	1.9	6.2	.01
Nervous and shaky	1.8	2.2	7.6	.01
Head aching	1.3	1.5	3.5	.06
Nauseous	1.4	1.6		
No appetite	1.7	1.9		
Dizzy	1.2	1.3		
Fainting	1.2	1.1		
Energized	1.6	1.6		
Sexually aroused	1.2	1.3		
Blood rushing	1.5	1.6		
Hands trembling	1.5	1.7		
Stomach cramps	1.2	1.3		
Stomach emptiness	2.0	2.2		
Nightmares	1.2	1.4		
Sleep problems	2.0	2.1		
Total of 20 items	1.5	1.7		

**Table 13. Mean Gender Differences in Emotional Reactions
to Jealousy**

Variable	Men Mean	Women Mean	F	p
Pain	2.0	2.6	14.7	.00
Vulnerability	2.1	2.5	6.9	.01
Fear of loss	2.2	2.6	7.3	.01
Inferiority	1.9	2.3	4.8	.03
Emotional exhaustion	1.9	2.3	4.8	.03
Self pity	1.9	2.2	3.5	.06
Trapped	1.4	1.6	3.5	.06
Excluded	2.0	2.3		
Low self esteem	1.9	2.2		
Resentment	2.1	2.4		
Grief	1.9	2.3		
Irritability	1.9	2.2		
Anger	2.2	2.4		
Aggression	1.8	1.9		
Anxiety	2.3	2.4		
Humiliation	1.8	2.1		
Frustration	2.1	2.3		
Depression	2.1	2.3		
Helplessness	2.1	2.3		
Envy	1.8	2.0		
Total of 30 items	1.9	2.1	7.8	.01

Table 14. Mean Gender Differences in Jealousy Correlates

Variables	Men Mean	Women Mean	F	p
Fantasized sex	4.8	4.1	6.4	.01
Believe in monogamy	4.1	5.0	4.1	.05
Relations ended	1.7	1.4	3.1	.08
Mate is jealous	3.8	3.2		
Control	4.3	4.0		
Security	5.7	5.6		
Were you unfaithful	2.2	2.0		
Partner unfaithful	1.9	2.1		
Expected length	5.7	5.5		
Relationship quality	6.0	5.0		
Would you leave?	5.8	5.8		
Would you tell?	4.9	4.9		
Would your mate tell?	5.2	5.1		

Table 15. Mean Gender Differences in Jealousy Elicitors

Variables	Men Mean	Women Mean	F	p
Don't know + low opinion	2.7	2.9		
Don't know + know nothing	2.6	3.3	3.6	.06
Don't know + think highly	3.3	4.1	4.2	.04
Know and distrust	3.3	4.3	5.4	.02
Know and consider similar	3.6	4.5	4.5	.04
Know and envy	3.8	4.6		
A family member	3.3	4.1	4.2	.04
Your best friend	3.6	4.0		
Know and consider friend	4.6	4.9		

Table 16.   Mean Gender Differences in Effects of Jealousy

Variables	Men Mean	Women Mean	F	p
Positive effects				
Forces examination	4.5	4.7		
A sign of love	2.7	2.8		
Not take for granted	2.7	2.8		
Induces commitment	2.3	2.6		
Brings excitement	2.0	2.4		
Partner desirable	2.3	2.3		
You feel alive	2.0	2.2		
Life more interesting	2.1	2.1		
Makes relations last	1.5	1.4		
Negative effects				
Distorts emotions	6.0	6.1		
Puts a strain	5.8	6.1		
Wastes time	5.7	6.0		
Causes physical distress	5.0	5.8	7.3	.01
Causes emotional distress	5.6	6.1	5.2	.02
May result in violence	4.9	5.3		
Drives away	4.9	5.1		
Causes guilt	4.5	5.1		
Restricts mate's freedom	5.2	5.5		

Table 17.   Mean Gender Differences in Attitudes toward Jealousy

Variables	Men Mean	Women Mean	F	p
Wants to get rid of it	5.8	5.9		
Jealousy is normal	5.0	4.5		
Is at times appropriate	4.7	4.5		
Believe someone who is not	3.8	4.4		
You can stop it	4.6	4.2		
Likes being jealous	5.9	6.2		
Likes partner to be jealous	2.3	2.8		
Jealousy is desirable	2.4	2.9		
One's jealousy is a problem	2.2	2.5		

Table 18. Mean Gender Differences in Jealousy Reasons

Variables	Men Mean	Women Mean	F	p
Fear of loss	5.8	6.1		
Result of insecurity	5.7	6.1		
Feeling excluded	4.7	5.6	8.2	.01
Losing control	4.9	5.3		
Threat to privacy	4.6	4.6		
Fear of losing face	4.6	4.5		
Competitiveness	4.5	4.3		
Relationship weakness	4.3	4.6		
Grief and pain	3.9	4.5		
Envy	4.0	4.1		
Immaturity	4.0	3.9		
Feeling inadequate	3.8	4.5	3.2	.07
Seeming inadequate	3.5	4.3		
Accompanies love	3.7	3.5		
Childhood deprivation	3.0	3.8	4.5	.04
Reaction to threat	3.4	4.0		
Self blame	2.9	3.3		
Ward off infidelity	2.5	3.1	3.0	.08
Ward off homosexuality	1.4	1.8		

Table 19. Mean Gender Differences in Jealousy in Response to Four Triggers

Variables	Men Mean	Women Mean	F	p
Length of affair:				
One night	4.5	4.8	1.5	.14
One year	4.8	5.0	1.3	.21
Main effect for length of affair: F = 30.7 p = .0001				
Gender × length of affair interaction: F = .01 p = .91				
Comparison to you:				
Worse than you	4.2	4.4	1.0	.31
Better than you	5.1	5.4	1.7	.09
Main effect for comparison: F = 302.2 p = .0001				
Gender × comparison interaction: F = .99 p = .58				
Outcome for the relationship:				
Improve things	4.4	4.7	1.1	.29
Leave the same	4.6	4.9	1.6	.10
Wants out	5.0	5.3	1.3	.19
Main effect for outcome: F = 34.7 p = .0001				
Gender × outcome interaction: F = 1.4 p = .25				
Type of affair:				
Sexual	4.9	5.1	0.8	.39
Emotional	4.4	4.8	2.0	.05
Main effect for type of affair: F = 118.6 p = .0001				
Gender × type of affair interaction: F = 7.7 p = .006				
Significant higher order interactions:				
Length × comparison × outcome × type interaction: F = 48.6 p = .0001				
Gender × length × comparison × outcome × type: F = 3.6 p = .03				

Notes

Chapter 1. The Green–Eyed Monster or the Shadow of Love?

1. Similar definitions were offered by other scholars, such as Buss (1994); Clanton & Smith (1986); Parrot & Smith (1993); Salovey (1991); White & Mullan (1989).

2. The psychological differences between envy and jealousy have been discussed by numerous scholars, including Anderson (1987); Haslam & Bornstein (1996); Hupka et al. (1985); Kreeger (1992); Parrott (1991); Parrot & Smith (1993); Salovey (1991); Salovey & Rodin (1986, 1991); Salovey & Rothman (1991).

   In the Hupka et al. (1985) study, the responses to jealousy and envy in Hungary, Ireland, Mexico, the USSR, Holand, Yugoslavia, and the U.S. were compared and found to be similar.

3. It may be worth noting that Nancy Friday's book *Jealousy* (1987) deals more with envy than with jealousy.

4. For a study addressing jealousy as a trigger of family murder followed by suicide, you may want to read Goldney (1977). For reports on jealousy as a trigger of murder, see Benezech (1984); Mowat (1966); and White & Mullen (1989) 218–246. White and Mullen report in their book that up to one in five murders is motivated by jealousy.

   For discussions of jealousy as a trigger of wife battering, see Adams (1990); Delgado & Bond (1993); Finn (1985); and Saunders & Hanusa (1986). Discussions of jealousy as a cause of the destruction of romantic relationships and as the trigger of aggression among dating couples, marital problems, and divorce can be found in Constantine (1976); Docherty & Ellis (1976); and Riggs (1993). For discussions of the relationship between jealousy and depression, suicidal thoughts, loss of self-esteem, anxiety, and anger, see Carson & Johnson (1985);

Mathes et al. (1985); and Everton & Tate (1990). For a discussion of jealousy as a trigger of violence, criminal behavior, and hatred, see Laner (1990) and Leong et al. (1994).

5. In eight different studies involving 1069 people, all of the respondents, including those who described themselves as not jealous, said that they experienced jealousy in some stage of their life. The first study (Aronson & Pines, 1980) involved fifty-four people. The second (Pines & Aronson, 1983) involved 103 people. The third (Pines, 1987a) involved fifteen commune members. The fourth (Pines, 1983) involved twenty-two male inmates. The fifth (Pines, 1996) involved fifty-eight people. The sixth (Pines, 1987b) involved 571 people. The seventh (chapter eight) involved twelve female inmates and twelve female noninmates. The eighth (Pines & Friedman, 1998) involved 222 American students.

6. The question of who is the target, the beloved or the rival, is a very interesting question addressed by Mathes & Verstraete (1993).

7. For a discussion of pathological jealousy, see for example Buunk (1994) and Coen (1987). For a discussion of pathological tolerance, see Pinta (1979).

8. Examples of studies that relate abnormal jealousy to different organic neurological and physical disorders include Achte et al. (1991); Breitner & Anderson (1994); and Hodgson et al. (1992).

9. Abnormal jealousy has been described as delusional, morbid, obsessional, and pathological. See for example Bishay et al. (1996); Buunk (1994); Egan et al. (1996); Stein, et al. (1994).

10. A normal distribution is bell-shaped:

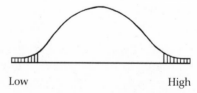

Low   High

Normalcy is defined as a characteristic of the majority that falls within two standard deviations above and below the mean. The middle range (the wide part of the bell) constitutes 95% of cases. This part is defined as normal. The lowest part of the scale (the left edge of the bell) comprises 2.5% of cases, and is defined as abnormally low. Similarly, 2.5% of cases fall in the highest part of the scale and are defined as abnormally high. If we think of a similar bell curve in relation to height, 95% of the population are of "normal" height, 2.5% are "abnormally" short, and 2.5% are "abnormally" tall. "Abnormal" in this case simply means the lowest and the highest ends of the scale.

11. For a discussion of the cultural determinants of jealousy, see Bhugra (1993); Hupka (1981, 1991); Hupka & Bank (1996); Hupka & Ryan (1990); Hupka et al. (1985); Mullen (1993); and Zummuner & Fischer (1995).

12. Abnormal jealousy has been found to be related to different psychiatric neurological and physical disorders including schizophrenia, paranoia, borderline personality disorder, mental handicap, alcoholism, brain damage and a variety of organic diseases. See for example Achte et al. (1991); Breitner & Anderson (1994); Cooper & Collacott (1993); Hodgson et al. (1992); Napier (1994); Shaji & Cyriac (1991); Soyka (1995); and Sokya et al. (1991).

13. This literature was presented in chapter two of Pines (1996). Additional references include Caspi & Herbener (1990); Kay et al. (1988); Marikagas et al. (1988); Taylor (1989); Taylor & Vandenberg (1988); and Wilson (1989).

14. The concept of "romantic image" was first introduced in chapter two of Pines (1996).

Chapter 2. Are You a Jealous Person?

1. The question "Are you a jealous person?" was answered by the 728 people who took part in three different studies on which this chapter is based. The first study (Aronson & Pines, 1980) was a pilot study involving fifty-four men and women. The second (Pines & Aronson, 1983) involved 103 men and women. The third (Pines, 1987b) involved 571 men and women.

   A study of the convergent validity of the Pines and Aronson Jealousy Question, together with five other jealousy scales, is described by Mathes et al. (1982). It reports a significant correlation between the question and the following variables: Interpersonal Jealousy ($r = .33$); Chronic Jealousy ($r = .61$); Self-Reported Jealousy ($r = .31$); Projective Jealousy ($r = .52$); Neuroticism ($r = .42$); and Insecurity ($r = .45$). ("r" indicates correlation. The higher the correlation, the more two variables tend to vary together.) For other data, see Appendix C.

2. Other jealousy researchers also distinguished these three compo-

nents of romantic jealousy. See for example Dolan & Bishay (1996b); Paul et al. (1993); and Sharpsteen & Kirkpatrick (1997).

3. The conclusion that jealousy has universal and identifiable features is supported by other studies, including Haslam & Bornstein (1996); Hupka et al. (1985); Parrot & Smith (1993), Salovey & Rothman (1991); Sharpsteen & Kirkpatrick (1997); Smith et al. (1988); and Spielman (1971).

4. Breitner & Anderson (1994) report in their study of seven cases of delusional jealousy that a previous experience of infidelity appears to be a common antecedent to extreme jealousy.

5. The finding of a positive correlation between belief in monogamy and jealousy seems to contradict the findings of a study by Weis & Felton (1987) in which it was found that single undergraduate females with most exclusive extramarital activities (those who rejected a higher number of extramarital activities) were most likely to score high on a measure of jealousy, to associate sex and love, to view themselves as conservative, and to attend church frequently. The results of our study suggest that when such women marry, they tend to marry men with conservative attitudes similar to their own, and thus create unions in which jealousy is less likely to be triggered.

6. Other researchers have also noted the relationship between dispositional proneness to experience jealousy and perception of jealousy in others. See for example Greenberg (1985), Mathes et al. (1982) also report a significant correlation between people's report on thier own level of jealousy and Projective Jealousy (r = .52).

7. Bringle (1991) is one of the theorists who view jealousy as a stable personality trait. See for example Bringle & Buunk (1985); Bringle & Evenbeck (1979); and Bringle & Williams (1979). Other scholars have noted that such traits as jealousy have a "family history" (Vinokur, 1986).

8. The results of a study by Downey & Vitulli (1987), for example, suggest that decreased jealousy in older people results from increased maturity and self-esteem.

9. The noted sociologist Bernard (1986) suggests that because of changes in the institution of marriage, jealousy is declining. The changes in the social and legal concept of jealousy across cultures and throughout history have also been discussed by Mullen (1993).

10. See, for example, Neill (1960).
11. Other scholars have also noted the effect of the family constellation on the child's jealousy. Neubauer (1983) contends that differences in the development of rivalry, jealousy, and envy depend on whether the child is an older or younger sibling, and that the sibling position may play a significant role in jealousy. See also Mandler (1991).
12. Zummuner & Fischer (1995), who studied the social regulation of emotions in jealousy situations, found significant discrepancies between felt and shared jealousy—all subjects regulated their jealousy response.
13. Other researchers have also noted the relationship between jealousy and self-esteem. For example, see Sharpsteen (1995) and Stewart & Beatty (1985). Mathes et al. (1982) also report a significant correlation between jealousy and Insecurity ($r = .45$). Other scholars, such as Gordon Clanton, claim that the direction of the relationship between jealousy and self-esteem is not clear. It is possible, they argue, that the humiliation of jealousy reduces people's self-esteem, and not the other way around.
14. The correlation between jealousy and one's mental state has been noted in other studies as well, for example, Carson & Johnson (1985); Mathes et al. (1985); and Tarrier et al. (1989).
15. The study is mentioned in Pines (1996).

Chapter 3. The Unconscious Roots of Romantic Jealousy

1. At a later stage of his writing, Freud gave up the idea of an Electra complex for girls, and talked about Oedipus complex for both boys and girls.
2. See White & Mullen (1989), pp. 78–79.
3. Examples of studies of organic causes of jealousy are discussed in the following: for a study of brain damage, see Achte et al. (1991); for a study of organic psychoses, see Soyka et al. (1991); for a study of alcoholism and alcohol psychosis, see Napier (1994) and Soyka et al. (1991); for a study of hyperthyroidism, see Hodgson et al. (1992); for a study of carcinoma, see Egan et al. (1996).
4. For a discussion of the relationship between delusional jealousy and schizophrenia, see Soyka (1995); for a discussion of the rela-

tionship between delusional jealousy and paranoia, see Achte et al. (1991) and Shaji & Cyriac (1991); for borderline personality disorder, see Sefedin (1992); and on mental handicap, see Cooper & Collacott (1993).

5. The following articles report successful application of pharmacological interventions in the treatment of delusional jealousy: Byrne & Yatham (1989); Gross (1991); Herceg (1976); Lane (1990); Munro et al. (1985); Stein et al. (1994); and Wright (1994).

6. For successful application of cognitive therapy in the treatment of delusional jealousy see Bishay et al. (1996); Dinesh (1993); Dolan & Bishay (1996a, 1996b); and Ellis (1996).

7. Writings on the application of the systems approach to the treatment of delusional jealousy include Friedman (1989); Im et al. (1983); Sluzki (1989); and Teisman (1979).

8. Papers describing individual psychotherapy for the treatment of delusional jealousy include Coen (1987); Docherty & Ellis (1976); Freud (1922/1955); and Pao (1969).

9. See also Horney (1937).

Chapter 4. Treating the Couple, Not the Jealous Mate

1. Writings on the systems approach to treating marital problems include Fisch et al. (1982); Guerin et al. (1987); Gurman & Kniskem (1981); Haley (1977); Sluzki (1978); Steinglass (1978); and Watzlawick et al. (1974). Writings on the systems approach to jealousy include Friedman (1989); Guerin et al. (1987); Im et al. (1983); Margolin (1985); Pam & Pearson (1994); Slonim–Nevo & Vosler (1991); Sluzki (1989); and Teisman (1979).

2. See Nichols (1984), p. 127.

3. See White & Mullen (1989), pp. 14–17.

4. A shorter version of this case was presented in chapter six of Pines (1996).

5. See Guerin et al. (1987), pp. 64–80.

6. See Guerin et al. (1987), p. 77.

7. See Barker (1987), pp. 79–81.

8. I would like to thank my dear friend and colleague Professor Murry Bilmes for his contribution to my understanding of the psychoanalytic perspective and this case.

9. Role–reversal was used as a technique for treating jealousy by others as well. For example, see deSilva (1987).
10. See Im et al. (1983).
11. Reframing was recommended by other psychologists as well as a technique for treating jealousy. For example, see Im et al. (1983) and Teisman (1979).
12. See Margolin (1985).
13. See Sluzki (1989).

Chapter 5. Men Get Angry, Women Get Depressed

1. Two examples of feminist psychoanalysts who have written about women's "self in relations" are Jean Baker Miller (1987) and Lillian Rubin (1983).
2. Writings describing evolutionary theory and research on sex differences in attraction include Buss (1985, 1989, 1994); Buss & Schmitt (1993); Daly & Wilson (1978); Small (1992); Symons (1979).
3. See Pines & Aronson (1983) and Pines & Friedman (1998).
4. In a study done by Gary Hansen (1985) on dating jealousy among college students it was found that there were no sex differences in response to jealousy–provoking situations. On the other hand, sex-role orientation was consistently related to jealousy—with traditional men and women being the more jealous. Other studies that did not find sex differences in jealousy are reported by McIntosh (1989) and White (1981a). Greg White and Paul Mullen (1989, pp. 127) report that most studies did not find gender differences in jealousy, and that those studies in which sex differences were found were not consistent in finding one gender to be more jealous than the other.
5. For both men (38%) and women (30%), the most frequent response was to "talk about it." For women, the second most frequent response (26%) was "try to ignore the whole thing." "Ignoring" was a far less frequent response (18%) for men. Men (25%) and women (24%) are similar in their likelihood to let their mate know that they are hurt. For most men (81%) and women (80%), these three responses (talking, ignoring, and expressing hurt) accounted for the majority of the total responses mentioned. Only a very small percentage of both men and women described themselves as either shouting (8% women and

5% men), getting away (5% of the men and 4% of the women), or resorting to violence (only three men and one woman out of 568).

6. See, for example, the works by Henley & Thorn (1977), and Tannen (1990).

7. A study investigating the reasons for dating violence discovered that jealousy caused men to become violent during a date more often than women (Stets & Pirog–Good, 1987). Another study of aggression toward partner and rival (Paul & Galloway, 1994) showed that men were more inclined to think about aggressive action against the rival, but women were more emotionally and behaviorally reactive to the rival.

   In a study by Bram Buunk (1984), it was found that the attribution of aggression was significantly related to jealousy among males but not among females. In a study of dangerousness associated with jealousy conducted by Gregory Leong and his colleagues (1994), all the dangerous patients (described as suffering from "the Othello syndrome") were men.

8. This observation is based on my clinical work, as well as the work of others. See for example Buunk (1982, 1995); Clanton & Smith (1986); Mullen & Martin (1994); Paul & Galloway (1994); and White & Mullen (1989), pp. 126–31.

9. Both my clinical work and studies with Ariella Friedman seem to support this notion. See Pines & Friedman (1998) and Mullen & Martin (1994). Paul Mullen and Judy Martin found in their community study of jealousy that women were more concerned with the effects of infidelity on the quality of the relationship.

10. See Pines (1996); Tavris (1992); and White (1981b).

11. See Darwin (1965/1988, 1970/1981).

12. See Buss et al. (1990, 1992); Cashdan (1993); Daly et al. (1982); Feingold (1992); and Wilson (1978).

13. See Goodwin (1942).

14. See Murdock (1949)

15. White & Mullen (1989), pp. 63–64.

16. The power perspective was discussed by White (1977, 1980). See also White & Mullen (1989).

17. See White & Mullen (1989), p. 58.

18. Clanton & Smith 1986.

Chapter 6. Romantic Jealousy in Different Cultures

1. My friend and colleague Ralph Hupka (1981), a cross-cultural psychologist at California State University, Long Beach, has summarized many of the anthropological reports relating to jealousy, and his articles are probably the best work written on the subject. See also Hupka & Bank (1996) and Buunk & Hupka (1987). Many of the examples quoted in this chapter are from Hupka's two papers. Another source is an article written by the noted anthropologist Margaret Mead (1931/1986). The sociological contribution to the chapter is mainly that of my dear friend Gordon Clanton (see Clanton & Smith (1986)).
2. See Weeks (1914).
3. See Turner (1884).
4. See Clanton (1989).
5. See Gouldsbury & Sheane, (1911).
6. See Hupka (1981).
7. See Powers (1877) and Weltfish (1967).
8. See Mirski (1937).
9. See Mead (1931/1986).
10. See Fawcett (1886–1889).
11. See Benedict (1934).
12. See Gouldsbury & Sheane (1911).
13. See Aronson & Pines (1980); Pines (1987a); Pines & Aronson (1983); Pines & Friedman (1998).
14. See Benedict (1934).
15. See Irons (1979); Kurland (1979); Mead (1931/1986); and Swartz & Jordan (1980).
16. See Mead (1931/1986).
17. See Hupka (1981).
18. See Mirski (1937).
19. See Mead (1931/1986).
20. See Warner (1937).
21. See Karsten (1925).
22. See White & Mullen (1989).
23. See Taplin (1879).
24. See Langsdorff (1813).

25. See Williams (1820).

26. See Thompson, (1859).

27. See Mishkin (1937).

28. See Davis (1936/1986).

29. See Gouldsbury & Sheane (1911).

30. See Matthews (1877).

31. See Rivers (1906).

32. See Goodwin (1942). See also Hupka (1981) for a comparison between the Toda and the Apache.

33. See Clanton (1989).

34. See Bernard (1986).

35. See Yankelovich (1981).

36. See Prochaska & Prochaska (1978).

37. See Crovitz and Steinman (1980).

38. The results of the Harris poll are quoted in Basow (1986).

39. See Basow (1986), p. 212.

40. See Davis (1936/1986).

41. See Rubin (1990).

42. See Thompson (1983) and Penn et al., (1997).

43. See Blumstein & Schwartz (1983). See also Pittman (1989) for reported findings about high rates of infidelity combined with a belief in monogamy.

44. See Whitehurst (1986).

45. See Paul et al. (1987).

46. See Buunk & Hupka (1987).

47. See Exodus 19: 3–5 RSV.

48. See Downing (1986).

49. See Clanton (1989).

50. See Harvey & Weary (1984) and Thompson & Snyder (1986).

51. See Hupka (1981).

Chapter 7. Romantic Jealousy in Open Relationships

1. "Sexual mate exchange" was formerly called "wife swapping." The new term avoids the sexist connotations of the older one. See Gilmartin (1986).

2. Swingers rated themselves as less jealous than did nonswingers in a study by Jenks (1985).

3. See O'Neill & O'Neill (1972).
4. See Smith & Smith (1973).
5. See White & Mullen (1989).
6. See Pines (1987a).
7. See Beecher & Beecher (1971) and White & Mullen (1989).
8. See Davis (1936/1986), whose position is elaborated in chapter six of the present book.
9. See Melamed (1991) and Neill (1960).
10. See Pines & Aronson (1981).
11. See Kanter (1972) and White & Mullen (1989), pp. 122–123.
12. See Buunk (1981) and Constantine & Constantine (1974).
13. See Denfeld (1974).
14. See Bartell (1970).
15. See Gilmartin (1986).
16. See DeBuono et. al (1990).
17. See Pines, (1996).
18. See Gilmartin (1986).
19. Similar findings were reported in a special session devoted to the subject of infidelity in the annual convention of the American Association of Marriage and Family Therapists, San Francisco, October 1989. See Gilmartin (1986). See also Pestrak et al. (1985) and Pittman (1989).

Chapter 8. Crimes of Passion

1. Paul Mullen (1996) discusses the relationship between jealousy and violence toward one's partner from both an evolutionary and a social construction perspective. In another paper, (Mullen & Maack, 1985), Mullen reports that an analysis of 138 crimes of passion discovered that 51% involved an attack on the loved one.

   See also Goldney (1977) and Mowat (1966). In Mowat's British study, 85% of the seventy–one murders and thirty–nine attempted murders triggered by jealousy that he analyzed involved the loved one.
2. The Federal Bureau of Investigation (1986). In an analysis of 195 murders, conducted almost forty years ago, jealousy was the underlying motive in 22% of the cases (Gibbens, 1959). Also, in an analysis conducted almost fifty years ago of 200 murders committed in England,

it was found that jealousy was the underlying motive in 23% of the cases (East, 1949).

3. For example, Gregory Leong and his colleagues (1994) report that people suffering from delusional jealousy ("Othello Syndrome") may present with hostility that ranges from verbal abuse to homicidal acts.

Ola Barnett and colleagues (1995) discovered significantly elevated levels of jealousy among maritally violent men.

David Riggs (1993) reports the results of a survey of 654 college students in which it was found that students who were aggressive toward their partners and those who were victims of partners' aggression reported more problems in their relationships than did students in nonaggressive relationships. Jealousy was one of the problems mentioned most often by the aggressive students.

For further studies on this topic see also Delgado & Bond (1993); Goodstein & Page (1981); Hafner & Boker (1982); Pines (1983); and White & Mullen (1989), chapter eight.

4. The study involving 607 people is described in Pines (1987b) and in Pines & Friedman (1998). The study involving 103 people is described in Pines & Aronson (1983).

5. In two different studies of homicide, West (1968) and Wolfgang (1958), jealousy was found to be the third most common cause

6. For characteristics of violent offenders, see Straus et al. (1980); Straus & Hotaling (1980); Taylor (1985); and Gove (1985). To review for characteristics of the violently jealous, see White & Mullen (1989), pp. 227–230.

7. I discuss romantic images extensively in chapter one of the present work, as well as in the second chapter of Pines (1996). The connection between childhood wounds and adult romantic relationship is nicely articulated by Hendrix (1988).

8. This point is also made by White & Mullen, (1989), pp. 223–227.

9. Studies of individuals who committed crimes triggered by jealousy show that most often such crimes are committed by males on female victims. For example, see Mowat (1966); see also Mullen & Maack (1985). Regarding other characteristics of violent offenders, see Gove (1985), and for other characteristics of the violently jealous, see White & Mullen (1989), pp. 227–230.

10. The study was conducted in a women's prison in California, with the help of specially trained University of California, Berkeley students.

11. The results of the comparison indicated that the women in prison described themselves as more jealous (3.4 vs. 2.7) and as perceived by their intimate partners to be far more jealous (4.9 vs. 2.7) than did the control group. When describing their most intense experiences of jealousy, the women in prison reported feeling more rage (6.9 vs. 4.9), more anxiety (5.1 vs. 4.4), humiliation (5.2 vs. 4.5), frustration (6.2 vs. 5.5), depression (6.0 vs. 4.9), grief (4.2 vs. 3.8), pain (6.5 vs. 5.1), and aggression (6.5 vs. 4.7). They also felt more possessive (6.0 vs. 4.3), self-righteous (5.7 vs. 3.8), and close to a nervous breakdown (3.1 vs. 2.8). When asked how they usually coped with their jealousy, they were far more likely to say that they used violence (3.4 vs. 1.6). They also reported being more likely to suffer silently but visibly (4.0 vs. 2.8) or to leave their mate (3.3 vs. 2.5). When asked about their child-hoods, the women in prison described a more troubled home life (3.7 vs. 4.9), a troubled relationship between the parents (2.9 vs. 4.6) marked by violence of father toward mother (2.8 vs. 1.2), having a jealous mother (4.3 vs. 2.1), and being beaten while growing up (2.8 vs. 1.1). They were also likely to feel less secure in their current intimate relationships (4.7 vs. 5.5).

12. See White & Mullen, (1989), p. 226.

13. For example, see Buunk (1994), who examines self-help books on jealousy as well as counseling and therapy for jealous individuals. Also, for advice on letting go of a relationship, see Wanderer (1989) and for a discussion of coping with jealousy, see White & Mullen (1989), chapter nine, as well as chapter nine of this book.

Chapter 9. Coping with Romantic Jealousy

1. For an example of treating jealousy with self-hypnosis, see Milne (1985). For examples of treating jealousy with pharmacological interventions, see Byrne & Yatham (1989); see also Gross (1991); Herceg (1976); Lane (1990); Munro et al. (1985); Stein et al. (1994); and Wright (1994). For examples of treating jealousy with cognitive therapy see Bishay et al. (1996) and Dolan & Bishay (1996a; 1996b). To review examples of treating jealousy with cognitive behavioral therapy, see Bishay et al. (1989), deSilva & Marks (1994), and Feist (1986). Albert Ellis (1986, 1996) provides two examples of treating jealousy with rational-emotive therapy. Also, for examples of the use of couples

therapy for the treatment of jealousy, see Glass & Wright (1997); Im
et al. (1983); Margolin (1985); Ridley (1996); and Verhulst (1985). For
examples of the use of systems therapy to treat a jealousy problem,
see deSilva (1987); Friedman (1989); Green & Bobele (1988); and Teisman (1979). The most famous treatment of jealousy using psychoanalysis is, of course, the work of Sigmund Freud (1922/1955). Other
publications include Fenichel (1953), Jones (1929/1950); and Riviere
(1932). The psychodynamic approach is described in the treatment of
the jealous spouse by T. L. Barker (1987). A combination of couples
and psychodynamic therapy is described by Baumgart (1990), and a
combination of couples and individual therapy is described by
Marks & deSilva (1991). For an integrated approach for treating jealousy, which includes a combination of the psychodynamic, systemic,
behavioral, social–psychological, and evolutionary perspectives, see
Pines (1992).

2. See Monat & Lazarus (1985).

3. Pines & Aronson (1988), chapter seven.

4. See Swami (1983).

5. The study involving 571 men and women was described in Pines
(1987b) and in Pines & Friedman (1997). The study involving 103 men
and women was described in Pines & Aronson (1983).

6. A version of this "talk and listen" exercise is offered by Bernie Zilbergeld (1992).

7. B. F. Skinner (1953) is considered the father of the behavioral
approach and its most well known spokesman.

8. See for example Cobb & Marks (1979); Marks (1976); and Wanderer
& Ingram (1992).

9. The technique of desensitization was introduced by Joseph Wolpe in
his classic 1958 book *Psychotherapy by Reciprocal Inhibition.*

10. See Ellis (1986, 1996).

11. See Wanderer & Ingram (1992).

12. The technique is described by Im et al. (1983).

13. Tsafy Gilad (personal communication), 1991.

14. Bernie Zilbergeld (personal communication), 1991.

15. This exercise was inspired by Hendrix (1988).

16. See, for example, Jacobson (1978, 1991); Segraves (1982); and Stuart
(1980).

Chapter 10. Can Any Good Come Out of Romantic Jealousy?

1. Other parts of this research were described in Pines & Aronson (1983).
2. See Pines (1996).
3. See Carter & Sokol (1988).
4. This case was first described in Pines (1996), chapter six.
5. This view of jealousy was the basis for workshops that I led with Gordon Clanton at the Esalen Institute, Big Sur, California.

References

Achte, K., Jarho, L., Kyykk, T., & Vesterinen, E. (1991). Paranoid disorders following war brain damage. *Psychopathology, 24* (5), 309–315.

Adams, D. (1990). Identifying the assaulting husband in court: You could be the judge. *Response to the Victimization of Women and Children. 13* (1), 13–16.

American Psychiatric Association. (1994). *DSM-IV Diagnostic and Statistical Manual of Mental Disorders* (4th ed.). Washington, DC: Author.

Anderson, R. (1987). Envy and jealousy. *Journal of College Student Psychotherapy, 1* (4), 49–81.

Aronson, E., & Pines, A. M. (1980). Exploring sexual jealousy. Paper presented at the annual meeting of the Western Psychological Association, Honolulu.

Barker, R. L. (1987). *The green-eyed marriage: Surviving jealous relationships.* New York: Free Press.

Barnett, O. W., Martinez, T. E., & Bluestein, B. W. (1995). Jealousy and romantic attachment in maritally violent and nonviolent men. *Journal of Interpersonal Violence, 10* (4), 473–486.

Bartell, G. D. (1970). Group sex among mid–Americans. *Journal of Sex Research, 6,* 113–130.

Basow, S. (1992). *Gender stereotypes and roles.* Belmont, CA: Wadsworth.

Baumgart, H. (1990). *Jealousy: Experiences and solutions.* Chicago: University of Chicago Press.

Beecher, M., & Beecher, W. (1971). *The mark of Cain: An anatomy of jealousy.* New York: Harper and Row.

Benedict, R. (1934). *Patterns of culture.* Boston: Houghton Mifflin.

Benezech, M. (1984). Homicide by psychotics in France. *Journal of Clinical Psychiatry, 45* (2), 85–86.

Bergman, M. S. (1995). On love and its enemies. *Psychoanalytic Review, 82* (1), 1–19.

Bernard, J. (1986). Jealousy and marriage. In G. Clanton & L. G. Smith (Eds.), *Jealousy*. Lanham, MD: University Press of America.

Bhugra, D. (1993). Cross cultural aspects of jealousy. *International Review of Psychiatry, 5* (2–3), 271–280.

Bishay, N. A., Petersen, N., & Tarrier, N. (1989). An uncontrolled study of cognitive therapy for morbid jealousy. *British Journal of Psychiatry, 154,* 386–389.

Bishay, N. R., Tarrier, N., Dolan, M., & Beckett, R. (1996). Morbid jealousy: A cognitive outlook. *Journal of Cognitive Psychotherapy, 10* (1), 9–22.

Blumstein, P., & Schwartz, P. (1983). *American couples*. New York: William Morrow.

Brainerd, E., Hunter, P. A., Moore, D. W., & Thompson, T. R. (1996). Jealousy induction as a predictor of power and the use of other control methods in heterosexual relationships. *Psychological Reports, 79* (3), pt. 2, 1319–1325.

Breitner, B. C., & Anderson, D. N. (1994). The organic and psychological antecedents of delusional jealousy in old age. *International Journal of Geriatric Psychiatry, 9* (9), 703–707.

Bringle, R. G. (1991). Psychological aspects of jealousy: A transactional model. In P. Salovey (Ed.), *The psychology of jealousy and envy* (pp. 103–131). New York: Guilford Press.

Bringle, R. G., & Buunk, B. (1985). Jealousy and social behavior. *Review of Personality and Social Psychology, 6,* 241–264.

Bringle, R. G., & Evenbeck, S. (1979). The study of jealousy as a dispositional characteristic. In M. Cook & G. Wilson (Eds.), *Love and attribution*. Oxford, England: Pergamon Press.

Bringle, R. G., & Williams, L. J. (1979). Parental–offspring similarity on jealousy and related personality dimensions. *Motivation and Emotion, 3,* 265–286.

Buss, D. M. (1985). Human mate selection. *American Scientist, 73,* 47–51.

Buss, D. M. (1989). Sex differences in human mate preferences: Evolutionary hypothesis tested in 37 cultures. *Behavioral and Brain Sciences, 12,* 1–49.

Buss, D. M. (1994). *The evolution of desire: Strategies of human mating*. New York: Basic Books.

Buss, D. M., Angleitner, A. A., & Asherian, A. (1990). International preferences in selecting mates: A study of 37 cultures. *Journal of Cross Cultural Psychology, 21* (1), 5–47.

Buss, D. M., Larsen, R. J., & Westen, D. (1996). Sex differences in jealousy: Not gone, not forgotten, and easily explained by alternative hypotheses. *Psychological Science, 7* (6), 373–375.

Buss, D. M., Larsen, R. J., Westen, D., & Semelroth, J. (1992). Sex differences in jealousy: Evolution, physiology, and psychology. *Psychological Science, 3,* 251–255.

Buss, D. M., & Schmitt, D. P. (1993). Sexual strategies theory: An evolutionary perspective on human mating. *Psychological Review, 100,* 204–232.

Buunk, B. (1981). Jealousy in sexually open marriages. *Alternative Lifestyles, 4* (3), 357–72.

Buunk, B. (1982). Strategies of jealousy: Styles of coping with extramarital involvement of the spouse. *Family Relations, 31,* 13–18.

Buunk, B. P. (1984). Jealousy as related to attributions for the partner's behavior. *Social Psychology Quarterly, 47,* 107–112.

Buunk, B. (1994). Pathological jealousy. *British Journal of Clinical Psychology, 33* (4), 577–578.

Buunk, B. P. (1995). Sex, self esteem, dependency and extradyadic sexual experience as related to jealousy response. *Journal of Social and Personal Relationships, 12* (1), 147–153.

Buunk, B. P., Angleitner, A., Oubaid, V., & Buss, D. M. (1996). Sex differences in jealousy in evolutionary and cultural perspective: Tests from the Netherlands, Germany, and the United States. *Psychological Science, 7* (6), 359–363.

Buunk, B., & Hupka, R. B. (1987). Cross-cultural differences in the elicitation of sexual jealousy. *Journal of Sex Research, 23* (1), 12–22.

Byrne, A., & Yatham, L. N. (1989). Pimozide in pathological jealousy. *British Journal of Psychiatry, 155,* 249–251.

Campbell, B. (Ed.). (1972). *Sexual selection and the descent of man.* Chicago: Aldine.

Carson, N. D., & Johnson, R. E. (1985). Suicidal thoughts and problem solving preparation among college students. *Journal of College Student Personnel, 26* (6), 484–487.

Carter, S., & Sokol, J. (1988). *Men who can't love.* New York: Berkeley Books.

Cashdan, E. (1993). Attracting mates: Effects of parental investment on mate attraction strategies. *Ethology and Sociobiology, 14,* 1–23.

Caspi, A., & Herbener, E. S. (1990). Continuity and change: Assortative marriage and the consistency of personality in adulthood. *Journal of Personality and Social Psychology, 58* (2), 250–258.

Chasin, C., Grunebaum H., & Herzig, M. (Eds.). (1990). *One couple four realities: Multiple perspectives on couple therapy.* New York: Guilford Press.

Clanton, G. (1989). Jealousy in american culture, 1945–1985. In D. D. Franks & E. D. McCarthy, (Eds.), *The sociology of emotions,* (pp. 179–193). Grenwich, CT: JAI Press.

Clanton, G. & Smith, L. G. (Eds.). (1986). *Jealousy*. Landham, MD: University Press of America.

Cobb, J. P., & Marks, I. M. (1979). Morbid jealousy featuring an obsessive compulsive neurosis: Treatment by behavioral psychotherapy. *British Journal of Psychiatry, 134*, 301–305.

Coen, S. J. (1987). Pathological jealousy. *International Journal of Psychoanalysis, 68* (1), 99–108.

Cohen, B. (1989). *The Snow White syndrome: All about envy*. New York: Jove.

Constantine, L. (1976). Managing jealousy. In D. H. Olson (Ed.), *Treating relationships*. Lake Mills, IA: Graphic Publishers.

Constantine, L. L., & Constantine, J. M. (1974). Sexual aspects of multilateral relations. In J. R. Smith & L.G. Smith (Eds.), *Beyond monogamy* (pp. 268–290). Baltimore: Johns Hopkins University Press, 268–290.

Cooper, S. A., & Collacott, R. A. (1993). Pathological jealousy and mental handicap. *Journal of Intellectual Disability Research, 37* (2), 195–199.

Crovitz, C., & Steinman, A. (1980). A decade later: Black–white attitudes toward women's familial role. *Psychology of Women Quarterly, 5*, 170–176.

Daly, M., & Wilson, M. (1978). *Sex, evolution and behavior*. North Scituate, MA: Duxbury Press.

Daly, M., & Wilson, M. (1988). *Homicide*. New York: Aldine De Gruyter.

Daly, M., Wilson, M., & Weghorst, S. J. (1982). Male sexual jealousy. *Ethology and Sociobiology, 3*, 11–27

Darwin, C. (1965/1988). *The expression of emotions in man and animals*. Chicago: University of Chicago Press.

Darwin, C. (1970/1981). *The descent of man and selection in relation to sex*. New York: W. W. Norton.

Davis, K. (1936/1986). Jealousy and sexual property. In G. Clanton & L. G. Smith (Eds.), *Jealousy*. Lanham, MD: University Press of America.

DeBuono, B., Zinner, S., Daamen, M., & McCormack, W. M. (1990). Sexual Behavior of College Women in 1975, 1986 and 1989. *New England Journal of Medicine, 322* (12), 821–825.

Delgado, A. R., & Bond, R. A. (1993). Attenuating the attribution of responsibility: The lay perception of jealousy as a motive for wife battery. *Journal of Applied Social Psychology, 23* (16), 1337–1356.

Denfeld, D. (1974). Dropouts from swinging: The marriage counselor as informant. In J. R. Smith & L.G. Smith (Eds.), *Beyond monogamy* (pp. 260–267). Baltimore: Johns Hopkins University Press.

deSilva, P. (1987). An unusual case of morbid jealousy treated with role reversal. *Sexual and Marital Therapy, 2* (2), 179–182.

deSilva, P., & Marks, M. (1994). Jealousy as a clinical problem: Practical issues of assessment and treatment. *Journal of Mental Health UK, 3* (2), 195–204.

DeSteno, D. A., & Salovey, P. (1996a). Genes, jealousy, and the replication of misspecified models. *Psychological Science, 7* (6), 376–377.

DeSteno, D. A., & Salovey, P. (1996b). Jealousy and the characteristics of one's rival: A self-evaluation maintenance perspective. *Personality and Social Psychology Bulletin, 22* (9), 920–932.

deWeerth, C., & Kalma, A. P. (1993). Female aggression as response to sexual jealousy: A sex role reversal? *Aggressive Behavior, 19* (4), 265–279.

Dinesh, A. K. (1993). Cognitive formulation for morbid jealousy (Othello syndrome). *Irish Journal of Psychological Medicine, 10* (3), 157–159.

Docherty, J., & Ellis, J. (1976). A new concept and findings in morbid jealousy. *American Journal of Psychiatry, 133* (6), 679–683.

Dolan, M., & Bishay, N. R. (1996a). The effectiveness of cognitive therapy in morbid jealousy. *Journal of Cognitive Psychotherapy, 10* (1), 35–40.

Dolan, M., & Bishay, N. R. (1996b). The effectiveness of cognitive therapy in the treatment of non-psychotic morbid jealousy. *British Journal of Psychiatry, 168* (5), 588–593.

Dolan, M., & Bishay, N. R. (1996c). The role of sexual behavior/attractiveness schema in morbid jealousy. *Journal of Cognitive Psychotherapy, 10* (1), 41–61.

Downey, J., & Vitulli, W. F. (1987). Self-report measures of behavioral attributions related to interpersonal flirtation situations. *Psychological Reports, 61* (3), 899–904.

Downing, C. (1986). Jealousy: A depth–psychological perspective. In G. Clanton & L. G. Smith (Eds.), *Jealousy*. Landham, MD: University Press of America.

East, W. (1949). *Society and the criminal.* London: H.M.S.O.

Egan, E. A., Lunn, B., Campbell, M., & O'Brien, J. T. (1996). Delusional jealousy in old age: Case presentation in association with previously undiagnosed carcinoma of the bronchus. *International Journal of Geriatric Psychiatry, 11* (6), 565–566.

Ellis, A. (1962). *The American sexual tragedy.* New York: Grove Press.

Ellis, A. (1986). Rational and irrational jealousy. In G. Clanton & L. G. Smith (Eds.), *Jealousy*. Lanham, MD: University Press of America.

Ellis, A. (1996). The treatment of morbid jealousy: A rational emotive behavior therapy approach. *Journal of Cognitive Psychotherapy, 10* (1), 23–33.

Enoch, M. D. (1991). Delusional jealousy and awareness of reality. *British Journal of Psychiatry, 159* (Suppl. 14), 52–56.

Everton, G. M., & Tate, D. T. (1990). Correlates of jealous behavior. *Psychological Reports, 66* (2), 601–602.

Fawcett, F. (1886–1889). On the Saoras (or Savaras). *Journal of the Anthropological Society of Bombay, 1,* 206–272.

Federal Bureau of Investigation (1986). *Uniform crime reports of the United States.* Washington, D.C: Department of Justice.

Feingold, A. (1992). Gender differences in mate selection preferences: A test of the parental investment model. *Psychological Bulletin, 112,* 125–139.

Feist, E. (1986). An innovative program for the treatment of panic attacks: A case study. *Australian Journal of Clinical Hypnotherapy and Hypnosis, 7* (2), 122–126.

Fenichel, O. (1953). A contribution to the psychology of jealousy. In *Collected Papers of Otto Fenichel* (pp. 349–62), collected and edited by Hanna Fenichel and David Rapaport. New York: W. W. Norton.

Finn, J. (1985). The stresses and coping behavior of battered women. *Social Casework, 66* (6), 341–349.

Fisch, R., Weakland, J. H., & Segal, L. (1982). *The tactics of change.* San Francisco: Jossey Bass.

Freud, S. (1922/1955). Certain neurotic mechanisms in jealousy, paranoia and homosexuality. In *Complete psychology works of Sigmund Freud.* (Vol. 18, pp. 223–340). London: Hogarth Press.

Friday, N. (1987). *Jealousy.* New York: Bantam.

Friedman, S. (1989). Strategic reframing in a case of delusional jealousy. *Journal of Strategic and Systemic Therapies, 8,* (2–3), 1–4.

Gagne, M. H., & Levoie, F. (1993). Young people's views on the causes of violence in adolescents. *Canada's Mental Health, 41* (3), 11–15.

Geary, D. S., Rumsey, M., Bow, T. C., & Hoard, M. K. (1995). Sexual jealousy as a facultative trait: Evidence from the pattern of sex differences in adults from China and the United States. *Ethology and Sociobiology, 16* (5), 355–383.

Gibbens, T. C. N. (1959). Sane and insane homicide. *Journal of Criminal Law, Criminology and Police Science, 49,* 110–115.

Gilmartin, B. G. (1986). Jealousy among the swingers. In G. Clanton & L. G. Smith (Eds.), *Jealousy.* Lanham, MD: University Press of America.

Glass, S. P., & Wright, T. L. (1997). Reconsrtucting marriage after the trauma of infidelity. In K. Halford & H. J. Markman (Eds.), *Clinical handbook of marriage and couple interventions* (pp. 471–507). New York: John Wiley & Sons.

Goldney, R. D. (1977). Family murder followed by suicide. *Forensic Science, 9* (3), 219–228.

Goodstein R., & Page, A. A. (1981). The battered wife syndrome: Overview of the dynamics and treatment. *American Journal of Psychiatry, 138,* 65–77.

Goodwin, G. (1942). *The social organization of the Western Apache.* Chicago: University of Chicago Press.

Gouldsbury, C., & Sheane, H. (1911). *The great plateau of Northern Rhodesia.* London: Edward Arnold.

Gove, W. R. (1985). The effect of sex and gender on deviant behavior. In Alice S. Rossi (Ed.), *Gender and the life course* (pp. 115–44). New York: Adeline.

Green, S., & Bobele, M. (1988). An interactional approach to marital infidelity. *Journal of Strategic and Systemic Therapies, 7,* 35–47.

Greenberg, J. (1985). Proneness to romantic jealousy and proneness to jealousy in others. *Journal of Personality, 53* (3), 468–479.

Gross, M. D. (1991). Treatment of pathological jealousy by fluoxetine. *American Journal of Psychiatry, 148* (5), 683–684.

Guerin, P. J., Fay, L. F., Burden, S. L., & Kautto, J. G. (1987). *The evaluation and treatment of marital conflict: A four-stage approach.* New York: Basic Books.

Gurman, A. S., & Kniskem, D. P. (Eds.). (1981). Part IV: Systems theory approaches. In *Handbook of family therapy.* New York: Brunner/Mazel.

Hafner, H., & Boker, W. (1982). *Crimes of violence by mentally abnormal offenders.* Cambridge, England: Cambridge University Press.

Haley, J. (1977). *Problem solving therapy: New strategies for effective family therapy.* San Francisco: Jossey Bass.

Hansen, G. L. (1985). Dating jealousy among college students. *Sex Roles, 12,* 713–721.

Harris, C. R., & Christenfeld, N. (1996a). Gender, jealousy, and reason. *Psychological Science, 7* (6), 364–366.

Harris, C. R., & Christenfeld, N. (1996b). Jealousy and rational response to infidelity across gender and culture. *Psychological Science, 7* (6), 378–379.

Harris, P. L., Olthof, T. J., Terwogt, M., & Hardman, C. E. (1987). Children's knowledge of the situations that provoke emotion. *International Journal of Behavioral Development, 10* (3), 319–343.

Harvey, J., & Weary, G. (1984). Current issues in attribution theory and research. *Annual Review of Psychology, 35,* 227–259.

Haslam, N., & Bornstein, B. H. (1996). Envy and jealousy as discrete emotions: A taxometric analysis. *Motivation and Emotion, 20* (3), 255–272.

Hendrix, H. (1988). *Getting the love you want.* New York: Holt.

Henley, N., & Thorn, B. (1977). Womanspeak and manspeak: Sex differences and sexism in communication, verbal and nonverbal. In A. Sargent (Ed.), *Beyond sex roles* (pp. 201–218). St. Paul: West.

Herceg, N. (1976). Successful use of Thiothirene in two cases of pathological jealousy. *Medical Journal of Australia, 1* (16), 569–570.

Hodgson, R. E., Murray, D., & Woods, M. R. (1992). Othello's syndrome and hyperthyroidism. *Journal of Nervous and Mental Disease, 180* (10), 663–664.

Horney, K. (1937). *The neurotic personality of our time.* New York: Norton.

Hupka, R. B. (1981). Cultural determinants of jealousy. *Alternative Lifestyles, 4,* 310–356.

Hupka, R. B. (1991). The motive for the arousal of romantic jealousy: Its cultural origin. In P. Salovey (Ed.), *The psychology of jealousy and envy* (pp. 252–270). New York: Guilford Press.

Hupka, R. B., & Bank A.. L. (1996). Sex differences in jealousy: Evolution or social construction? *Cross Cultural Research, 30* (1), 24–59.

Hupka, R. B., Buunk, B. P., Falus, G., Fulgosi, A., Ortega, E., Swain, R., & Tarabrina, N. V. (1985). Romantic jealousy and romantic envy: A seven-nation study. *Journal of Cross Cultural Psychology, 16* (4), 423–446.

Hupka, R. B., & Ryan, J. M. (1990). The cultural contribution to jealousy: Cross cultural aggression in sexual jealousy situations. *Behavior Science Research, 24,* 51–71.

Hyde, J. S. (1993). Sex, love and psychology. Paper presented at the annual convention of the American Psychological Association, Toronto, Canada.

Im, W. G., Wilner, W. R., & Breit, M. (1983). Jealousy: Interventions in couples therapy. *Family Process, 22,* 211–219.

Irons, W. (1979). Investment and primary social dyads. In N. A. Chagnon & W. Iron (Eds.), *Evolutionary biology and human social behavior* (pp. 181–221). North Scituate, MA: Duxbury Press.

Jacobson, N. S. (1978). Specific and nonspecific factors in the effectiveness of a behavioral approach to the treatment of marital discord. *Journal of Consulting and Clinical Psychology, 46,* 442–452.

Jacobson, N. S. (1991). When and why couples change in marital therapy. Paper presented at the annual convention of the American Psychological Association, San Francisco.

Jacobson, N. S., & Christensen, A. (1996). Diversity in gender, culture, ethnicity, class, and sexual orientation: Clinical implications. In *Integrative couple therapy* (pp. 212–230). New York: Norton.

Jenks, R. J. (1985). Swinging: A test of two theories and a proposed new model. *Archives of Sexual Behavior, 14,* 517–527.

Jones, E. (1929/1950). Jealousy. In *Papers on Psychoanalysis*. London: Baillieve, Tindall, and Cox.

Joseph, B. (1986). Envy in everyday life. *Psychoanalytic Psychotherapy*, 2 (1), 13–15.

Joyce, J. (1969). The dead. In *Dubliners*. New York: Viking.

Kanter, R. M. (1972). *Commitment and community*. Cambridge, MA: Harvard University Press.

Karsten, R. (1925). The Toba Indians of the Bolivian Gran Chaco. *Acta Academiae Aboensis*, 4 (4), 1–126.

Kay, P., Fulker, D. W., Carey, G., & Nagoshi, C. T. (1988). Direct marital assortment for cognitive and personality variables. *Behavior Genetics*, 18 (3), 347–356.

Kenrick, D. T., Groth, G. E., Trost, M. R., & Sadalla, E. K. (1993). Integrating evolutionary and social exchange perspectives on relationships: Effects of gender, self appraisal, and involvement level on mate selection criteria. *Journal of Personality and Social Psychology*, 64, 951–969.

Klein, M. (1986). A study of envy and gratitude. In J. Mitchell (Ed.), *The selected Melanie Klein*. New York: Free Press.

Kreeger, L. (1992). Envy preemption in small and large groups. *Group Analysis*, 25 (4), 391–408.

Krug, R., Finn, M., Pietrowsky, R., & Fehm-Horst, L. (1996). Jealousy, general creativity and coping with social frustration during the menstrual cycle. *Archives of Sexual Behavior*, 25 (2), 181–199.

Kurland, J. A. (1979). Paternity, mother's brothers, and human society. In N. A. Chagnon and W. Iron (Eds.), *Evolutionary biology and human social behavior* (pp. 181–221). North Scituate, MA: Duxbury Press.

Lane, R. D. (1990). Successful fluoxetine treatment of pathological jealousy. *Journal of Clinical Psychiatry*, 51 (8), 345–346.

Laner, M. R. (1990). Violence and its precipitators: Which is more likely to be identified as a dating problem? *Deviant Behavior*, 11 (4), 319–329.

Langsdorff, G. H., Von (1813). *Voyages and travels in various parts of the world*. London: H. Colburn.

Leong, G. B., Silva, J. A., Garza, T .E. S., & Oliva, D. (1994). The dangerousness of people with the Othello syndrome. *Journal of Forensic Sciences*, 39 (6), 1445–1454.

Lester, D., Deluca, G., Hellinghausen, W., & Scribner, D. (1985). Jealousy and irrationality in love. *Psychological Reports*, 56, (1), 2–10.

Lumpert, A., & Friedman, A. (1992). Sex differences in vulnerability and maladjustment as a function of parental investment: An evolutionary approach. *Social Biology*, 39, 65–81.

Lusterman, D. (1995). Treating marital infidelity. In R. H. Mikesell, D. Lusterman, and S. H. McDaniel (Eds.), *Integrating family therapy: Handbook of family psychology and systems theory* (pp. 259–270). Washington, DC: American Psychological Association.

Mandler, G. (1991). Some thoughts on sibling rivalry and competitiveness. *British Journal of Psychotherapy, 7* (4), 368–379.

Margolin, G. (1985). Building marital trust and treating sexual problems. In A. S. Gurman (Ed.), *Casebook of marital therapy* (pp. 271–301). New York: Guilford Press.

Marikagas, K. R., Weissman, M. M., Prusoff, B. A., & John, K. (1988). Assortative mating and affective disorders. *Psychiatry, 51,* (1), 48–57.

Marks, I. M. (1976). The current status of behavioral psychotherapy, theory and practice. *American Journal of Psychiatry, 133,* 253–261.

Marks, M., & deSilva, P. (1991). Multifaceted treatment of a case of morbid jealousy. *Sexual and Marital Therapy, 6* (1), 71–78.

Mathes, E. W., Adams, H. E., & Davies, R. M. (1985). Jealousy, loss of relationship reward, loss of self-esteem, depression, anxiety and anger. *Journal of Personality and Social Psychology, 48* (6), 1552–1561.

Mathes, E. W., Roter, P. M., & Joerger, S. M. (1982). A convergent validity study of six jealousy scales. *Psychological Reports, 59,* 1143–1147.

Mathes, E. W., & Verstraete, C. (1993). Jealous aggression: Who is the target, the beloved or the rival? *Psychological Reports, 72,* 1071–1074.

Matthews, W. (1877). *Ethnography and philology of the Hidatsa Indians.* Washington, DC: Government Printing Office,

McIntosh, E. G. (1989). An investigation of romantic jealousy among black undergraduates. *Social Behavior and Personality, 17,* 135–141.

Mead, M. (1931/1986). Jealousy, primitive and civilized. In G. Clanton & L. G. Smith (Eds.), *Jealousy.* Lanham, MD: University Press of America.

Melamed, T. (1991). Individual differences in romantic jealousy: The moderating effect of relationship characteristics. *European Journal of Social Psychology 21* (5), 455–461.

Miller, J. B. (1987). *Toward a new psychology of women* (2nd ed.). Boston: Beacon Press.

Milne, G. (1985). Horse sense in psychotherapy. *Australian Journal of Clinical and Experimental Hypnosis, 13* (2), 132–134.

Mirski, J. (1937). The Eskimo of Greenland. In M. Mead (Ed.), *Cooperation and competition among primitive peoples.* New York: McGraw-Hill.

Mishkin, B. (1937). The Maori of New Zealand. In M. Mead (Ed.), *Cooperation and competition among primitive peoples.* New York: McGraw-Hill.

Monat, A., & Lazarus, R. S. (1985). *Stress and coping.* New York: Columbia University Press.

Mowat, R. R. (1966). *Morbid jealousy and murder*. London: Tavistock Publications.

Mullen, P. E. (1993). The crime of passion and the changing cultural construction of jealousy. *Criminal Behavior and Mental Health, 3* (11), 1–11.

Mullen, P. E. (1996). Editorial: Jealousy and the emergence of violence and intimidating behaviors. *Criminal Behavior and Mental Health, 6* (3), 199–205.

Mullen, P. E., & Maack, L. H. (1985). Jealousy: Pathological jealousy and aggression. In David P. Farrington & John Gunn (Eds.), *Aggression and dangerousness* (pp. 103–126). New York: Wiley.

Mullen, P. E., & Martin, J. L. (1994). Jealousy: A community study. *British Journal of Psychiatry, 164,* 35–43.

Munro, A., O'Brien, J. V., & Ross, D. D. (1985). Two cases of 'pure' or 'primary' erotomania successfully treated with Pimozide. *Canadian Journal of Psychiatry, 30* (8), 619–622.

Murdock, G. P. (1949). *Social structure*. New York: Macmillan

Napier, H. A. (1994). Effects of ethanol and self concept on self report measures of romantic jealousy. *Dissertation Abstracts International, 54* (8–B), 4432.

Neill, A. S. (1960). Jealousy at Summerhill. In *Summerhill: A radical approach to child-rearing* (317–320). New York: Hart.

Neubauer, P. (1983). The importance of the sibling experience. *The Psychoanalytic Study of the Child, 38,* 325–236.

Nichols, M. (1984). *Family therapy: Concepts and methods*. New York: Gardner Press.

O'Neill, G., & O'Neill, N. (1972). *Open marriage: A new lifestyle for couples*. New York: Evans.

Pam, A., & Pearson, J. (1994). The geometry of the eternal triangle. *Family Process, 33* (2), 175–190.

Pao, P. N. (1969). Pathological jealousy. *Psychoanalytic Quarterly, 34* (4), 617–701.

Parrott, G. W. (1991). The emotional experience of envy and jealousy. In Peter Salovey (Ed.), *The psychology of jealousy and envy*. New York: Guilford Press.

Parrot, W. G., & Smith, R. H. (1993). Distinguishing the experience of jealousy and envy. *Journal of Personality and Social Psychology, 64,* 906–920.

Paul, L. H., Olthorf, T. J., Terwogt, M., & Hardman, C. E. (1987). Children's knowledge of the situation that provoke emotions. *International Journal of Behavioral Development, 10,* 319–343.

Paul, L., Foss, M. A., & Galloway, J. (1993). Sexual jealousy in young women and men: Aggressive responsiveness to partner and rival. *Aggressive Behavior, 19* (6), 401–420.

Paul, L., & Galloway, J. (1994). Sexual jealousy: Gender differences in response to partner and rival. *Aggressive Behavior, 20* (3), 203–211.

Penn, C. D., Hernabdez, S. L., & Bermudez, M. (1997). Using a cross-cultural perspective to understand infidelity in couple therapy. *The American Journal of Family Therapy, 25* (2), 169–185.

Pestrak, V. A., Martin, D., & Martin, M. (1985). Extramarital sex: An examination of the literature. *International Journal of Family Therapy, 7* (2), 107–115.

Pestrak, V., Martin, D., & Martin, M. (1986). A brief model of jealousy: A threat of loss of power and identity. *Counseling and Values. 31* (1), 97–100.

Pines, A. M. (1983, August). Sexual jealousy as a cause of violence. Paper presented at the annual convention of the American Psychological Association, Anaheim, California.

Pines, A. M. (1987a). Polyfidelity—an alternative to monogamous marriage? In Y. Gorni, Y. Oved, & I. Paz (Eds.), *Communal life* (pp. 622–626). Israel: Yad Tabenkin Transaction Books.

Pines, A. M. (1987b). Sexual jealousy. *Chadashot* (Israel), April 5, 3–11.

Pines, A. M. (1992a). Romantic jealousy: Five perspectives and an integrative approach. *Psychotherapy, 29,* 675–683.

Pines, A. M. (1992b). *The shadow of love: Romantic jealousy* (chap. 8). Tel Aviv: Tcherikover (Hebrew).

Pines, A. M. (1996). *Couple burnout.* New York: Routledge.

Pines, A. M., & Aronson, E. (1980). The jealousy question scale. *Psychological Reports, 50,* 1143–1147.

Pines, A. M., & Aronson, E. (1981). Polyfidelity: An alternative lifestyle without sexual jealousy. In G. Clanton (Ed.), Jealousy. *Alternative Lifestyles, 4,* 373–392.

Pines, A. M., & Aronson, E. (1983). The antecedents, correlates and consequences of sexual jealousy. *Journal of Personality, 51,* 108–136.

Pines, A. M., & Aronson, E. (1988). *Career burnout: Causes and cures.* New York: Free Press.

Pines, A. M. & Friedman, A. (1998). Gender differences in romantic jealousy. *Journal of Social Psychology, 138,* 54–71.

Pinta, E. (1979). Pathological tolerance. *American Journal of Psychiatry, 135* (6), 698–701.

Pittman, F. (1989). *Private lies: Infidelity and the betrayal of intimacy.* New York: W. W. Norton.

Powers, S. (1877). *Tribes of California*. Washington, DC: Government Printing Office.

Prochaska, J. & Prochaska, J. (1978). Twentieth-century trends in marriage and marital therapy. In T. J. Paolino & B. S. McCrady (Eds.), *Marriage and marital therapy* (pp. 1–24). New York: Brunner/Mazel.

Radecki-Bush, C., Farrell, A. D., & Bush, J. P. (1993). Predicting jealous responses: The influence of adult attachment and depression on threat appraisal. *Journal of Social and Personal Relationships, 10* (4), 569–588.

Ridley, J. (1996). Couples presenting with jealousy: Alternative interventions. *Journal of Cognitive Psychotherapy, 10* (1), 63–73.

Riggs, D. S. (1993). Relationship problems and dating aggression. *Journal of Interpersonal Violence, 8* (1), 18–35.

Rivers, W. H. (1906). *The Todas*. London: Macmillan.

Riviere, J. (1932). Jealousy as a mechanism of defense. *The International Journal of Psychoanalysis, 13*, 414–429.

Rubin, L. (1983). *Intimate strangers: Men and women together*. New York: Harper and Row.

Rubin, L. (1990). *Erotic wars*. New York: Farrar, Straus and Giroux.

Salovey, P., (Ed.). (1991). *The psychology of jealousy and envy*. New York: Guilford Press.

Salovey, P., & Rodin, J. (1986). Coping with envy and jealousy. *Journal of Social and Clinical Psychology, 7*, 15–33.

Salovey, P. & Rodin, J. (1991). Provoking envy and jealousy: Domain relevance and self esteem threat. *Journal of Social and Clinical Psychology, 10* (4), 395–413.

Salovey, P., & Rothman, A. J. (1991). Envy and jealousy: Self and society. In Peter Salovey (Ed.), *The psychology of jealousy and envy* (pp. 271–286). New York: Guilford Press.

Saunders, D. G., & Hanusa, D. (1986). Cognitive–behavioral treatment of men who batter. *Journal of Family Violence 1* (4), 357–372.

Sefedin, R. (1992). The borderline self and the jealous object. *Journal of Contemporary Psychotherapy, 22* (2), 131–145.

Segraves, R. T. (1982). *Marital therapy: A combined psychodynamic behavioral approach* New York: Plenum Medical Book Company.

Shaji, K. S., & Cyriac, M. (1991). Delusional jealousy in paranoid disorder. *British Journal of Psychiatry, 159*, 442.

Sharpsteen, D. J. (1995). The effects of relationship and self–esteem threats on the likelihood of romantic jealousy. *Journal of Social and Personal Relationships, 12*, 85–101.

Sharpsteen, D. J., & Kirkpatrick, L. A. (1997). Romantic jealousy and adult romantic attachment. *Journal of Personality and Social Psychology, 72* (3), 627–640.

Shengold, L. (1994). Envy and malignant envy. *Psychoanalytic Quarterly, 63* (4), 615–640.

Skinner, B. F. (1953). *Science and human behavior.* New York: Macmillan.

Slonim-Nevo, V., & Vosler, N. R. (1991). The use of single-system design with systemic brief problem-solving therapy. *Families in Society, 72* (1), 38–44.

Sluzki, C. E. (1978). Marital therapy from a systems theory perspective. In T. J. Paolino & B. S. McRady (Eds.), *Marriage and marital therapy.* New York: Brunner/Mazel.

Sluzki, C. E. (1989). Jealousy. *Networker,* May/June, 53–55.

Small, M. (1992). The evolution of female sexuality and male selection in humans. *Human Nature, 3,* 133–156.

Smith, R. H., Kim, S. H., & Parrott, G. W. (1988). Envy and jealousy: Semantic problems and experiential distinctions. *Personality and Social Psychology Bulletin, 14,* 401–409.

Smith, J. R. & Smith, L. G. (1973). Co-marital sex and the sexual freedom movement. *Journal of Sex Research, 6,* 131–142.

Soyka, M. (1995). Prevalence of delusional jealousy in schizophrenia. *Psychopathology, 28* (2), 118–120.

Sokya, M., Naber, G., & Volcker, A. (1991). Prevalence of delusional jealousy in different psychiatric disorders: An analysis of 93 cases. *British Journal of Psychiatry, 158,* 549–553.

Spielman, P. M. (1971). Envy and jealousy: An attempt at clarification. *Psychoanalytic Quarterly, 40,* 59–82.

Stein, D. J., Hollander, E., & Josephson, S. C. (1994). Serotonin reuptake blockers for the treatment of obsessional jealousy. *Journal of Clinical Psychiatry, 55,* 30–33.

Steinglass, P. (1978). The conceptualization of marriage from a systems theory perspective. In T. J. Paolino & B. S. McRady (Eds.), *Marriage and marital therapy.* New York: Brunner/Mazel.

Stets, J. E., & Pirog-Good, M. A. (1987). Violence in dating relationships. *Social Psychology Quarterly, 50,* 237–246.

Stewart, R. A., & Beatty, M. J. (1985). Jealousy and self-esteem. *Perceptual and Motor Skills, 60* (1), 153–154.

Straus, M. A., Gelles, R., & Steinmetz, S. K. (1980). *Behind closed doors: Violence in the American family.* Garden City, NY: Doubleday.

Straus, M. A., & Hotaling, G. T. (Eds.). (1980). *The social causes of husband-wife violence.* Minn: University of Minnesota Press.

Stuart, R. B. (1980). *Helping couples change: A social learning approach to marital therapy*. New York: Guilford Press.

Swami, A. V. (1983). Jealousy and the abyss. *Journal of Humanistic Psychology, 23* (2), 70–84.

Swartz, M. J., & Jordan, D. K. (1980). *Culture: The anthropological perspective*. New York: Wiley.

Symons, D. (1979). *The evolution of human sexuality*. Oxford, England: Oxford University Press.

Tannen, D. (1990). *You just don't understand: Women and men in conversation*. New York: William Morrow.

Taplin, G. (Ed.). (1879). *The folklore, manners, customs and languages of the South Australian Aborigines*. Adelaide: Spiller.

Tarrier, N., Becket, R., Harwood, S., & Ahmed, Y. (1989). Comparison of a morbidly jealous and a normal female population. *Personality and Individual Differences, 10*, 1327–1328.

Tavris, C. (1992). *The mismeasure of women*. New York: Simon & Schuster.

Taylor, C. G. M. (1989). Spouse similarity for IQ and personality convergence. *Behavior Genetics, 19* (2), 223–227.

Taylor, C. G. M., & Vandenberg, S. G. (1988). Assortative mating for IQ and personality due to propinquity and personal preference. *Behavior Genetics 18*, (3), 339–345.

Taylor, G. (1988). Envy and jealousy: Emotions and vices. *Midwest Studies in Philosophy, 13*, 233–249.

Taylor, P. J. (1985). Motives for offending among violent and psychotic men. *British Journal of Psychiatry, 147*, 491–498.

Teisman, M. W. (1979). Jealousy: Systemic problem–solving therapy with couples. *Family Process, 18*, 151–160.

Thompson, A. S. (1859). *The story of New Zealand* (Vol. 1). London: John Murray.

Thompson, A. (1983). Extramarital sex: A review of the research literature. *The Journal of Sex Research, 19* (1), 1–22.

Thompson, J. S., & Snyder, D. K. (1986). Attribution theory in intimate relationships: A methodological review. *The American Journal of Family Therapy 14* (2), 123–38.

Todd, J., Mackie, J. R., & Dewhurst, K. (1971). Real or imagined hypophallism: A cause of inferiority feelings and morbid sexual jealousy. *British Journal of Psychiatry, 119*, 315–318.

Turner, G. (1884). *Samoa*. London: Macmillan.

Verhulst, J. M. (1985). The jealous spouse. *Medical Aspects of Human Sexuality, 19* (5), 110–20.

Vinokur, G. (1986). Classification of chronic psychoses including delusional disorders and schizophrenias. *Psychopathology, 19*, 30–34.

Wagner, J. (1976). Jealousy, extended intimacies and sexual affirmation. *E.T.C., 33* (13), 269–288.

Wanderer, Z. (1989). *Letting go.* New York: Warner Books.

Wanderer, Z., & Ingram, B. L. (1992). Treatment of phobias with physiologically monitored implosion therapy (PMIT). *Journal of Behavior Therapy and Experimental Psychiatry, 22* (1), 31–35.

Warner, A. (1937). *Black civilization.* New York: Harper & Row.

Watzlawick, P., Weakland, J., & Fisch, R. (1974). *Change: Principles of problem formation and problem resolution.* New York: W. W. Norton.

Weeks, J. H. (1914). *Among the primitive Bakongo.* London: Seeley Service.

Weis, D. L., & Felton, J. (1987). Marital exclusivity and the potential for future marital conflict. *Social Work, 32*, 45–49.

Weltfish, G. (1967). *The lost universe.* New York: Basic Books.

West, D. J. (1968). A note on murders in Manhattan. *Medicine, Science and the Law, 8*, 249–255.

White, G. L. (1977). Inequality of emotional involvement, power, and jealousy in romantic couples. Paper presented at the American Psychological Association convention, San Francisco.

White, G. L. (1980). Inducing jealousy: A power perspective. *Personality and Social Psychology Bulletin, 6*, 222–227.

White, G. L. (1981a). Coping with romantic jealousy: Comparison to rival, perceived motives, and alternative assessment. Paper presented at the American Psychological Association convention, Los Angeles.

White, G. L. (1981b). A model of romantic jealousy. *Motivation and Emotion, 5*, 295–310.

White, G. L., & Devine, K. (1991). Romantic jealousy: Therapists' perception of causes, consequences and treatment. Quoted in G. L. White & P. Mullen (1989). *Jealousy: Theory, research and clinical strategies.* New York: Guilford Press.

White, G. L., & Mullen, P. (1989). *Jealousy: Theory, research and clinical strategies.* New York: Guilford Press.

Whitehurst, R. N. (1986). Jealousy and american values. In G. Clanton & L. G. Smith (Eds.), *Jealousy*, Lanham, MD: University Press of America.

Williams, D. H. (1820). *A journal of voyages and travels in the interior of North America.* Andover, MA: Flagg & Gould.

Wilson, E. D. (1978). *On human nature.* Cambridge, MA: Harvard University Press.

Wilson, W. (1989). Brief resolution of the issue of similarity versus complementarity in mate selection using height preference as a model. *Psychological Reports, 65* (2), 387–393.

Wolfgang, M. E. (1958). *Patterns in criminal homicide.* Philadelphia: University of Pennsylvania Press.

Wolpe, J. (1958). *Psychotherapy by reciprocal inhibition.* Stanford, CA: Stanford University Press.

Wright, S. (1994). Familial obsessive–compulsive disorder presenting as pathological jealousy successfully treated with fluoxetine. *Archives of General Psychiatry, 51,* 430–431.

Yankelovich, D. (1981). New rules in American life: Searching for self fulfillment in a world turned upside down. *Psychology Today,* April, 35–92.

Zilbergeld, B. (1992). *The new male sexuality.* New York: Bantam.

Zummuner, V. L., & Fischer, A. H. (1995). The social regulation of emotions in jealousy situations: A comparison between Italy and the Netherlands. *Journal of Cross Cultural Psychology, 26* (2), 189–208.

Index